Peter Mann was born in the UK and read English at Exeter College, Oxford. In 1976 he came to Hong Kong as a police inspector before joining the colonial government's Administrative Service, serving in the fields of transport, housing, security, environment and tourism. He also served as District Officer, Wan Chai. He is currently chairman of the Royal Commonwealth Society, Hong Kong Branch.

SHERIFF OF WAN CHAI

by

Peter Mann

BLACKSMITH BOOKS

SHERIFF OF WAN CHAI

ISBN 978-988-13765-6-5 (paperback)
Text and photographs © 2016 Peter Mann

Published by Blacksmith Books
Unit 26, 19/F, Block B, Wah Lok Industrial Centre,
31–35 Shan Mei St, Fo Tan, Hong Kong
www.blacksmithbooks.com

Typeset in Adobe Garamond by Alan Sargent
Printed in Hong Kong

First printing November 2016

Contents

Acknowledgements

This book was mainly written in Xinhui, Guangdong province, from 2013–16. I would like to thank my wife, Zoe; my good friends John Carmichael, Rachel Cartland, Tim Collard, Mark Godfrey, John Hoffmann, Ian Howard, Antoine Laurent, Ophelia Macpherson, Sue Page, Guy Shirra, Andrew Wells, Michael Wells, Robert Whitehead and Julia Woolland for their advice; Paul & Grace Yung and Leo Chow in China; and finally my dear mother, Margaret, who always had a passionate faith in the future.

PROLOGUE

As the midnight hour approached on 30 June 1997, the Union Jack was lowered for the last time and the red and yellow-star Chinese flag unfurled. Old friends in the police stripped the royal insignia from their uniforms. We, who had made Hong Kong our home, looked down from the top of the Furama Hotel over the glittering harbour. The 'Pearl in the Dragon's mouth' was about to be swallowed and things would never be quite the same again. We saw *Britannia* and her escorting frigate haul up their anchors and prepare to cast off. The strains of *Rule Britannia* and *Land of Hope and Glory* drifted off in the monsoon and mist. The guns of HMS *Chatham* fired a salute which echoed off the mountains on either side. Through the tears in our eyes, we watched the convoy as it sailed slowly through the harbour to Lei Yue Mun, where it disappeared into the darkness. This was the night when Britain finally shut down its once-mighty empire. Exactly fifty years had passed since the relentless process had been set in motion by that other 'midnight hour' when the jewel of India had been prised from its setting in the Imperial Crown, while a full century earlier Queen Empress Victoria had celebrated her Diamond Jubilee surrounded by eleven colonial prime ministers.

A poem by Rudyard Kipling, written for that event and reflecting on the transient nature of power – our 'dominion over palm and pine' – came forcefully to mind:

> *Far called, our navies melt away,*
> *On dune and headland sinks the fire,*
> *Lo, all our pomp of yesterday*
> *Is one with Nineveh and Tyre!*

The return of the Pearl of the Orient and its magnificent harbour to the Dragon after being ceded to the Lion at the Treaty of Nanking a century-and-a-half earlier now ushered in the end of empire and the dawn of the third millennium. The last post had sounded, the final flag was folded as the sun set, as it must, on the largest empire in history.

CHAPTER ONE

England

I WAS BORN in 1953 (Year of the Water Snake in the Chinese calendar), the youngest of three children. Winston Churchill was once again prime minister and we had a new young queen on the throne. My parents, Jack and Margaret, had managed to fall in love and get married in the middle of the war. My mother's family claimed descent from Matthew Boulton, the early industrialist and iron magnate who helped build James Watt's steam engine. Jack's family hailed from Northamptonshire where his forbears were yeoman farmers. He fought in a tank regiment in Normandy after D-Day and was taken prisoner at the Battle of Caen.

Britain in the 1950s was emerging from a catastrophic war in which her green and pleasant land had been bombed and bank-rupted, and she was now under political pressure to divest herself of what remained of her far-flung empire. Her global power was effectively broken and if a stark reminder was needed, 'Big Brother' America pulled the plug on our Suez adventure in 1956. As US secretary of state, Dean Acheson, famously observed, 'Britain has lost an empire and not yet found a role.' In 'Blighty' there were bombsites everywhere and rationing was still in force. On the other hand, we had successfully held out against the Nazis, our children had not been forced to speak German or Japanese and prosperity was slowly beginning to return.

Margaret's family was connected to the church; her great-grand-father was a Welsh missionary who had spent a half-century in India and met his wife in Agra Fort during the mutiny. Thomas Evans was a formidable figure with a long white beard and, like most Victorians, could see very little value in native culture or religion.

However, he was a charismatic speaker and preached to large enchanted crowds in Hindi. As a Baptist, he did much temperance work and sat on the Opium Commission. He particularly enjoyed buying cases of alcohol, gathering crowds to sing hymns and then, as a vivid testament to his feelings, smashing all the bottles and pouring the evil liquor down the drain. I hope in my lifetime I have compensated a little for his excessive zeal. He made himself rather unpopular by confiscating the gin of a wounded officer in Agra Fort, claiming that 'Drink is the devil's own net to catch poor souls!' Decency forbade him from reporting the comments of the unfortunate soldier. One day, a Brahmin informed him that someone had stolen his household god. 'You worship a god that a thief can steal?' asked the missionary, in amazement. In his later years he was known as the 'Grand Old Man of India' and was buried there in 1906 after a lifetime on the subcontinent.

Evans' daughter married David Hooper, government botanist in Madras, who was helping to develop quinine as a treatment for malaria and who was later appointed curator of the Indian Museum in Calcutta. My grandmother, Elsie, was born in the hill station of Ootacumund (Snooty Ooty as it was known) and returned to England shortly before the First World War to marry a country parson. She had a rich fund of stories about life in India, such as the time she entered the kitchen unexpectedly to find the cook filtering the coffee through a sock. Seeing the horror on her face, he stammered, 'Memsahib should not worry, I am not using clean socks – these are old, dirty socks!' Another time the family was riding in a tonga when they saw a wedding party on the street. One of the guests was wearing a white vest with Elsie's father's name clearly visible on the back. The outraged man dismounted to demand his vest back. It was, of course, the practice of Indian laundries to rent out clothes for special occasions.

Margaret grew up in vicarages and rectories in the West Country with her brother and sister where she played Tarzan in the large, rambling gardens. When Margaret was sixteen, the family went up to visit her brother who was studying at Oxford. It was a difficult journey, starting with their drive to the station in the family Austin Seven. As the vicar tried to get up the first hill without stalling, Elsie said, 'Herbert, I'm getting out!' She then proceeded to walk up the hill while the poor vicar ground the gears behind. When they finally arrived at the station, the train was about to depart. 'Hurry up!' shouted Elsie as the family raced onto the platform. Margaret was carrying a tin of cakes for her brother which burst open, sending them cascading onto the platform. 'Leave them!' ordered Elsie. As the steam train was starting to move, Elsie raised her voice and shouted, 'Stop the train!' The driver was so surprised that he did. Then one of the passengers told her that it was not the London train at all but one bound for Bristol.

As the vicar's wife and head of the Mother's Union, Elsie controlled the social life of the village. At one tea party, the vicarage dog was attacked by a bull terrier. Elsie, who had dealt with rabid dogs in India, grabbed a poker from the fireplace and struck the terrier on its head. It dropped the vicarage dog and staggered unsteadily to the gate. Shortly afterwards, having been told the story, the owner of the dog came to complain. Elsie glowered at him and said, 'We will not bother the constable today but don't you ever allow your horrid dog anywhere near the vicarage again!' On Sundays, Margaret and Rachel sat at the back of the church listening to their father preaching. You can still see the marks on the wall of the church where the two girls used to twist their sixpences for the collection.

Though it was unusual for a woman to enter higher education in those days, in 1938 Margaret went on to study Social Sciences at Bristol University and developed a love of books which was to propel her to become a writer herself. Here she enjoyed her first romantic kiss with a fellow student at the top of the Wills Tower. When the outbreak of war cut short her studies, she joined the Nursing Reserve and met Jack at a village dance near Salisbury Plain where he was doing his tank training. They married shortly before he was sent to France. A few months later, and pregnant, she received a telegram from the War Office saying that Jack was 'Missing believed captured'. Luckily, he did return from a German POW camp, although a bit the worse for wear. A few months before his release, the camp received some Red Cross parcels and he described a cup of Horlicks as 'tasting like nectar'. Having had a few of his tanks blown up, he subsequently suffered from claustro-phobia and hated enclosed spaces like cinemas.

After the war, Jack managed a cider works in Hereford which was owned by Margaret's Uncle Clare, an eccentric clergyman who flew a biplane in the thirties and used to land on beaches such as Weston-Super-Mare to preach to holidaymakers. He was known as 'The Flying Vicar' until questions were asked in Parliament about the safety of such antics and prohibitive regulations intro-duced. His flying days were anyway numbered as soon afterwards he went blind and decided to marry his chambermaid.

Our family's religious tradition was strong. Margaret's younger sister, Rachel, was an accomplished poet who had published verse, including some dedicated to Haile Selassie, emperor of Ethiopia and 'Lion of Judah', during his English exile. However, she had a highly developed social conscience and made herself ill by worrying about people starving in Africa. Eventually, she decided to become a nun and after serving in a mission in Basutoland (now Lesotho) she retired to a convent near Malvern.

In the mid-fifties, Jack was offered a job managing a company in Manchester and the family moved to a pleasant house with a large garden in Cheshire. Aged seven, I was packed off to St Chad's, a prep school in North Wales. The Harry Potter films faithfully depict life at British boarding schools in the 1960s, replete with 'back to school' scenes involving steam trains disgorging children in blazers bearing trunks and tuck-boxes – though no owls or giants.

My mother thought of me as a budding Yehudi Menuhin and encouraged me to learn the violin although I was less than happy with the taunts of the other boys. My musical career almost came to an end when I managed to break my violin bow over the headmaster's daughter's bottom. The minx had claimed somewhat provocatively that she would not feel a thing if whacked while wearing her new *lederhosen*. Matron was not amused. After a decent interval I was allowed to continue with the Spanish guitar. My favourite subjects were history, taught by an ex-Army officer who had fought in Malaya, and scripture, taught by a Welsh preacher with a halo of white hair. Our dormitories were named after British national heroes, such as Nelson and Wellington, and every night we would have long, whispered conversations at the end of which we played a game to see if we could retrace all the conversational threads to their source. Just before we fell asleep we would hear the distinctive sound of the Emerald Isle express as it huffed its way to Holyhead.

In 1966, I went to Monkton Combe School near Bath, set in a verdant valley in the Somerset hills, where I rowed and took my 'A' levels. We had initiation ceremonies, like all public schools, such as being made to walk through a disused railway tunnel without a torch, but generally it was a very happy and liberal school. There were the usual traditions of not being able to unbutton your jacket in your first year and having to wear cufflinks and detachable collars with studs. True to family tradition the school had a special Christian character, a fine chapel and was famous for producing missionaries. The dining hall had a set of large wooden boards hanging on the wall entitled 'Monktonian Missionaries'. As we ate our porridge, we could take note that J.P. Carruthers had departed for the Gold Coast in 1883.

However, puberty was now knocking on the door, and it was difficult to meet girls at an all-boys school. Luckily we had activities with local girls' schools in the form of debates, plays and concerts. So we would find ourselves stealing a kiss from a young soprano during the interval of Bach's *B Minor Mass* or backstage during a Richard Rodney Bennett opera. In 1968, we held our Centenary Service in St Paul's Cathedral and I remember well a romantic walk with a girlfriend in Regent's Park afterwards just as the autumn leaves were making a crunching, red and yellow carpet on the ground.

In class we studied ancient history, the Tudors and Stuarts, the French classics and lots of Shakespeare. I managed to avoid Greek but we all had to do Latin. We also put on regular school plays and my favourite role was Mosca (the fly) in Ben Jonson's *Volpone*. In the summer, I would run down to the River Avon every day for outings in fours or eights. The First Eight raced at Henley Regatta. Our coach would ride along the towpath with a megaphone. 'Next stroke, give it a Moriarty!' he would say, referring to the famous scene where Sherlock Holmes heaves his nemesis, Moriarty, off the cliff. We also had a very keen Combined Cadet Force and had to parade and drill once a week in full uniform with rifles. Becoming fed up with polishing boots and brass, I joined the RAF section, which was not so 'spit and polish'. I was rewarded with a training flight, including a loop-the-loop and barrel roll, in a Chipmunk trainer over the Severn Bridge. After that, I thought it would be fun to become a conscientious objector and was allowed to do community service instead, such as visiting old people's homes and picking apples on the school grounds.

This idyll was interrupted in late 1970 by the death of my father aged fifty-eight from prostate cancer, which was a great blow to the family. The following year, I was lucky enough to be offered a place at Exeter College, Oxford to read philosophy and theology (due to family tradition) but later I changed to English language and literature as the original course comprised Christian theology and dry Oxford philosophy – such as logical positivism – and not the philosophy of religion, which was my field of interest.

Prior to going up to Oxford, I had helped my mother move from Cheshire to Bath, as my brother was working for the BBC in Bristol and we had friends in the West Country. We bought a house in Abbey View Gardens, which had a panoramic view of the lovely city, with the Abbey in the foreground, the honey-coloured Georgian squares and terraces spread all around and the spires of Lansdown Hill beyond.

Oxford in the early seventies was a city of dreaming spires with a tang of political radicalism fanned by the Vietnam War and the Cultural Revolution in China. The hippie movement was in full swing, creating a heady culture of drugs, sex and rock 'n' roll. We would sit in our rooms and listen to music full of creativity and imagination such as Pink Floyd's *Meddle,* Supertramp's *Crime of the Century* and Caravan's *In the Land of Grey and Pink.* We also listened to Bach, Beethoven and Mozart. Like students everywhere, we chased girls, stayed up late, drank and smoked, and generally tried to put the world to rights. We loved to go punting on the Cherwell with pretty girls from the sixth-form colleges, such as St Clare's, taking a chilled bottle of champagne. After a heavy night out, we would be found in Browns in the market, tucking into a large and greasy cooked breakfast. Occasionally, we would have a drink with Tony Blair in the White Horse on Broad Street. He was the same year as us, yet far more sensible, and when after a few pints we started playing Dead Ants, which meant falling over backwards in our chairs, he was out the door.

Exeter College was founded in 1314, the same year as the Battle of Bannockburn, and its pleasant quadrangles lie between Turl Street and Broad Street. Its front quad is framed by an early seventeenth-century dining hall with some excellent portraits, including one of King Charles, and the Gilbert Scott chapel, modelled on Sainte Chapelle in Paris, filled with tapestries (the Adoration of the Magi) and stained glass by Exeter undergraduates William Morris and Edward Burne-Jones. At the back of the college sit the library and Fellows' Garden from which you can look out onto All Soul's College and the Radcliffe Camera. When I first arrived, you could still occasionally see J.R.R. Tolkien walking around the garden in a thick tweed jacket.

I rowed for my college, which in those days was an unfashionable concession to fitness and health, and was reluctantly persuaded to become Captain of Boats. The best time was summer Eights Week when girls would come down to the boathouses on the Isis to drink Pimms and watch the bumping races. The worst thing you could possibly do was 'catch a crab' or get your oar stuck in the water, which brought the boat to a shuddering halt and earned you the extreme opprobrium of your fellow oarsmen. The best thing you could do was be in a winning eight that managed to make a bump right in front of your boathouse, thus improving your position for the next race and your chances of a hot date that evening. Our cox, who looked like Oscar Wilde with hair parted in the centre, wore the college flower, a purple peony, in his blazer buttonhole and a gold medal in the shape of a chrysanthemum which had been presented to the college by Crown Prince Hirohito before the war.

The highlight of the year was the Boat Club Dinner, which was a black-tie affair with lots of heavy drinking. Sometimes, if the First Eight had had a good season and if an old boat was to be retired, then we would burn the boat in the quad and leap over the flames like Vikings. After the dinner, it was traditional to go out and play tricks on nearby colleges, like letting off a few fire extinguishers in Jesus College across the road. On Christmas Day it was the tradition to call that college, and when the porter answered, 'Hello, this is Jesus' to say 'Happy Birthday!' and stifle our sniggers.

I was also a keen thespian and played an anchorite monk, complete with beard and rattling chains, in Peter Barnes' *Noonday Demons* and the title role in the Marowitz *Macbeth* for the Experimental Theatre Company. I loved acting and in those days could effortlessly remember huge chunks of lines. One day, I was walking to a play rehearsal with a friend when we observed a very eccentric gentleman carrying two plastic bags walk unsteadily to a park bench. The man had an impossibly lined face as if he had taken on all the cares of the world. We watched as he pulled out a bottle of gin from one bag and a glass and tonic from the other. Having mixed a drink to his satisfaction and taken a large gulp, he took out a book and buried his nose in it.

'Have you any idea who that is?' asked my friend.

I shook my head.

'Believe it or not, that is the famous poet, W.H. Auden,' he replied.

Every few weeks, I would drive my green Mini Cooper to Bath to visit my mother and enjoy the weekend ambience of the Georgian city, but it was during the long summer holidays that we indulged our passion for travel.

In the summer of '72 a friend and I decided to follow in the footsteps of Alexander the Great on his epic journey to the East. We flew to Istanbul and took the 'Magic Bus' all the way to Delhi. In Istanbul, I visited the famous Turkish baths and suffered a brutally painful massage from a man who looked like a prison guard from the film *Midnight Express*. My sadistic masseur kept muttering, 'English boy!' as he pounded my flesh as if to pummel the sin out of me. Our overland journey took us across Turkey to Ankara and Erzurum, from where we could see the snow-capped peak of Mount Ararat, entering Iran at Tabriz.

Then we motored through the breathtaking vistas of the Great Salt Desert towards Teheran, which was surrounded for hundreds of miles by oil pipelines. Here the Shah still ruled, having been propped up first by the British and then the Americans as a source of cheap oil and a bulwark against the Russians. The year before, with great hubris, the Shah had staged a spectacular and extravagant celebration of 2500 years of Persian monarchy at Persepolis, the ancient capital which had been burnt to the ground by Alexander. Just a few years later, in 1979, the Iranian people were to rise up against the Shah's oppressive regime and drive him out of the country. However, champagne was still flowing then and one evening we ventured into the bar of the Hilton Hotel to admire the city's Western sophistication and its beautiful, intelligent women.

A few days later we arrived at the holy city of Mashhad which was dominated by the turquoise domes of the tomb of Imam Reza. The next day we crossed into Afghanistan near Herat and had to endure groups of little boys along the road throwing stones at our bus. We stopped to stare at the famous pillars which were said to have been erected by Alexander a couple of millennia earlier, and recited the immortal lines from Shelley's *Ozymandias:* 'Look upon my works, ye mighty, and despair!'

The most macho guy on our bus was a large Australian rugby player with a fierce red beard. We were all a bit scared of him until we arrived at a guest house run by two weird Afghan brothers who took a fancy to the Aussie and wanted to stroke his beard. This drove the big guy crazy and we had a good laugh as the brothers chased him around the verandah.

We took the southern route to Kabul via Kandahar as we were not sure that our bus could manage the passes of the Hindu Kush. Much of our time was spent in seedy hostels thick with hashish smoke. Afghanistan has always been a rather dangerous place for the British, never more so than during the military catastrophe of 1842 when due to a disastrous series of mistakes an entire British army was annihilated. However, I did manage to board a bus at 3 a.m. one morning in Kabul to travel up-country to visit the famous, huge rock Buddha at Bamiyan. Just as well, as it was later blown up by the Taliban.

Leaving Kabul, we descended through the Khyber Pass into Pakistan at Peshawar and then through the Punjab to Lahore. At that time India and Pakistan were fighting in Kashmir and the border between Lahore and Amritsar was open for only one morning a week. Due to the fact that many travellers were cooped up in one place for days on end, Lahore at that time probably boasted the best con-men on the planet. We were introduced to a local fellow called David, who seemed the quintessential English gentleman, replete with blazer and cravat, speaking flawless English and claiming to have been at Cambridge. On the day we met him he insisted on taking us to lunch at his club. The next day (the day before the border opened) I luckily missed his second invitation to lunch when he received a call from a 'business associate' after the banks had shut and just needed to borrow a few hundred dollars until the next day. My friends were glad to oblige with their holiday money. How could they refuse? The next day David had disappeared and my friends were informed that if they wanted to make a report to the police then they would need to wait in Lahore for another week.

Notwithstanding the prevailing anti-imperialist climate, I was politically incorrect enough, doubtless thinking of my great-grand-father in Calcutta, to buy a pith helmet as soon as I arrived in India. My travelling companion went to Kathmandu but I chose Kashmir and spent a few weeks on a houseboat on Dal Lake, with the occasional trip up to the hill station and glacier at Gulmarg. I remember the owner of the houseboat asking me a strange question.

'Why did you British leave India?'

'I thought you kicked us out!' I replied.

'No, no,' he spluttered, 'That was the mad fools in Delhi!'

Note that this was only twenty-five years after independence. Returning to Delhi and being hugely impressed by the Moghul grandeur of the Red Fort, I decided that I could not leave India without seeing the Taj Mahal. However, as long-distance travellers often do, I had now run out of money. Begging my mother by letter to send funds to American Express in Delhi, I had just enough rupees left for a third-class return railway ticket to Agra.

Arriving at the Taj Mahal wearing a kaftan, with long hair and beard and sleeping bag on my shoulder, I looked the archetypal hippie. As luck would have it, there was a full moon that night and the immortal marble form of that famous monument to Love glowed like a moonstone. Embedded in the marble walls were semi-precious stones that sparkled like red, green and blue fireflies on a translucent lake. It was a magical experience which on its own would have justified the danger and discomfort of the whole trip. As the last remaining tourists left the site, I realised that I did not have enough money for even a modest hotel. Luckily, while walking around the gardens, I had spied a discreet spot that was protected from the eyes of the security guards on patrol through the night. It was here that I laid out my sleeping bag and fell asleep next to the moonlit Taj Mahal.

Back in Delhi, I found a kindly hostel owner who allowed me a bunk until my money arrived. When it did (bless my mother's heart) I began to calculate how on earth I was going to return the two-thousand-odd miles to Istanbul, from where I had a return ticket to London. I wanted to fly from Delhi to Teheran but in the event could only afford to fly to Kabul. I shall never forget the terror of my short flight on Air Afghanistan, nor the interminable, bumpy way home through Iran and Turkey, often suffering from diarrhoea. The experience of roughing it certainly made you realise first how lucky you were in your safe, middle-class existence, and when you returned, how suburban and provincial England was compared to the spectacular sights of Asia.

The next summer I fancied something more relaxing and went to the Greek islands. I spent a blissful few weeks on Ios, sleeping on the beach, swimming in the fresh, turquoise water and sipping retsina or ouzo with a plate of grilled squid in small seaside tavernas. The high point of that trip was listening to classical music high, both on the mountain and acid, as the sun sank into the Aegean Sea, and finding the whole thing a profoundly religious experience as the sky turned crimson and the stars and moon ventured forth.

A few weeks later, after a visit to the volcanic island of Thera, and having again run out of money on the island of Crete, I decided to try my hand at picking grapes. At dawn, I went to the market place, as advised, and said in my best Greek, *'Thelo thulia!'* (I want work). To my surprise my offer was taken up by a local woman who drove me to her vineyard. The first few hours of cutting grapes were all right. However, as the sun rose high in the sky and you had to carry the grapes further and further and then wash them in permanganate solution which stung your cut fingers and the sweat ran into your eyes, you realised that this was real man's work. By the end of the day I could hardly walk. The Greek woman took a look at this student with soft hands who was so unaccustomed to manual labour, paid me and said, 'I don't think you will be back tomorrow.' She was right.

Given my religious background and spiritual interests, I had always wanted to visit Mount Athos, in the northeast of Greece, a peninsula near to Thessalonika. The Holy Mountain, or Agios Oros, is a theocratic state filled with monasteries and retreats and forbidden to women visitors. You need a special visa to get in and one of my friends at Athens University had vouched for me as a student of Byzantine Art. I hiked around for a week, staying in monasteries at night, climbing the 8,000 foot Holy Mountain and visiting some hermits in their caves. The icons and religious artwork were stunning. The monasteries served hearty fish broth with chunks of bread and flagons of red wine for breakfast. The monks ranged from fat lecherous types to the deeply spiritual. All wore chimney-pot hats and sported full beards. One night I stayed in a mountain retreat run by an intense monk called Father Dimitri who spent the whole night singing and praying. I asked myself whether I could become a monk but thought that perhaps I was too caught up with pleasure and the material world.

Later, upon the advice of a wise friend, I went to spend a few days all by myself on a small uninhabited island near Paros. Most people never voluntarily spend time alone and when they have no choice they retreat into TV or music because they find the enormity of their own presence in the 'now' rather embarrassing. Sleeping on the beach by a camp fire, walking and swimming by day, eating some bread and fruit in the evening, it proved a magical time. I remember meeting a Greek fisherman who just could not believe I was there by myself. 'You are alone?' he kept repeating, 'All alone?' I wanted to reply, 'Aren't we all?' but I just nodded. Once I awoke in the middle of the night to see a pair of glittering eyes looking at me. I cried out and a wildcat ran away, more frightened than I. The real demons, indeed, are usually in our own minds.

It was around this time that I became interested in Buddhism. The message of the Buddha seemed very similar to that of Christ, when removed from the heavy framework of organised religion. The Kingdom of Heaven is within! We should try to practise meditation and observe our mind and develop compassion for other beings, which is the best motivation for anything we might wish to undertake. The beauty of nature, as many poets have discovered, is also a great inspiration.

With this in mind, my second year at Oxford was spent at a farmhouse in the Cumnor hills, where Matthew Arnold's 'Scholar Gypsy' used to roam, a few miles from town. There were sheep in the fields and a nearby river where one could walk, breathe fresh air and daydream. It took some effort to rouse oneself from this country idyll to drive into town for a tutorial on, say, the poetry of Andrew Marvell. My English literature tutor, appropriately named Wordsworth, would mutter, 'I don't know what you think you are doing, living out there like a hippie. Your brain is becoming addled!'

For my third year, I came back to town and worked hard for a month or so to learn all the things I should have learnt in the preceding two years. In those days, we had to wear *sub-fusc* complete with white bow tie and gown to take our final exams. In order to wake up on time, I fixed my stereo to play the alarm clock sequence from *The Dark Side of the Moon* every morning at 7 a.m., much to the irritation of my flatmates. When it was all over, as was traditional, my friends came to the Examination Schools building with champagne and a few joints for good measure.

It never occurred to me that getting a job might be a problem. My practical father was no longer around to push me and when I asked my mother, she would respond, 'Whatever you like, darling.' For sure, we laughed at fellow students who cut their hair and dressed up in suits to visit the Careers Advisory Office. Why should we worry about finding a job? After all, we had degrees from Oxford! However, we did not reckon with the Oil Crisis of 1973 which sent the world's economy into a tailspin. The UK was a grim place to live in 1974. Edward Heath's confrontation with the miners caused a strike which led to the 'three-day week' in order to conserve energy. It was a time of gloom and power-cuts. As this was also the height of the Cold War, it was also possible that at least some of Britain's industrial unrest was being orchestrated from Moscow.

As I had always enjoyed acting, I applied to do a drama course at the Bristol Old Vic, but they didn't seem to be interested in Oxford graduates. I also went for an interview with a dog-food company. In truth, I just wanted a summer job to earn enough money for more exotic travel. However, when I arrived at the interview there were all these keen types from red-brick universities who, unlike me, actually knew everything about the company and the job on offer. I even considered joining the army. In a panic, I went to see an uncle who was a senior civil servant. 'What do you want to do?' he barked. Well, I didn't feel a strong vocational pull in any direction at the time. What I really wanted to do was to carry on living a happy student life. 'You've got no fire in your belly,' he growled, 'I can't help you.'

I had already written my epitaph: 'Too late for the Empire, too early for Space, here lies Peter in disgrace.' My mother disliked this and suggested 'state of grace'. 'Anyway,' she said, 'there's still some Empire left; it's called Hong Kong!' Not long before, I had seen Bruce Lee's new film *Enter the Dragon.* It painted a wonderful picture of the mysterious East and I was particularly impressed with the scene in the typhoon shelter where whole families, including girls in pyjamas, together with dogs and chickens, were living on boats. Eastern promise indeed! My wanderlust was piqued and I decided that maybe I should look for a job in the exotic Orient.

Another friend suggested that we both apply to join the Royal Hong Kong Police. The recruiting brochure showed a smart officer with a cap, whose silver badge portrayed a couple of dodgy Victorian gentlemen inspecting what looked like cases of opium on a wharf. I applied, even though my Oxford tutor declined to give me a reference as he thought the job was beneath me. At the interview in the Hong Kong Government Office in Grafton Street, an old colonial asked me if I played rugby. I said I did but preferred rowing.

A fortnight later I received an offer of appointment as inspector of police. My friend, however, reneged on his part of the deal. Short of joining the Foreign Legion, it was the most outrageous thing I could think of doing. I was just twenty-three years old.

When I told my girlfriend, Julia, the news, she was tearful but supportive. The week before I left, my mother humorously gave me a copy of Kipling's famous lines:

> *Take up the White Man's burden*
> *Send out the best of your breed*
> *Go bind your sons to exile*
> *To serve your captives' need.*

My letter of appointment included an allowance to buy a tropical suit. There was also a fact sheet on Hong Kong which stated that the colony was hot, noisy and overcrowded and that it wasn't everyone's cup of tea. However, for a young man with no clear career path aside from getting away from England's gloomy skies and industrial unrest, it was just the ticket.

Although it is no small thing for a young man to leave behind his family, friends and home country and start a new life on the other side of the world, as the saying goes: 'Nothing ventured, nothing gained'. It was to prove a marvellous venture with much to gain.

CHAPTER TWO

Arrival in Hong Kong

I ARRIVED IN HONG KONG on a warm October afternoon in 1976, a few weeks after the death of Chairman Mao. In those days it was a twenty-eight-hour flight via Rome, Bombay and Bangkok, and the famous landing at Kai Tak involved a hair-raising last minute right turn over the rooftops of Kowloon City before the plane thumped down on the runway stretched out into the harbour. As we disembarked from our British Airways jet and took leave of the stern and matronly stewardess who had glowered at us during the journey, we blinked in the strong sunshine and speculated coarsely on the source of the odour issuing from what looked like a stagnant waterway beside the runway. When Bob Hope first arrived in Hong Kong and made a similar comment, he was informed that the cause was basically shit. 'Yes,' he replied, 'but what have they done to it?'

Having cleared Immigration and Customs, our band of young opportunists was met by an impressive chief inspector, elegantly turned out in a crisp, green summer uniform replete with shining black leather Sam Browne belt. Our eyes lingered for a moment on his service revolver. 'Right lads,' said he, 'let's be having you in the bus for the Police Training School.' The old blue Bedford transport lurched out of Kai Tak Airport and was soon threading its way through the densely-packed streets of Kowloon. As we paused at a traffic light on a busy intersection, a fat Chinese hawker dressed in a T-shirt and shorts, selling some dubious-looking foodstuff, looked up at my alien white face, gave a guffaw of laughter and spat a definitive wad of mucus onto the pavement. So this was Hong Kong!

Ramshackle tenements with shops at street level pushed and bullied themselves into prime positions along the roadsides. Above them a multitude of colourful signs of different shapes and sizes advertised all sorts of products and wares. One that made me wonder about the local weather and the suitability of my attire was the Lee Kee Boot Company. Higher up, I could see row upon row of washing drying on poles. The other thing one noticed was the crowds. Both pavements were heaving with humanity, most of them wearing T-shirts, shorts and flip-flops. The girls were pretty and sported long, lustrous, black hair. I wondered idly why the Asians had better hair than us. Although it was nominally autumn, it was still hot and humid. The humidity was cloying and sweat-inducing. Suddenly the bus braked sharply, causing us to grab the seats in front. The driver uttered an incomprehensible Cantonese oath as a red taxi in front of us turned left without a signal. As I settled back before the next veering swerve, I took comfort in the reassuring familiarity of the English road signs, red pillar-boxes and urban layout.

Even though the Cross-Harbour Tunnel had recently been opened, the chief inspector explained that it was policy to take the cheapest route, which meant crossing the harbour on the Jordan Road Ferry. It was also good luck, evidently, to arrive by sea. Moments later, we drove up a ramp onto a large ferry boat. Scrambling off the bus in the twilight, we crowded together at the bow to survey with astonishment the choppy water of the blue-green harbour, dotted with junks and shipping, and the impressive bulk of Hong Kong Island, festooned with dazzling skyscrapers, all lit up and twinkling, the New York of Asia. It looked like a huge dynamo or pulsating beehive radiating energy and prosperity. 'That's the Connaught Centre, headquarters of Jardine Matheson and the tallest building in Asia,' our guide announced authoritatively, pointing at a glittering steel tower which appeared to be covered in portholes. 'In Chinese,' he added wryly, 'it's known as the building of a thousand arseholes.' He did not clarify whether this referred to the building's appearance or the people who worked in it.

Having made our first crossing of Victoria Harbour, we drove off the ferry towards Central District, which was the headquarters of business and government. Our guide pointed out the impressive colonial buildings: the Indian-inspired General Post Office, the majestic Hong Kong Club and classically colonnaded Supreme Court. There was also the imposing Hongkong and Shanghai Bank protected by two snarling imperial lions, still bearing scars from Japanese shelling, and next door the Bank of China which, for reasons of face, had to be just a little bit taller.

Then we headed up the hill for Wong Chuk Hang, which means 'Yellow Bamboo Stream', near Aberdeen on the south side of Hong Kong Island. Entering the impressive main gate of the Police Training School, which was flanked by turreted pill-boxes (a relic of the '67 leftist disturbances, we were informed), it was something of a surprise to see a number of young men lying face down in the compound with their hands clasped behind their necks. In answer to our anxious questions, we were informed that these cadets were being disciplined.

While digesting the ominous import of these words, we were shown to our dormitory where we dumped our suitcases and began to unpack. Just as we were beginning to relax after our long journey, we heard the sound of angry voices and boots pounding up the stairs. Moments later, the door was kicked open and in burst a half-dozen officers in full uniform.

'What do you think this is, a bloody tea party?' shouted their leader, a dark-haired Scotsman with a missing front tooth and ruddy face. They then proceeded to upturn all of our cases, dumping our precious belongings on the floor. The Scotsman noticed a girlie magazine lying amongst the junk.

'Right, whose is this?' he bellowed, his face purpling with anger.

No one moved.

'I think it's time you jokers were taught a lesson,' he added unpleasantly.

Still wearing our clothes from the plane, we were marched straight out into the compound to be drilled for a good hour in the warm tropical evening. Then, to see what we were made of, we were put over an assault course complete with ropes to climb, ditches to ford and trenches to wriggle through. The poor fellow next to me was asked to do fifty press-ups and he did his best before collapsing.

'Pathetic!' said the drill sergeant, 'my granny could do better than that.'

As we stood gasping and sweating in the humid air, the Scotsman started to warm to his theme.

'You guys thought this would be easy, didn't you?' he asked rhetorically.

'You thought this would be a Sunday school picnic, eh?'

As he ranted, he walked up and down our bedraggled ranks, fixing one or another of us with a withering, basilisk stare. He leered into my face.

'Did you hear what I said?'

'Yes sir!' I replied.

He stretched his ugly, implacable face very close to mine.

'Do you see those blocks over there?' he growled.

My eyes flicked away to take in the high-rise public housing estate on the other side of the camp.

'There are ten thousand Chinese over there, and they all hate your guts!'

By this time, our disorientation was complete. In unfamiliar surroundings, exhausted and jet-lagged, we were at their mercy.

Then an older gentleman appeared who was introduced as the force chaplain. The Scotsman saluted him and said, 'Seems like London have let us down again, Sir! A pathetic bunch, a complete rabble.'

The chaplain spoke to each of us in turn, asking about our religious convictions and alluding darkly to the moral problems we would face if we fraternised with the local Chinese girls. He then asked whether any of us had had sexual relations with another man. We stood silent in an ecstasy of embarrassment. He took a step forward and looked me in the eye. The Scotsman poked me in the chest with his swagger stick.

'Answer the chaplain,' he barked.

'Er . . . no, sir,' I stammered. The chaplain leaned forward and gave me a big wink.

'Feel free to come and see me if you have any problems,' he beamed.

Then he asked if any of us could sing as there was a service the next morning and he was short of choir members.

'Squad, take two paces forward!' barked the Scotsman. 'They all volunteer, Sir!'

'Right you lot,' he said. 'Sing *Onward Christian Soldiers!*'

And we did. We all sang *Onward Christian Soldiers* at the top of our voices.

After another hour of being drilled and harangued, a large tropical moon rose in the night sky, under which we were marched to some steps outside a darkened room. I thought I caught the sound of stifled laughter from within. We were given the order, 'About turn!' At that moment, the room suddenly blazed with light and a torrent of guffawing cadets poured out of the door, each bearing pints of beer. The whole thing had been an elaborate colonial initiation ceremony. After an hour or so, we were all taken down to the bars of Wan Chai to get properly drunk.

I should add that one of our group, another surly Scot, later confided in me that he had been profoundly disappointed that our training was not to proceed in the fashion of the initiation. His favourite film was *The Hill* with Sean Connery and Harry Andrews set in a prison.

'Life's too soft, these days,' he sighed.

On Monday morning we went for a run up Brick Hill, which was at the back of the school near Ocean Park. I was feeling fit and led the pack up the hill. As we climbed higher, I looked out over the coastline of green bays and was suddenly struck down by wave after wave of appalling vertigo. I don't know whether it was the humidity or alien terrain, but I had to sit down and wait for the worst to pass, enduring the jeers of my squad-mates as they passed me. That week we toured the colony (or 'territory' as it was euphemistically called), were issued with uniforms and kit, visited Police HQ and played a bit of cricket. There was also rowing at Middle Island.

At the weekend, we were lucky enough to see the annual 'Beating of the Retreat', which was held on our parade ground. Attended by the great and the good, including His Excellency the Governor in full colonial rig topped by his ostrich plumes, the ceremony commemorated the surrender of Hong Kong to the Japanese on Christmas Day 1941. It was a splendid occasion, like a tattoo, with two marching bands; one of Chinese bagpipers, who criss-crossed the square under the illumination of coloured spotlights. We all stood as the Union Jack was lowered to the strains of the *Last Post,* and a piper came forward to sing the *Twenty-third Psalm* in a beautiful tenor voice. Then, far away on the mountainside, a lone piper played *Amazing Grace.* There was scarce a dry eye on the parade ground that evening. I was half expecting ghostly Imperial Japanese troops to emerge in the moonlight.

Over the next few months we learned Cantonese, criminal law, firearms and drill. I thought I would hate the drill but actually it was quite relaxing and, like rowing, once the squad was up to speed, there was an exultant feeling of many people moving in unison. The only problem was that we had to drill without shirts so sunburn was always a threat. Later in the course we inspectors were required to drill an unfortunate squad of constables. It was quite a challenge getting them from A to B on the parade ground, requiring planning and anticipation to give the right command at the right time. Some of us made an absolute hash of it, leaving the poor constables in a complete mess. At our passing-out parade, we asked the band-master to play the Souza march made famous as the theme to *Monty Python's Flying Circus.* It was great music to march to, while we enjoyed the subversive undertone.

In the evenings, we would congregate in the officer's mess for a few pints or gin-and-tonics. The fans whirred overhead and outside the cicadas clicked in the tropical foliage. It all felt very Graham Greene or Somerset Maugham. Occasionally, there were female visitors who were doubtless flattered by the attention they received from all the single men. It was not a good idea to take your girlfriend there lest she be devoured by lustful male eyes. In any case, especially on Fridays and Saturdays, most of the expatriate inspectors were by 9 p.m. preparing to depart for the fleshpots of Wan Chai for a so-called nightcap.

Our Chinese colleagues were friendly but had (what appeared to us) some strange habits. Early in the morning we would have the 'dawn chorus' – loud hawking of mucus in the bathroom to get rid of what the locals called 'the evil spit monster'. We would also find shoe-prints on the toilet seats as most of them still used 'squat and drop' facilities at home such as one might find in parts of Europe. They were strictly forbidden from gambling at the school, which must have been difficult as most Chinese will gamble on anything at the drop of a hat. Not as accustomed to drinking as us, they would often turn red-faced after a glass of beer as most East Asians lack the enzymes to metabolise alcohol. The advantage of this condition was that there was less chance of alcoholism, whereas this was a major problem for many Europeans in the tropics. It took us a while to get used to sleeping in the heat as we only had fans, air-conditioning being regarded as extravagant.

As for spoken Cantonese, it is very difficult to master a language that has eight tones. Foreigners (or *'gwai lo'* – ghost people – as we are known) are forever getting the tones wrong and it is only by constant practice that we can become nearly fluent. I will not even go into the concept of 'classifiers' which are used to designate various categories of noun. Many is the time I have been certain that what I have said is correct only to be greeted by a gawping stare of complete incomprehension. Indeed, our teacher impressed upon us the importance of first saying, *'M Goi!'* or 'Please!' whenever we attempted to speak to cue the listener that a foreigner was attempting to speak the vernacular. The pitfalls are legion. As Cantonese has a limited range of phonemes, meaning is signified by subtle variations in tone, which can be very confusing to foreigners. One must avoid talking about crabs or shoes as these words sound very much like a part of the female anatomy. Similarly, if one mispronounces the words for nine or dog, then one is referring to a part of the male anatomy. One day at a formal dinner I tried to tell a conservative Chinese matron that I had been diving and succeeded in communicating that I had been 'shitting in the sea'. The best thing about the lessons was that we had one very pretty female teacher, and we all mooned over her.

Our Cantonese instruction books had been written by a venerable Chinese gentleman called Sidney Lau. They contained some marvellous old sayings and proverbs, such as 'A man will not cry until he has seen his own coffin'; whereas a crafty person would 'pose as a pig to eat a tiger'. Then there were obscure proverbs like 'Three monks will not drink water', the explanation being that one or two monks can carry water but three will argue endlessly over who does what. The Chinese have some very colourful expressions, often delivered in two parts with the meaning given as a pun, 'An African monk – an annoying person', where the second part of the expression sounds like *'black man'*.

While Cantonese can be very eloquent and subtle, it also has a profound store of profanity related to people's mothers and ancestors and dropping dead on the street, enough to make a navvy blush, as anyone riding on a bus or tram in Hong Kong and listening in on seemingly casual conversation will attest.

The written language is also complex and fascinating. It is best learned early and Chinese children normally start at five or six years old with an hour's homework a day. The simple pictographic characters become increasingly and accumulatively more complex, some being written with as many as twenty different strokes. You need to know about 2,000 of them to read a Chinese newspaper. Many are surprisingly expressive – for example, the character for an 'official' has two mouths.

Towards the end of our course, each of us was given a Chinese name. There was a special section in the Language Division that undertook this task. The aim was to provide a convincing Chinese name that was similar to the sound of the English name, but not a simple transliteration. These names were so authentic that if they appeared in a local newspaper report, a reader could assume that the bearer of the name was a local officer. My Chinese name is Man Pui-dak, 文沛德, which means 'Man of Great Virtue'. Although I make no comment on its aptness, local people all seem to appreciate the sound of this name.

In my study of criminal law, I had the misfortune to have an instructor who not only looked like an octopus but also appeared to be permanently hung over and was therefore extremely cantankerous. My being an Oxford graduate led to theories that I was a plant for the Independent Commission Against Corruption (ICAC) so I was given a particularly hard time. 'Let's ask smarty-pants,' he would drawl, 'Mann, define "conspiracy"!' No matter how well I did, he was always finding excuses to fail me and put me on guard duty for the weekend, which I accepted philosophically.

On the other hand, weapons' training (or 'musketry' as it was called) was a lot of fun. Following the riots of 1967 when the Cultural Revolution spilled over the border into Hong Kong, the police had established riot squads that consisted of a platoon with four ranks, each representing an increased use of force, to meet the threat of serious civil disturbance. In the front rank, police carried batons and rattan shields; in the second, Webley Smoke Pistols firing gas canisters (but watch the wind direction or it might blow back on you); in the third, Federal Riot Guns firing baton shells (which bounced off the ground and broke legs); and finally a rank with alternate Remington pump-action shotguns and AR15 assault rifles (semi-automatic versions of the M16) for rooftop snipers. We had to fire all these on the range, in addition to the Colt 38 which was the standard police handgun. We also learned to fire Sterling sub-machine guns, which had an alarming tendency to rise up as they were discharged. This was all good *Boy's Own* stuff.

Another highly enjoyable exercise we carried out was testing airport security. The challenge was for us cadets to find ways of breaching security at the airport, thus exposing any flaws that might exist in the present system. In those pre-terrorist days you could get away with almost anything whereas today we would have been cut down in a hail of machine gun fire. Probably the best training for this sort of thing had been my undergraduate days at Oxford when we prepared to crash a college ball. My tactics were fairly simple. I arrived at HAECO (the aircraft engineering facility next to the airport) wearing my tropical business suit and holding a briefcase in which I had secreted a pair of blue overalls, a clipboard and a toy gun. Approaching the security guard with confidence, I informed him that I had a meeting with a member of staff whose name I had found in the telephone directory. I was asked to wait so went for a little stroll. I could see the runway outside so I walked out and ducked behind a wall where I opened my briefcase, took off the suit and put on the blue overalls.

With the clipboard in my hand, I looked just like an airport worker. Feeling very pleased with the way things were going I walked over to the nearest plane and up the steps into the aircraft. Walking to the front, I arrived at the cockpit where a pilot was doing a pre-flight check. His surprise turned to alarm when I raised my toy gun and said, 'Luckily for you this is just a drill!' Moments later I heard the wail of sirens and the airport police arrived and boarded the plane. I put my hands up and was rather roughly handcuffed and escorted off the aircraft. I shall never forget the look on the tourists' faces as I was dragged through immigration controls by a posse of angry policemen.

The high spot of the month was payday. We would grab our few thousand dollars and head for town. The most popular shopping attraction was the newly opened Ocean Terminal which had a plethora of shops selling cameras and electronic goods. Coming from an austere UK, our jaws dropped at the incredible selection of consumer goods. We all emerged clutching the latest stereo and Pentax or Nikon. We also quickly learned about Chinese food and that quintessential Hong Kong gastronomic experience, *yam cha* (literally 'drink tea') where many small, delicious dishes known as *dim sum* (little bits of heart) served in bamboo steamers were wheeled around on trolleys by ladies who would call out their melodious names (*'ha gau, siu mai, ma lai go*) before plonking them on your table and noting the details on a slip of paper, while you drank many cups of tea, or in our case bottles of San Miguel beer. Chinese restaurants are brilliantly lit, often with screaming children running wild. We soon discovered that the Cantonese are probably the noisiest people on the planet and that just a few of them can make a truly extraordinary clamour.

We also made expeditions to the garish, crimson Jumbo Floating Restaurant in the middle of Aberdeen Harbour, which had caught fire a few years before with some loss of life. Based on Tanka (boat people) wedding boats, her exterior was a riot of writhing dragons with flashing eyes and inside was a maze of multi-coloured dining halls and private rooms complete with panelling, scrolls and ceramics. She even had her own pier on the shore and a ferry service provided by boats which were small replicas of the mother vessel. Once seated at our table, the waiters would bring a half-dozen bottles of cold San Miguel beer and two plates heaped with big juicy steamed prawns, followed by more seafood. After our meal, we would hire a sampan and tour the typhoon shelter to marvel at the boat people living on hundreds of vessels, with families cooking under awnings, dogs and chickens wandering around the decks and young children tied to ropes to stop them falling over the side. This was the end of an era as within ten years, most of the boat dwellers were rehoused on dry land.

On Friday nights, after a few drinks in the mess, we would jump into taxis or cars – there were no breathalysers in those days – and head down to Wan Chai. One time we nearly didn't make it as my friend crashed his MGB into a lamp post on the way down the hill. The police were called and I had to hide in the bushes with a handkerchief tied round my head to staunch a cut brow, looking for all the world like a left-behind Japanese soldier. We were lucky as traffic fatalities were not uncommon. There were still many girlie bars on Lockhart Road (named after an intrepid colonial ad-ministrator) and in the seventies the US fleet was frequently in town. The Vietnam War had ended with the fall of Saigon in April 1975 and Pol Pot was rampaging in Cambodia. The bars were all playing the Eagles' new hit single *Hotel California.* One of the great sports of the time was bar brawls between British soldiers (known as squaddies) and American sailors. However, the white-clad American shore patrol was always quick to arrive and restore order.

We all had our favourite bars and sweethearts: there were, for example, the Pussycat, Ocean, Winner and Back Door. One of our favourite tactics was to head into a back street, buy a bottle of cheap Chinese wine from a store and knock it back quickly, thus getting well tanked up before we hit the bars, where beer was more expensive and the price of girlie drinks exorbitant. You had to be careful not to get too drunk or your friends would take you across the road to the Pinky Tattoo Parlour to get a nice tattoo. For each girlie drink you bought, the girl got 40 per cent, the bar kept 40 per cent, and the Mamasan 20 per cent. The Mamasan was the boss of the bar, would match the girls with customers and her word was law. The 'bar fine' to buy a girl out went to the bar but the girl could keep extra tips. Most of the girls came from poor back-grounds and were working to support their families.

Other favourite watering holes were the Godown, which had a Shandong doorman with a bulldog and a back bar with a live

Filipino band, and the Bull and Bear, which was the first Western-style pub in Hong Kong and was run by an old English harridan with a beehive hairstyle. She was a racist and disliked Chinese customers. When you brought in a local girl she would watch you like a hawk and if you laid a hand on the girl, or heaven forbid, kissed her, then you were both unceremoniously thrown out. After a heavy night out, you inevitably became hungry and there were a number of enterprising places serving early-morning greasy break-fasts to sop up the alcohol. One of these was called the Horse and Groom, which we referred to as the 'House of Doom'.

On Sundays, when not on guard duty, some of us would go to ride trial motorbikes at the Castle Peak Range track on the western side of the New Territories. We would ride with our bikes in the back of an old police Bedford lorry. It was a long journey and we would tell stories in the back and laugh as we passed the Freezing-Hot thermos flask factory in Tsuen Wan. The bike track was near the Castle Peak Firing Range used by the army so we needed to check first that no firing practice was going on. The art of trial-bike riding is to negotiate a vertiginous circuit of steep hills and gullies, putting your foot down for balance as little as possible. I was not a very skilful rider and one time I managed to jar the bike into my groin, much to the amusement of my laconic Scottish friend close behind.

'Ow, my balls!' I wailed.

'You haven't got any!' was his cheerful reply.

One of the highlights of our training was the traditional Mess Night. Resplendent in our uniforms of short white mess jackets with silver insignia and black trousers with buff stripes, we sat down to a fine dinner with plenty of beer, wine and speeches. The only problem was that you were not allowed to leave the table until after the loyal toast at the end, which was a serious issue if you had had a couple of pints before you sat down, so the old hands would have an empty bottle handy under the table. The high point of the evening was the 'Trooping of the Duck' which was our regimental mascot. The duck, dressed in his own little mess jacket walked along the tables and had to be kissed by all the females present. Afterwards there was the usual singing and jokes and much later, when I staggered upstairs, I found that my bed had been moved by some friends down to the parade ground, where I went and simply got in and fell asleep. No matter what you had been up to the night before, however, you had to be on parade bright-eyed and bushy-tailed for roll call at 7 a.m. sharp, and woe betide those who were late.

There was a very nice touch at Christmas. As we single Brits had no family in Hong Kong, there was a quaint tradition where families from the *hongs* (the old trading companies, like Jardines and Swire) volunteered to invite young inspectors to their homes for lunch on Christmas Day. I went to a beautiful apartment in the upmarket residence called Tregunter where I was treated to a delicious lunch with an expatriate family and also given a present. I have never forgotten this kind gesture. I was also invited to dinner with another senior civil servant who had been at Monkton Combe. He reassured me that I would soon settle down and get the hang of things.

Before we passed out of the training school we went on a camp in the wilds of the Sai Kung Country Park. We put up our tents in a remote paddy field and set off for long marches in the pouring rain. There were huge mosquitoes there but luckily we had plenty of incense coils to keep them at bay. One evening we went to the local village for some noodles and discovered that they had a fridge full of Tsingtao beer. One of the Chinese inspectors had never drunk beer before. After three or four bottles, he amazed us by doing a perfect handstand against the wall before rushing out and vomiting copiously. The toothless old Hakka woman who ran the store thought this was hilarious.

The time was fast approaching when we would be reporting for duty to our new posts and actually be responsible for the policing of this weird and wonderful place. I decided that I needed to do more research on exactly what the Brits were doing in Hong Kong in the first place. It appeared that the loss of the American colonies in 1776 had been substantially due to local resistance to British taxes. By the late eighteenth century, around 25 per cent of British government revenue was derived from taxes on tea. British overseas expansion subsequently moved eastwards, with India becoming the main focus, while the East India Company also carried on a lucrative China trade through Canton. By 1800, Europe had developed an insatiable appetite for Chinese products, mainly tea, silk and china (porcelain) – our grannies all had Willow Pattern tea services.

The problem was that Qing China required cash – or silver bullion – for these commodities and would not accept barter trade. Qing officials said there was nothing the foreigners could supply that China needed. Indeed, samples of the latest military and commercial technology brought to the Qing court by British envoy Lord Macartney in 1793 had all been packed away in boxes and never looked at again. This policy caused a serious balance of payments crisis for the East India Company. The problem was to find a product that the Chinese would buy and which would offset the huge cost of the goods shipped west. The answer was Indian opium, which soon balanced the budget. In 1831, $12m of China tea was imported to England and $13m of Indian opium was exported to China.

By the late 1830s the outflow of cash from China and the increasing scourge of opium addiction was becoming a serious problem for the Qing government. So they sent one of their best and brightest mandarins, Lin Zexu, governor of Hunan, to sort out matters. Lin was incorruptible and his policies were brutally effective, including the seizure and burning of 20,000 cases of British opium. However, he seriously underestimated the resolve of the British merchants. William Jardine (known to the Chinese as 'Iron-headed Rat') sailed to London and harangued the Foreign Secretary, Lord Palmerston, with tales of the affront to British trade and honour. Consequently, an expeditionary force, including sixteen men-of-war, the aptly-named iron warship, *Nemesis* and 3,000 troops from India, was despatched in the name of free trade to avenge the insult and open up the country. The Chinese proved no match for the firepower of the Royal Navy, which had been battle-hardened in the struggle against Napoleon.

After a campaign along the coast the Qing court was forced to sign the Treaty of Nanking in 1842 (the first of the so-called 'unequal treaties') in which Hong Kong was ceded in perpetuity to the British Crown and five treaty ports, including Shanghai, were opened to foreign trade. Some thought that gunboat diplomacy was striking a blow for free trade, but others, such as Gladstone, lamented that, 'A war more unjust in its origin, a war more calculated in its progress to cover this country with permanent disgrace, I do not know and have not read of.' Subsequently, the Kowloon peninsula was ceded in 1860 after the Second Opium War, started for specious reasons to improve the terms of the first treaty, over the seizure of a Chinese junk (supposedly British registered) called the *Arrow*.

The big question is why, when Hong Kong Island and Kowloon had been ceded in perpetuity, was the New Territories only leased for ninety-nine years in 1898? The year before, the Russians at Port Arthur and the Germans at Tsingtao had been granted ninety-nine-year land leases by the weak Qing government. The British military in Hong Kong pointed out that a larger hinterland was needed for the colony's defence, especially as the latest artillery had a range of 30,000 yards. Although the new Tory government in London did not want to encourage other powers to take advantage of China's weakness and were more concerned with increasing trade, they reluctantly agreed. This new acquisition was regarded as essentially temporary and the *status quo* of the Chinese villages was therefore preserved. Subsequently, it was foreseen that the lease might one day become a problem and Governors May, Lugard, Stubbs and Clementi all vehemently recommended that it should be converted to freehold. However, it never was and the rest is history.

In any case, Lord Palmerston was unhappy with the result in 1842, describing Hong Kong as 'a barren rock with scarce a house upon it'. Moreover, it did have one of the finest harbours on the China coast so, after a shaky start, the little settlement soon grew into a prosperous town and entrepôt for the China trade, which a few decades later would become known as the 'Pearl of the Orient'. The name Hong Kong (literally 'Fragrant Harbour') derives from the local incense tree (*Aquilaria sinensis*) which provided incense to the whole region. The prevailing trade winds were perfect for the China trade. Ships arrived from Europe on the summer south-westerly and returned in the winter with the north-easterly. Commercial godowns (warehouses) were quickly built, including the Jardine Matheson's headquarters at East Point, and the land leases provided the early government with revenue. Disease was endemic and life-expectancy for Europeans in the colony's early years was short. Only those with strong constitutions who had adopted a prudent lifestyle (not too many mutton chops and bottles of claret for breakfast) could expect to survive for long.

A flat and attractive site under the Peak was the subject of fierce bidding at the first land auction between different commercial and military factions. As a compromise the site was granted to the Church of England, as no one could complain of favouritism shown to God. Up to this day, St John's Cathedral is the only freehold property in town. Missionaries poured in from England and America, excited at the prospect of a bridgehead into China with its millions of souls ripe for conversion. By the end of the century, Lord Curzon was able to describe Hong Kong as 'the furthermost link in that chain of fortresses which from Spain to China girdles half the globe'.

So that was how the Crown Colony of Hong Kong came into being. How about its police force? In 1841, Hong Kong had a population of around 7,000 fishermen and farmers when Captain William Caine was appointed Chief Magistrate with a force of thirty-two constables. In 1844, a proper colonial police force was set up following the establishment of the Metropolitan Police in London a decade earlier. In 1857, the expatriate population was threatened by a plot to put arsenic in the bread. Fortunately, too much arsenic was used and those who ate it immediately vomited it up. Shortly afterwards, the Secretary for Chinese Affairs, Daniel Caldwell, who was one of the first Englishmen to marry a Chinese wife, was accused of being a brothel keeper and pirate by Attorney-General Thomas Anstey. There may have been some substance in these allegations as it was suspected that only those pirates who did not pay protection were hunted down by the Royal Navy. Governor Bowring, however, defended Caldwell saying that he 'was one of our most valuable public servants while Anstey is a chronic pest'. The initial Chinese population was made up of coolies, boatmen and other workers, which led to a fair amount of criminal activity.

During the 1850s the colony's population doubled to 80,000 due to the outbreak of the Taiping Rebellion, allegedly provoked by the colourful preaching of an American Baptist missionary, and led by Hong Xiuquan, who believed himself to be Jesus Christ's younger brother. This led to an influx of wealthy Cantonese families who went on to found local social institutions such as the Tung Wah Hospital and the Po Leung Kuk, which protected young girls. By 1865, the increasing success of Hong Kong as a mercantile centre with the best deep-water harbour in the region, protected from typhoons and having two entrances so that sailing ships could enter and leave whatever the wind direction, had caused the population to rise to 125,000. In 1880, the first local Chinese was appointed to the Legislative Council.

A few years later, Charles May, an Irishman, presided over a police force of 171 Europeans, Chinese and Indians. May, who it was alleged could neither speak the local language nor recognise Chinese faces, was also suspected of running a brothel, to which the attorney general had been a regular visitor. In 1893, he was succeeded by another Irishman, Francis May, who went on to become governor. By 1900, Hong Kong was the third port of Empire after Liverpool and London. In 1916, the population was 530,000 and by 1940 had risen to over one million. The force was decimated during the Japanese occupation and subsequently had to cope with the influx of a million refugees at the end of the civil war in China. In 1967, the Cultural Revolution spilled over the border and caused serious civil disturbances, including bombing, looting and arson attacks. The Hong Kong Police performed so well that it was given the honorific 'Royal'.

However, due to low salaries, there was increasingly widespread corruption in the police and civil service generally. The new Commissioner of Police, Charles Sutcliffe, was determined to break the power of the staff sergeants who controlled the system. In 1973, he challenged a senior officer, Chief Superintendent Peter Godber, with evidence of his disproportionate wealth. Godber, who controlled assets of over $4 million, or six times what he had earned since joining the force, then fled the colony, walking through Customs and Immigration at Kai Tak using an expired airport security pass, thus causing significant public outrage. In 1974, supported by Governor Sir Murray MacLehose, the ICAC was set up. Police salaries and conditions of service were subsequently improved and the Royal Hong Kong Police, which affectionately became known as 'Asia's Finest', matured into a highly professional force policing a very crowded, complex city. The establishment of the ICAC, moreover, helped Hong Kong over the next two decades grow into a major international financial hub.

CHAPTER THREE

Asia's Finest

AFTER PASSING OUT from the Police Training School, I was posted as a sub-unit commander to Yau Ma Tei Division. This was an area of Kowloon sandwiched between the glitzy tourist area of Tsim Sha Tsui and the busiest and most densely populated part of the colony, Mong Kok. A commercial and residential area comprising mainly shop houses, the district boasted a hospital and schools, the Jordan Road ferry pier, a typhoon shelter packed with fishing boats, the Temple Street hawker bazaar and a main thoroughfare running right through its centre, Nathan Road. The police station was a substantial colonial building with white colonnades and balconies.

Our district superintendent, a veteran of police service in Palestine and Malaya was fond of his grog, as were many police officers in those days. He frequently started his day at 8 a.m. with a couple of large bottles of San Miguel beer in the mess to 'set himself up for the day'. His second in command was a competent but intense officer nicknamed 'Crazy Knife', a stickler for discipline who would tolerate no funny business. As a sub-unit commander, my job was to take charge of one eight-hour shift of uniformed police providing beat coverage for the whole division. The day was divided into three shifts, namely 'A' shift from 8 a.m. to 4 p.m., 'B' shift from 4 p.m. to midnight and 'C' (graveyard) shift from midnight to 8 a.m.

To familiarise us with the beats, new inspectors were driven around the district for a few days in Land Rovers, to be shown the landmarks and briefed on crime hot spots and street life. The jeeps were hot and uncomfortable but had fans to cool us down a little and were equipped with radio. We were accompanied by experienced locals, and although our Cantonese was improving, it was always good to find a local junior officer who spoke good English. You could tell who did because they wore red tabs under their RHKP shoulder flashes. We were reminded about police procedures, our powers of arrest and the system of police bail. We were taught how to use beat radios and how to call for emergency assistance when needed.

There was a duty officer in the station to receive reports and handle administration and there were cells for those arrested and charged with offences, awaiting court appearances. The sub-unit consisted of one station sergeant, three sergeants and around thirty constables. Upon arrival at the station, and having donned uniform and Sam Browne belt, we drew our revolvers and six bullets from the armoury and beat radios (a recent innovation) and paraded in the square. Having allocated beat duties and discussed special instructions, the constables would march off to their beats. Summer uniform was made of comfortable green cotton whereas winter uniform was thicker dark blue wool. We looked very smart with our polished boots, pressed uniforms, leather belts and holsters and peaked caps, at the front of which was the silver badge of the Royal Hong Kong Police, which depicted the aforementioned sailing ships and possible opium traders.

Traditionally, there had been a reluctance in Hong Kong to report crime. It was considered extremely dangerous to enter any government office. Indeed, there was a famous Chinese saying, 'When alive, do not enter the Mandarin's door; when dead, do not enter the gates of Hell'. Through the good offices of the Fight Crime Committee, citizens had been encouraged to report crime and friendly neighbourhood police posts had been established all over town. Junior Police Call had also done sterling service in winning over young minds and portraying police officers as friends who were there to help and improve their quality of life.

Our job was to patrol the streets conspicuously and in force to deter crime, to warn and sometimes arrest people committing nuisances and, upon receiving reports of serious crime, to arrest the perpetrators and hand them over to the CID. Sometimes we had to give evidence in court and even prosecute cases. One of the main nuisances in a busy commercial area was illegal hawking of food, clothes and other goods, often by recently arrived immigrants who were still pouring into Hong Kong from across the border. If not constantly tackled, the situation would deteriorate and pavements and streets would become blocked. We had a special hawker control force called the Nuisance Squad, together with Urban Services Department staff, who chased hawkers around the streets, arresting those they caught and confiscating their goods and barrows. After receiving a small fine in court, these fellows would often be back on the street the next day; but we had to show willing. Our senior divisional inspector had made it very clear to us that under no circumstances were hawkers to be allowed on the main thorough-fare, Nathan Road.

I remember one illegal hawker, who spoke good English and called himself a 'merchant', coming to see me to complain about how all his cassette tapes had been confiscated by an unkempt Hawker Control Officer who looked like *Lap Sap Chung,* the 'Litter Monster' of government propaganda. He said he did not mind being arrested by proper officers like 'Ah Sir' but resented being detained by shabby youths with long hair.

Most of the licensed hawkers worked in the mile-long night bazaar in Temple Street where they sold every imaginable item from hats to handbags and clothes to cutlery. There were also areas for Chinese opera and stalls selling noodles and snake soup. There was a whole quarter devoted to music cassette tapes which made a deafening racket. However, in order to 'give face' to the inspector when he patrolled with his sergeant, they would turn down the noise as I walked past, thus providing a sort of rolling Doppler effect as one walked down the street. In those days, I was head and shoulders taller than most locals on the street, although thanks to a better diet, or maybe too many McDonald's hamburgers, Hong-kongers are generally much taller these days.

It was quite an experience to imbibe the sights, sounds and smells of Kowloon's exuberant street life. The 'wet markets' packed with every kind of meat and offal, the tanks of live fish and their freshly sliced cousins, hearts still beating on the wooden slabs; the incredible diversity of fruit and vegetable and the sharp smell of local herbs such as coriander. There were also displays in the Chinese medicine shops of exotic items such as tiger bones, rhinoceros horn, bear bile, turtle shells, dried snakes, seahorses and scorpions, human placenta, ginseng and *lingzhi* (spirit mushrooms) and the unmistakably acrid smell of brewing Chinese medicine that patients drank before eating a sweet to remove the bitter taste.

One day, having the night before been reading about Napoleon's military campaigns, I devised an ingenious plan to channel all the illegal food hawkers, including those selling the notorious *chau dao fu* or deep-fried stinking bean curd, into a narrow street where they were ambushed by hidden officers. You had to be very careful, however, that they did not attempt to flee into crowded places where their hot oil might splash innocent bystanders, because this had happened recently and a small child had suffered third-degree burns. This time, finding themselves comprehensively surrounded, a half-dozen food and clothes hawkers surrendered their carts without a struggle and were marched back to the station for booking. Much of the time, however, our patrols came up empty handed. The hawkers employed scouts with radios and knew when we left the police station and seemed to be well briefed on all of our movements.

One notorious location was the Jordan Road Ferry, where illegal fish hawkers occupied the whole pier. When they saw us coming, they would grab their fish, step onto boats moored near the pier and thumb their noses at us from a safe distance. The Napoleon in me one day decided to execute a pincer movement. When the hawkers had jumped into their boats, they were dismayed to see a Marine Police launch closing in on them and forcing them back to the pier. As we moved to arrest them, a scuffle broke out and I tried to grab a basket of fish held fast by a fat fisherwoman.

My sergeant had frequently told me to stand back and not get involved in such physical contact. He was absolutely right, as during the scuffle the fisherwoman slipped and fell with a great splash into the harbour. Her floundering movements alerted us to the fact that she could not swim. Luckily, one of the constables, having taken off his hat and revolver, dived in and dragged her out. I then became the focus of immediate hostility.

'I think we'd better leave now,' said the sergeant insistently. Back at the station, I was informed that an ugly mob had gathered, was talking angrily about police brutality and baying for my blood. Crazy Knife summoned me to his office.

'Did you push that woman into the harbour?' he enquired.

'Good Lord, no!' I said. 'We were conducting an illegal hawking operation and during the scuffle she slipped and fell.'

'Right,' he said decisively, 'We'll charge her with resisting arrest.'

Some inspectors were very hard on their constables, but I believed in encouragement wherever possible. One Friday night shift I was patrolling with my sergeant on Nathan Road, and when passing a small hotel through the window I saw what looked like a pair of police boots. Entering the hotel lobby, I discovered two constables taking a nap on a sofa. Sleeping on the job was a serious breach of duty and when roused, the two PCs were literally shaking with fear lest they lose their jobs. I told them to report to me in my office on Monday, thus giving them a very unpleasant weekend. One of the PCs was quite smart and had good potential so when they came to see me I told them I was very disappointed but was prepared to give them a chance if such behaviour was never repeated and if they performed well over the next month. They were very relieved and I was later pleased that one of them went on to become an inspector.

Another of our duties was to visit Queen Elizabeth Hospital, which was one of the largest hospitals in Kowloon. A constable was always on duty at the casualty ward in case someone came in with gunshot wounds or an axe in his head. We paid special attention to the custodial ward, which is a hospital ward with high security, including police guards, for sick prisoners, or those injured during crimes, or those on bail and awaiting a court appearance. Here one met some very colourful characters: one was an Indian 'merchant' who had been charged with 'obtaining property by deception' who gave me the same speech every time I visited.

'Sahib, this is all a big mistake!' he would say. 'I am a very respectable merchant who has been wrongly accused.' He looked like one of Ali Baba's forty thieves, with wicked eyes and a curly red beard, and I had no doubt that he was as guilty as sin.

'Yes, Ahmed,' I would say in a placatory way, 'I'm sure it will all be sorted out soon.'

As all the inmates wore striped pyjamas, the ward had the appearance of 'One Flew Over the Cuckoo's Nest'. One evening there was a pretty English girl who had been involved in some drunken fracas who sought my protection. Where possible, I did what I could to help, such as checking the facts with the officer in charge of the case. As a result of my intervention, the girl was released the next day and insisted on inviting her 'white knight' out on a date to show her gratitude. Being a police officer is not always a thankless job.

Licensing checks made a pleasant change from our more onerous duties. We would visit all the district restaurants and bars to check their restaurant and liquor licences. Doubtless in the past this had provided opportunities for fine wining and dining, but we were keen young officers who would never dream of drinking on duty. We were also required to check the licences of massage parlours, which made us extremely unpopular with the customers who sat up blinking in the bright lights and were sometimes asked to show their ID cards. Some of the massage girls also turned out to be illegal immigrants.

The worst thing that could happen was to find a dead body. The scene needed to be secured, CID and senior officers called, and lots of paperwork had to be filled out. In fact, it was not unknown for corpses to find their way from one district to another. One time, one of my constables was called to a squatter hut to investigate a bad smell. Inside was found an old street sleeper who had been dead for a few days. Although during our training we had been taken to a morgue, it was never a pleasant business. However, in this case, I was relieved to note that our duty was almost over, so we were able to hand the case over to the inspector on the next shift. It was the opposite story when some genuine villains were caught. Everybody wanted to take credit for the arrests. One time we arrested some robbers with help from Emergency Unit Kowloon West. My sergeant handcuffed them but so did Kowloon West, so we spent some time arguing over who had arrested them and whose crime figures would look better.

We also had to undertake some traffic duties. Each week we received a book of fixed penalty tickets (in Cantonese, parking tickets are called *ngau yuk gon* because they come in plastic wrappers and look like packets of dried beef). Having been on the receiving end of many parking tickets, it is a very therapeutic experience to be able to give them out yourself. We also lay in wait for motorists jumping red lights, stopped them further down the road and gave them tickets. Here our beat radios came in very useful as we could call the sergeant and tell him to stop the red Mercedes which had accelerated through the red light. Sometimes the Auxiliary Police (part-time officers who came on duty in the evenings and at weekends) helped with these duties as well as patrolling high-rise buildings.

One day, I was on 'A' shift duty when I received notice that the Chief Secretary, Sir Denys Roberts (who enjoyed the distinction of being the only colonial civil servant ever to hold the three key posts of attorney general, chief justice and chief secretary in one place) was coming to attend the opening of a new sports complex. I posted myself outside the venue and when Sir Denys stepped from his official limousine, I snapped to attention and gave him a smart salute. The great man, with his Mephistophelean eyebrows, smiled and gave me a wink. Later he married an attractive and much younger government lawyer whose nickname was 'Tits'. At one party another government lawyer exclaimed, 'Oh look, it's Tits!' The sharp reply came back, 'Lady Tits to you!'

Once a week we would have to act as Duty Officer (DO) in the Report Room. The DO was responsible for the running of the police station during a shift, logging all crime reports, supervising the armoury, gate guards and police transport, and taking charge of the safe with all its bail money and other cash which might have been seized in criminal cases. The station sergeant normally performed this role and was very nervous when young inspectors did the job, given the potential for trouble should the bail money be miscounted or misplaced. Indeed, there had been a famous case where a senior inspector who had unwisely borrowed the bail money overnight was caught out by a snap inspection.

As expatriate police inspectors we could get away with almost anything in those days. One night I was driving home from a night out on the town in my red Mini Cooper with a colleague when we came upon a police roadblock. I was driving too fast and came to a screeching halt having knocked down a few bollards. A sergeant came running towards me and I thought that attack was the best form of defence, so I jumped out holding my police warrant card and shouted in Cantonese,

'Sergeant, this road block is very poorly set up and badly lit!'

Taken aback, he looked me up and down and to give him credit he was not going to give up so easily.

'Sir, have you been drinking?' he asked.

'Of course not, sergeant!' I replied, looking him in the eye. Before he could say anything more I jumped back in the car and drove off. These days you would be immediately breathalysed, regardless of rank.

Soon after, we had a visitation from His Excellency the Governor, Sir Murray MacLehose, affectionately known as 'Jock the Sock'. He inspected the station and came up to the mess for a drink, accompanied by his smartly turned-out ADC. All officers were required to attend and the DS was visibly nervous lest any of us disgrace ourselves. Sir Murray, a formidable six foot four inches tall and the quintessential patrician colonial governor, although a diplomat by training, was indeed a great man. Among his many achievements was the commissioning of the Mass Transit Railway to solve Hong Kong's transport problems, the building of new towns in the New Territories to relieve the city's chronic overcrowding, the establishment of country parks, the introduction of representative government in the shape of District Boards and last, but not least, the setting up of the Independent Commission Against Corruption to stamp out the corruption that had traditionally blighted Hong Kong's public service. The great man sipped a gin and tonic, asked a few questions and then left.

Sir Murray made civil servants nervous. His height, superior bearing and sharp mind discouraged vague replies to questions or half-baked notions. I heard one story of an official in the Housing Department who had been called in to explain some policy and had been so discomfited by his cross-examination that upon leaving the gubernatorial office he had been violently sick.

A few months later, towards the end of October 1977, I returned to the station one morning at 7 a.m. for 'A' shift duty to be met by a white-faced inspector.

'They've all been arrested,' he declared.

'Who has?' I asked.

'Well, there's not much left of your sub-division,' he replied.

It transpired that at 4 a.m. that morning, half the police officers in this and other divisions had been arrested by the ICAC, including my station sergeant, two sergeants and seventeen constables in my sub-unit.

'It's something to do with a protection racket in the Shek Lung fruit market,' he stammered. 'The gloves are off. It's open season against the police.'

Of course, we young inspectors had no idea what was going on because we had joined after the ICAC had been set up and there was a natural disinclination on the part of the older officers to discuss the subject. In the sixties it had become normal practice in most police districts for officers to accept 'brown packets' stuffed with banknotes, which were proceeds from syndicates who were under police protection. There was a strict hierarchy of payment depending on rank. Not all officers accepted the packets. The saying was 'you could either get on the bus, watch the bus go by or get run over by the bus'. The whole system was controlled by the district and divisional staff sergeants, in both the uniformed branch and CID.

That day very little policing was done in Hong Kong. If the villains had known, they could have had a field day. We inspectors retired to the mess and drank all day. By evening there were hundreds of empty San Miguel bottles. We preferred the brown ones as the rumour was that the green ones let in too much light when stored and tasted funny. The next morning, around 2,000 disgruntled police officers marched to Police Headquarters in Arsenal Street to deliver a petition to Brian Slevin, the commissioner of police. Slevin decided to slip out of the rear entrance and head for the safety of the Hong Kong Club, and that entrance is still known as 'Traitor's Gate.' After a senior officer had accepted the petition, a hard core of mainly expatriate officers went over to ICAC Headquarters in Hutchison House and had a good punch up with ICAC staff, many of whom were former UK policemen. This affray was shown on the main evening news. Sir Murray was mortified, and faced with a police mutiny, decided a few days later to declare an amnesty. In all fairness, the police felt that they were being victimised as corruption was hardly limited to the force alone. However, it was agreed that you had to start with the police before you could move on to the rest of the government. What was important was that the message had been received loud and clear by the public service. Any more funny business and you were going down.

After life had returned to normal, I was transferred to run the district vice squad. We worked in plain clothes but carried a snub-nosed 38 Special under our shirts or in an ankle holster. I used to keep the gun in my bedroom drawer under my underpants and the bullets under the socks. Our duties were to take enforcement action against gambling, drugs trafficking and prostitution. However, our problem was that we no longer had any reliable criminal intelligence as this had all disappeared with the staff sergeants who had fled to Canada and Taiwan after the establishment of the ICAC. As a result many of our so-called tip-offs turned out to be duds. We would raid flats said to be used for drug dealing or gambling only to find that nothing illegal was going on. We had many ways of getting in, such as using the answerphone to say we were delivering food or had lost our keys. We also had the 'smart stick' of the day – an ingenious contraption with a hook that could unfasten any metal security door.

Occasionally we would find a few small packets of heroin (either white powder or the cheaper 'brown sugar') but not the hauls we had expected. A consequence of outlawing opium in Hong Kong was that it led to the mass consumption of heroin, which is frankly a more dangerous commodity. Most of the addicts took heroin using a method called 'chasing the dragon'. This meant heating up the white powder on a piece of silver foil and then inhaling the fumes, often using a straw. It was thought that the undulating patterns of smoke resembled a dragon's movement. Heroin addiction is difficult to break and tends to turn the addict into a thief or a prostitute in order to support the habit. There is a form of treatment using the less dangerous substitute, methadone, but this has limited success. The most effective, but painful, treatment is 'cold turkey'.

One day I was ahead of the squad in a squatter area which had a stream flowing through it. In a secluded spot was an old man with a white beard sitting on a rock. He looked like something out of a Chinese painting. Although I spotted a small white packet near him, he looked so peaceful and dignified that I took pity on him and kicked the packet into the stream as my squad came sweating up behind me.

'Nothing here,' I said.

Another time we were searching a high-rise building when we came upon a suspicious-looking man on the staircase of the twentieth floor. He did a runner and I chased him relentlessly down seventeen flights of stairs until I caught him on the third floor. He had ten packets of heroin on him. It felt good to catch this man but it was the big dealers that we were really after.

Then there were the illegal casinos or *daai dongs* where local punters played games for high stakes in flats or restaurants rented by the night. Gambling seems to be hard-wired into the Chinese DNA, whether horse-racing, football, *mahjong* or casino games such as *fan tan* or *pai gau*. *Fan tan* is played with an upturned bowl full of white buttons. When all the bets have been placed, the croupier lifts the bowl and uses a bamboo stick to separate the buttons into groups of four. The winning bet predicts how many buttons will be left over at the end. *Pai gau* is a game using thirty-two dominoes in which a score of nine is the winning hand.

We heard much gossip about the big casinos but could never find the real thing. One night, however, acting on a tip-off that proved correct for once (someone probably bore the operator a grudge) we found our Holy Grail. At about midnight, four of us were checking a large apartment with a lot of noise coming from inside. I sent two of the squad to the rear door and upon a signal we kicked the door in. Imagine our surprise to find the flat filled with at least fifty people.

The next thing I saw was two muscular and tattooed triad enforcers moving towards us.

I drew my pistol and shouted, *'Mo yuk!'* 'Don't move!'

The triads looked at us and decided it was not worth the trouble. We hastily called for backup and arrested the whole lot. We also seized a few hundred thousand dollars in cash.

The triads were regional criminal gangs who had existed in China since the seventeenth century and were originally formed to support the Ming dynasty against their northern Manchu enemies. Under the Qing, they became underground societies and migrated to Hong Kong with other Chinese immigrants. The most famous societies were the Sun Yee On (founded by Chiu Chow immigrants), 14K (former KMT from Canton) and the Wo Shing Wo (based in Sham Shui Po). Their regular business was drug- running, prostitution, and protection rackets. Whenever a Chinese opened up a new shop or restaurant, some dodgy guys would appear and say that it would be a pity if there was a fire or an attack but they could prevent this in return for a regular payment or percentage of profits. This was known as 'fragrant oil'.

The police had their own Triad Society Bureau which was meant to have experts on these matters and keep things under control but turf wars and street fights persisted. *Kung fu* societies and lion dance clubs were often thinly-veiled triad organisations. It was a police joke that when you saw a lorry full of lion dancers driving around beating their drums, you could charge them with multiple offences: being a member of a triad society, possession of offensive weapons, overloading and lack of vehicle insurance.

Hong Kong's laws on the subject of prostitution are complex. You have to prove that soliciting by girls is taking place on the premises whereas one-girl apartments – *yat lau, yat fung* as the locals say, 'one flat, one phoenix' – are exempt. So when the business takes place outside the bar or premises, the girls are safe unless they are caught soliciting on the street.

In the old days, brothels were regulated to provide services for soldiers and sailors and to minimise infection. These days, the most common front is a massage parlour or sauna. The quest for evidence aside, it is fairly shameful, though not unprecedented, for undercover police to be offered a sexual service, to accept it and then arrest the poor girl. However, as with hawkers, the police have to be seen to be doing their job as a deterrent to keep vice activities spiralling out of control. Many was the time late at night that the police station report room was a veritable cathouse of pouting girls who had been lifted from an unlicensed massage parlour.

When my time with the vice squad ended, and not being inclined to don a uniform again, I applied to join CID and was sent to the Detective Training School, which was in the old Aberdeen Police Station up on a hill overlooking a harbour with its community of boat people, floating restaurants and noisy putt-putting sampans. We had interesting lectures on forensic evidence, terrorism, surveillance and drugs from the Golden Triangle. One morning we jumped on a Customs launch and helped to search a Panamanian cargo ship in the harbour. God, it was hot down in the bowels of that ship and the experience gave us huge respect for the Customs officers whose job was like looking for a needle in a rice bucket.

We also brushed up on criminal law and learned how to conduct a proper criminal investigation, including compiling a murder file, which is probably the most complicated aspect of police work. However, I was subsequently posted to CID/Tsim Sha Tsui, which is the main tourist area, so the majority of my cases involved pickpockets or simple theft. We were based in the Marine Police HQ, which was a delightful colonial building on top of a hill with a popular mess called the 'Mariners' Rest'. It has since been 'renovated' by Hong Kong's richest man, lost its trees and charm, and been turned into a monument to French and Italian name-brand vulgarity.

My boss was a jovial fellow who had been a star in the recently filmed TV series, *The Hong Kong Beat*. It was not shown in Hong Kong where it was considered too close to the bone. To watch some of the episodes today is to be shocked by how politically incorrect it all seems. Officers say things like, 'Whack that suspect a few more times and he will confess!' Police may sometimes be suspected of impropriety in the commission of their difficult jobs but seldom are things stated so baldly.

One night we were called out to investigate a fight at one of Tsim Sha Tsui's most famous bars, 'Bottoms Up', which had featured in a recent James Bond movie. Run by a languid English lady, the bar boasted beautiful topless girls who sat in the middle of circular bars to serve drinks, including a stunning American black girl called Velvet. That night there was a fracas involving three or four Chinese men, some damage and smashed glasses and a few black eyes. Having got them back to the station, my boss suggested that we charge them with everything we could think of. So we charged them with assault, GBH, possession of an offensive weapon, membership of a triad society (they had tattoos) and unlawful possession (of their expensive Rolex watches). However, I'm not sure that we got all of the charges to stick. We spent all night in our office where most of the furniture seemed to have been seized in various drugs or gambling raids. In the corner was a shrine to Kwan Daai, a red-faced ancient bearded warrior who is the patron saint of Chinese soldiers and policemen.

Being in plain clothes, I could grow my hair and beard, which was a luxury not allowed in the uniformed branch. My boss often came in to my office and made snide comments about my appearance.

'Peter', he would say, 'You're a detective inspector. You are not supposed to wear a kaftan and flip-flops like a bloody hippie! What will the poor tourists think?'

My girlfriend, Lilian, an attractive Thai-Chinese medical student, and more practical than I, thought that I should display some ambition and join the private sector or the elite government Administrative Service. It was Easter and we had wangled a week's holiday on the lovely island of Lantau, which is twice the size of Hong Kong Island and then sparsely populated by farmers and fisherfolk. A number of Buddhist monasteries nestle in the hills and there is excellent walking. We had rented an idyllic little cottage in Pui O overlooking the sea, and while she revised for her medical exams I went for long treks into the mountains, armed only with a hat, stick, sandwiches and a water bottle. I discovered some remote rural communities and very nearly got eaten by packs of village dogs. The chows could be quite aggressive to strangers and it was necessary to carry a stout stick. If all else failed, you could look for a stone to throw. Actually, you didn't really need to throw one because the very act of reaching to the ground was well understood by the village dogs.

In one village, some Hakka ladies invited me to drink tea. They appeared to speak no Cantonese but the toothless old crones laughed a lot and were very friendly. Then I climbed up to a misty mountain pass which, apart from the cooing of Chinese wood pigeons and the splash of a waterfall, was uncannily quiet. I could almost feel the spirit of place and would not have been surprised if some goddess had stepped out of the rock. Upon climbing a long flight of stone steps, I discovered a deserted Chinese mansion set in a classical Chinese garden with a pond crossed by a zig-zag bridge (angled to stop spirits from crossing). I later discovered that this isolated hideaway had been built by a rich Chinese businessman. Further up the mountain, I came upon a small Buddhist monastery where to my surprise I found an American monk who was practising Tai Chi. He offered me tea and we had an interesting discussion about spiritual matters. That evening, Lilian cooked me a delicious dinner and we opened a bottle of wine.

'Peter, I think you're wasting your time in the police force,' she began, with that characteristic blend of gentle enforcement. 'I know you don't consider it to be a long-term career, and while you've had your fair share of fun, you really must consider your future. After all, you have a good degree and joining the Administrative Service would be a smart career move.'

I had to admit that she had a good point.

I was living in government quarters in Kadoorie Avenue, Kowloon and it so happened that my neighbour was the local bureau chief of *Time* magazine. He was extremely well briefed on the current political situation in Hong Kong and the knowledge he passed on served me well in the administrative grade examination and subsequent interview.

In December 1978, on a cold morning, I went to take my exam in a government school on Braemar Hill overlooking North Point. There were over a hundred Chinese there and I was the only *gwai lo*. The interview board was quite challenging and I was asked, *inter alia,* what I thought about democratic reform in Hong Kong. I replied that it would be a good thing but difficult to manage. In fact, my experience of politicians led me to believe that the introduction of adversarial politics might be a disaster, but I kept my mouth shut.

We spent Christmas in the old Tai O Police Station where my friend was the inspector. He had handsome quarters with a few bedrooms and a mess. Tai O is a fishing village on the extreme western side of Lantau Island and on a rocky headland stands an old whitewashed colonial police station looking out to sea. My friend's predecessor had been a stout rugby player who was fond of his beer. Having been posted to another district, the fishermen had taken him out for a final binge at which he had become hopelessly drunk. They had therefore found it necessary to return him to the police station in a bellicose state on a trolley in a pig basket, lest he fall off and hurt himself.

Above the police station on the top of the hill was a Royal Naval station whose job was to report on Chinese shipping entering or leaving the Pearl Delta. Today the old police station has been converted into a boutique hotel but the casual tourist may not know that the place is said to be haunted and you can still see bullet holes in the iron shutters. In 1916, a Sikh policeman accused of theft shot dead a European crown sergeant and set fire to the station. Luckily, the sergeant's wife and baby were rescued from an upper room, but the sergeant is rumoured to walk the compound, like the ghost of Hamlet's father, seeking revenge.

Having been offered a job in the Administrative Service, and shortly before I went on home leave, I visited Fan Ling to attend a passing-out parade of the Police Tactical Unit, which is the paramilitary arm of the police. Seeing me dressed outlandishly with long hair and a beard, one of the senior officers was speechless with rage after discovering that I was a police officer.

'We'll have that joker up here at PTU,' he fumed, 'and teach him a thing or two!'

Unfortunately for the old boy it was not to be: I was moving on.

CHAPTER FOUR

China

L IVING IN HONG KONG in those days, one was hardly aware of the
vast and mysterious country to the north. One of our weekend
pastimes was to drive up to the China border at Lok Ma Chau
where there was a lookout pavilion which offered a panoramic view
of the Mainland north of the border (which has now been transformed into the skyscrapers of Shenzhen) with farmers in their
paddy fields or by their fishponds and one or two Red Guards
patrolling up and down. It was a tantalising glimpse of a forbidden
land, and that lookout post was a 'must' for every tourist visiting
the colony.

China! A vast and ancient land that had fascinated Westerners for
centuries, ever since Marco Polo had returned to Venice with exotic
tales of dragons and pagodas that many regarded as tall stories. In
eighteenth century England, *chinoiserie* became the height of fashion
and stately homes all had their Chinese rooms. The three commodities that Europe craved above all were tea, silk and porcelain
and this drove the China trade right up to and beyond the Opium
Wars. Her ancient civilisation stretches back into the mists of time
with recorded history from the second millennium BC, and she is
credited with the invention of gunpowder, paper, printing and the
compass, among other things. While Britain was still in the Dark
Ages, China had a sophisticated mercantile economy, art and
literature, astronomy, medicine and refined cuisine.

Around the time of the English Civil War, the ruling Ming were
defeated by Manchurian invaders who established a new dynasty,

the Qing. Two hundred years later, the Qing Empire had become corrupt, supremely arrogant and inward-looking. Lord Macartney, whose 1793 embassy to the court of Emperor Qianlong had been spurned, partly by his refusal to *kowtow*, wrote that, 'The empire of China is like an old, crazy man-of-war that has been kept afloat for the past 150 years to overawe neighbours by her bulk and appearance.' It was their treatment as tribute-bearing barbarians that provoked the foreign powers, especially the British, who since 1815 had become the pre-eminent power in Europe. Incidentally, Macartney's embassy was not entirely a waste of time as one of the ships accompanying him, HMS *Jackall*, completed the first survey of Hong Kong's harbour, which became a major factor in the choice of a suitable anchorage during the First Opium War. This clash of cultures between a profoundly conservative, hide-bound empire that had spent several hundred years in splendid isolation and the foremost military and industrial power of the day forced China to open herself to international trade but also fatally weakened the ruling dynasty.

A long period of decline in Chinese power and prestige followed. The loss of Hong Kong and the treaty ports and subsequent looting and burning of the summer palace in the cynically manufactured Second Opium War were grave affronts to national pride, and accentuated the fault lines between the Manchu rulers and their Han Chinese subjects. Indeed, the Taiping, Nien and Hui rebellions of the mid-nineteenth century, in which 50 million perished, were mainly due to the loss of authority and confidence of the ruling Qing following the humiliation of the Opium Wars. The decline in imperial prestige was partly mitigated by the efforts of Prince Gong, Zeng Guofan and Li Hong-zhang, a senior mandarin who enlisted the help of 'China' Gordon to defeat the Taiping and then attempted to play the foreign 'barbarians' off against each other. Squeezed between the Western powers, Russia and Japan, Li attempted to reform and modernise the government and army but was opposed by the traditionalists, led by the Empress Dowager. At the same time, Sir Robert Hart managed to set up and run the Imperial Maritime Customs Service, which more or less provided sufficient revenue to run the Qing government in its shaky last few decades.

In 1894, Japan defeated the Chinese fleet on the Yalu River, the Empress Dowager having stolen the money intended to modernise China's navy in order to rebuild the Summer Palace. Japan then gobbled up Korea and Taiwan, and Russia occupied large parts of Manchuria. This led to further land grabs by both the British (New Territories) and the French (Indochina). The Boxer Rebellion of 1901 released a great outburst of anti-foreign and anti-missionary feeling that was only put down with difficulty. Supported by the Empress Dowager, the Boxers, who believed they had magical powers, and Imperial troops besieged the foreign community in Beijing's Legation Quarter. The siege lasted fifty-five days and was only relieved by the Eight-Nation Alliance (Britain, France, Russia, us, Germany, Italy, Japan and Austria) who sent 20,000 troops to lift the siege. The Empress Dowager then fled to Xian. The Alliance made China pay huge war reparations of 450 million taels of silver. The us used their share to found Tsinghua University and the British, Hong Kong University. So some good did come out of the Boxer Rebellion.

Following the fall of the Qing and declaration of the Republic of China in 1912, there followed a period of intense instability. The founding father of the Republic and Nationalist Party (KMT), Sun Yat-sen, had cited Hong Kong as his inspiration for good government in China. Unfortunately, he was persuaded unwisely to step down as president after just six weeks due to the mistaken belief that General Yuan Shi-kai stood a better chance of unifying the country. Yuan then tried to proclaim himself emperor and upon his death in 1916 feuding warlords were quick to fill the power vacuum. A flawed hero, Sun died prematurely of liver cancer in 1925 and his place was taken by his protégé Chiang Kai-shek.

A few years later, most of China was under the control of the KMT or allied warlords, except Manchuria under Marshal Zhang and Jianxi under Mao and the communists. The Chinese Communist Party (CCP) had been founded in Shanghai in 1921 with Soviet support. Chiang then decided to establish a new capital in Nanking, which was regarded as a safer location. Now an intense struggle developed between the KMT and the communists and many innocent Chinese were caught in the middle. In 1927, with the support of the Green Gang, Chiang launched an all-out attack on labour unions and communists in Shanghai and throughout China. He is reported to have said that the Japanese were China's 'skin disease' while the communists were China's 'heart disease'. If Chiang Kai-shek had been able to absorb the leftists, and had taken concrete steps to fight the corruption which characterised KMT government, China could have been saved much suffering.

Worse was to come. Japan, which had reformed and Westernised itself during the Meiji Restoration, was actively trying to expand its empire, looking hungrily at Chinese territory, especially Manchuria. Distracted by the First World War, the European powers allowed Japan to increase its influence in east Asia. At the Treaty of Versailles in 1919, in return for its naval assistance, Japan had been given the old German concession of Tsingtao. In 1932, they established themselves in Manchuria and set up the last Qing emperor, Pu Yi, as a puppet king. In 1937, they embarked on a series of military adventures all over eastern China. During the Second World War, Japan occupied huge chunks of China and at the war's end around two million Japanese soldiers needed to be repatriated.

Ordinary Chinese endured terrible hardships with great loss of life, especially in Nanjing. Chiang Kai-shek, whom FDR called 'Cash my Cheque' and General (Vinegar Joe) Stillwell nicknamed 'Peanut', was ineffectual in fighting the enemy as he seemed to be keeping his powder dry to eliminate the communists once the allies had defeated the Japanese. His wife, Madam Soong Mei-ling, had tried to make FDR promise to force the British to give Hong Kong back to China and when an American official reproved her for allowing lepers to roam the streets, she allegedly replied that 'China had a great culture when your ancestors were living in trees and painting themselves blue'. Unfortunately for Peanut his corrupt administration and incompetent military forces were about to lose out to the highly disciplined communists, so having stolen all China's gold and most of its priceless works of art, he embarked for Taiwan.

During the Long March and subsequent fighting, Mao's communist army had been able to win the confidence of Chinese peasants by displaying moral values that were conspicuously lacking in the KMT In October 1949, in Tiananmen Square, Mao proclaimed that 'the Chinese people have stood up'. Yet for all his achievements in unifying the country at last, and in later recognising the essentially sinister nature of Russian friendship, the dawn of a New China was swiftly overshadowed by misguided policies flowing from his concept of non-stop revolution. The Great Leap Forward led to countless millions of people starving to death due to poor planning and confused priorities. Mao's apologists called this a necessary evil while others saw it as a humanitarian disaster of the worst order.

Then, just as things were starting to stabilise, along came the Cultural Revolution, where extreme leftist ideology propagated by the Gang of Four, with Mao's connivance, led to chaos all over the country, the destruction of vast amounts of old buildings and cultural objects and the mass exile of people suspected of 'reactionary' background to the countryside for re-education through labour. Although the PLA was never infiltrated, Mao decided in 1968 to disband the Red Guards before they destroyed the CCP. The party's official view is that Mao was 70 per cent right and 30 per cent wrong. Others say that Deng's reforms could not have succeeded without the purging of the Great Leap Forward and the Cultural Revolution.

It was against this backdrop of intense suffering that hundreds of thousands of refugees poured into Hong Kong, which was perceived as a relative haven of peace and security. Most of them had a deep fear of communism and a kind of love/hate relationship with the colonial British who ruled Hong Kong. Squatter settlements blossomed on the hillsides and the British authorities had little choice but to accept them, for humanitarian reasons and also because Hong Kong had become a manufacturing centre in the sixties and its factories needed manpower. For many of the newcomers, Hong Kong was also a stepping-stone to emigration abroad, if they could afford it.

However, China was about to undergo a remarkable transformation. Following the downfall of the Gang of Four led by Mao's ex-film star wife, Jiang Qing, a major influence behind the Cultural Revolution, Deng Xiaoping had by the late seventies consolidated his hold on power and was determined to put an end to leftist lunacy in China. To the profound shock of the party, Deng famously said: 'It is glorious to get rich', and:'It doesn't matter if the cat is black or white as long as it catches mice'. This supreme pragmatist was largely instrumental in reversing centuries of isolation and economic decline. He emphasised that 'poverty is not socialism' and favoured modernisation through foreign technology and expertise.

Visiting America in 1979, Deng thrilled the world by donning a cowboy hat in Texas and enjoying not one but two landings in a space shuttle simulator. In 1980, he unveiled his first major economic experiment, the Shenzhen Special Economic Zone, north of Hong Kong. It should be noted, however, that some Chinese idealists say that this was the moment when the essence of the communist dream was traded for a descent into ugly capitalism. The fact that China, some thirty years later, was to become the second largest economy in the world, having grown at a steady 10 per cent per year, is largely due to his vision. Sadly, Deng never managed to visit Hong Kong. He always said he would come when China had regained sovereignty but he died a few months too early.

It is interesting to reflect on maps. When I was a boy growing up in England we used the Mercator projection (suitably shaded in imperial pink) which showed Great Britain, although physically small, to be in the centre of the world with the Americas to the west and Asia to the east. When I first visited China, I was surprised to see their map projection showing the Middle Kingdom firmly in the centre of the world with Europe and Africa to the west and the Americas to the east. These days the Chinese projection perhaps more accurately reflects geopolitical reality.

I have always been fascinated by Chinese history and philosophy. At Oxford it was fashionable to read the *I-Ching* (Book of Changes) and Lao Tze's *Tao Te Ching*. It was clear that the three traditional philosophies of China: Taoism, Confucianism and Buddhism, were profoundly interconnected. Confucianism is traditionally concerned with moral and social values and has recently been revived, perhaps unsuitably, as the intellectual face of modern China. There are now over 300 Confucian Institutes worldwide. Taoism is equally ancient, and embraces profound philosophical concepts, traditions of immortality and longevity, the martial arts, herbal medicine and *fung shui*.

Buddhism was introduced from India during the Han dynasty in the first century AD where it was strongly influenced by Taoism. Indeed, the Sanskrit sutras were translated into Chinese using mainly Taoist vocabulary. Given the similarities between the two philosophies, including meditation and breath control, Buddhism at that time was seen as a form of Taoism. Both philosophies share insight into the concept of 'emptiness', that being is the product of non-being: 'It is in the space between the spokes that that usefulness of the wheel depends' (*Tao Te Ching*.) Although Taoism remained the official religion of the Tang and Sung dynasties, Buddhism had become very influential by the ninth century, especially the Chan (Zen) sect. Tang dynasty pilgrims managed to collect a treasure-trove of knowledge from India, where Buddhism was in sharp decline, and transmit it to China. They also passed on this learning to Japanese monks who returned home to promote a cultural transformation in their own country. Buddhism suffered a great suppression in 845 when over 4,000 temples were destroyed. Apart from Taoist rivalry, it was felt that monastic Buddhism did not contribute to the livelihood of the empire in terms of providing soldiers and farmers, and there was also concern about the ultimate loyalty of monks to the emperor. During the Ching dynasty, Taoism was unofficially dropped as the state religion in favour of Tibetan Buddhism.

Christianity was introduced into China in the seventh century but was also repressed. It was the Jesuits who revived it in the seventeenth century while introducing new ideas in science and education. Two hundred years later, the Christian Taipings almost overthrew the Qing dynasty. However, Christianity was seen as a form of colonialism, especially after the Opium Wars, and was the object of violent attacks by the Boxers, among others. It is interesting to note that two significant Chinese figures of the twentieth century, Sun Yat-sen and Chiang Kai-shek, were both Christian converts.

When Mao established the New China in 1949, all religion was banned as the Communist Party was officially atheist. During the Cultural Revolution there was terrible destruction of religious sites throughout China. Most of Tibet's monasteries were destroyed by artillery (except the Potala which was spared on the orders of Zhou En-lai) and its most holy site, the Jokhang Temple, was turned into a pig slaughterhouse. However, China's 1978 constitution guaranteed freedom of religion, and subsequently many Buddhist and Taoist temples were rebuilt. Chinese intellectuals have once again become interested in Confucianism (even though Confucius's grave had been razed by Red Guards in 1967) and in 2006, China hosted the World Buddhist Conference. It is estimated that over 300 million Chinese citizens now practise some form of religious belief.

Eager to see this ancient and mysterious land, Lilian and I visited Mainland China for the first time in 1978. The only senior Hong Kong official to visit the People's Republic since its foundation in 1949 had, in 1973, been required to go via London and I needed to apply for special permission to make this trip. It had been less than two years since the death of Chairman Mao and China was still a most unusual place. Everyone wore blue or green Mao jackets, most people still worked on the land and there were huge agricultural communes. What few vehicles were on the road belched strange-smelling fumes. People were cheerful and extremely polite. The communist dream was still alive. Folk looked after each other and crime was unheard of. If you left an old toothbrush in a hotel bathroom, it would be returned to you wrapped in paper. As there was little industry there was no pollution.

We took the train to Lo Wu and walked over the old railway bridge which was the border. On the other side was a red flag, and a PLA soldier in a green cap with a red star stood under a large sign which proclaimed LONG LIVE THE PEOPLE'S REPUBLIC OF CHINA! We boarded a train to Canton and passed through pristine countryside with thousands of peasant farmers working in the fields. These were scenes almost unchanged since the Qing dynasty. Our hotel, the White Swan, was on Shamian Island where the original foreign factories had stood before the Opium Wars. We enjoyed a traditional Chinese banquet with lots of beer before being whisked off to the Sun Yat Sen Theatre for a splendid concert. We were entertained for over two hours by Chinese singers, musicians, acrobats, magicians and jugglers. Those in the front rows could also order snacks and beer to drink during the show, which was highly appreciated and seemed rather Shakespearian.

The next day, we visited a huge commune where cheerful farmers were working the fields. Deng had recently introduced agricultural reforms, which encouraged families to cultivate private plots in their free time and to sell the extra produce. This type of economic incentive showed a profound understanding of human nature and was probably why these farmers seemed so cheerful. I could almost see them marching off to the fields in the morning singing, '*Hey ho! Hey ho! It's off to work we go!*' like the Disney dwarfs. We also visited the commune's primary school, where rows of red-faced young children in Mao jackets and caps sat learning their lessons. As we entered the classroom, all the children stood up and intoned the greeting '*Ni hao, ni hao!*' with such piping voices that it left a strong impression. The following morning, we left China thinking what truly enormous potential the country had.

It is never wise to underestimate China. In late 1978, when Deng was visiting Singapore, Lee Kuan Yew remarked that China would recover from the Cultural Revolution and get ahead because his people were the descendants of landless peasants from Fujian and Guangdong, whereas China had the progeny of scholars, mandarins and literati. At the turn of the century, a prominent Hong Kong financier, Sir Paul Chater, made a similar observation: that although late Qing China appeared defeated and humiliated, 'that Empire is too intrinsically strong, too full of resources, too patient and persevering ever to remain for any length of time in her present condition'. How right both men were to be proved.

Having tasted the exotic flavour of China, I felt compelled to return a number of times in the eighties. My next trip was to Shanghai to attend the China Coast Ball held in the old Peace Hotel on the Bund. This was probably the first such white-tie event to be held in Shanghai (or anywhere in China) since before the war. The famous colonial buildings on the Bund were unchanged with the Peace Hotel on one side and the old Hongkong and Shanghai Bank on the other. Many of these former banks and offices were occupied by the Shanghai People's Government. The Peace Hotel (former China Hotel) was its old art-deco self and the famous jazz band was once again in residence, although the musicians were noticeably older. The hotel boasted a number of pre-war suites that had been extravagantly refurbished and one of my friends was staying in the India Suite, which looked like a miniature version of the Taj Mahal.

The ball itself was an over-the-top event that could only have been organised by Hong Kong people. Starting with a champagne reception, the over-dressed guests were surprised to find some tall and attractive local girls, who described themselves as models, but were probably call-girls slipped in for the benefit of single men. Shanghai had always led the way in the old China and it appeared also to be doing so in the new. A sit-down banquet ensued, followed by much vigorous dancing to the hotel jazz band, who were clearly as amazed as anyone else to see the capitalists at play again after a pause of around thirty years. Local eyes also popped when an exuberant Australian drag act, the Crystal Queens, took to the stage. The band played all night and as dawn broke, the hard core of party guests walked out on to the Bund still dressed in their white tie and tails. I called my sleeping friends to see if they wanted to join us but was given short shrift. I will never forget the look on the faces of the early morning walkers as they took in these strange creatures from another planet. Nor could I resist doing some Tai Chi for the benefit of the locals, although my frock coat was a tad restrictive.

A few years later we went to Tibet. One of our friends was writing a book called *Stone Routes* and had spent some time on the Roof of the World since its opening to foreigners in 1984. Incidentally, that book is still not finished. From Chengdu we flew to Lhasa over the three mighty rivers, the Yangtze, Mekong and Salween rivers, which flow down from the Himalayas. The view of those mighty cascades cutting down from the snow mountains into the jungles of south Asia was awesome. There were then only two hotels in Lhasa, the Holiday Inn and the Yak and Yeti, but we were booked into the former. I remember making the mistake of running up the stairs, which is not a good idea when you have just arrived at an altitude of 4,000 metres. Our friend had also asked us to bring all sorts of equipment but we had mainly concentrated on spirits and wine. We also discovered that drinking too much alcohol at that altitude can be a mistake.

In those days, there were few tourists and Lhasa was still quintessentially Tibetan as wholesale Sinification and Han immigration had not yet started. I was starting to become interested in Tibetan Buddhism and so there was much to see, starting with the Potala Palace and its incredible collection of images, mandalas and thankas. We visited the Jokhang Temple, the holiest in Tibet, where the statue of Sakyamuni Buddha brought by (Tang) Princess Wencheng for King Songtsan Gampo in 641 is displayed. It was here that I tried my first cup of yak butter tea and surprisingly quite liked it. Outside there were many Tibetans performing full prostrations around the Barkhor Square. Tibetan men look like cowboys with Stetson hats, in spite of their long hair and turquoise earrings, and the women wear colourful aprons and jewellery. Both have red cheeks due to the weather and high altitude.

The next day we visited the great Gelugpa monasteries of Sera, Ganden and Drepung which were being rebuilt following their destruction in the Cultural Revolution. We were welcomed by a high lama at Sera and 'bonked' on the head with a sacred sutra, which is a traditional blessing. Everywhere we went we were asked for pictures of the Dalai Lama. Later, we boarded a Land Cruiser and drove east to the first and most famous monastery in Tibet, Samye, founded by Padmasambava. In order to reach it, you need to cross the Brahmaputra River and navigate its many sandbanks. We spent the night at Samye, which is an architectural mixture of Tibetan, Indian and Chinese styles, and in the morning toured its hallowed grounds and saw the ancient inscription raised by King

Trisong Detsen, who promised to protect and sponsor Buddhism in Tibet. There is also a celebrated portrait of Padmasambava from the seventh century called 'Looks Like Me', because that is what the great guru said when it was shown to him. In 795, Samye was the scene of a great debate between the Indian 'gradual' enlightenment school and the Chinese 'sudden' enlightenment school, which the Indians won, setting the future tone of Tibetan Buddhism. The message was that there was no shortcut to liberation, which could only be achieved after extensive practice and meditation.

Nearby is the ancient fortress of Yungbulakang, the burial mounds of the early kings and a sacred mountain that we climbed. Then we drove hundreds of kilometres southeast towards Bhutan to visit the magical turquoise-coloured Lake Yamdrok surrounded by snow clad peaks, which was a stunning sight. Our friend encouraged us to throw a valuable personal possession into the lake for good luck. I don't think I have ever been in a more photogenic country and must have taken thousands of photos. On our way home we stayed another night in Chengdu at the Jinjiang Hotel and enjoyed a delicious Chinese banquet, improved by the fact that we had not found much good food in Tibet.

On one of my mother's visits to Hong Kong in the mid-eighties, she said that she wanted to visit the beautiful landscape of picturesque hills and river she had seen in a magazine. I racked my brain to understand what she meant before I realised she was talking about Kweilin in Guangxi, where the Li River winds its way through sculpted limestone hillocks, forming a landscape that Westerners consider to be quintessentially Chinese. At that time, Dragonair had started to fly to many destinations in China so we jumped on a flight and spent a few days in Kweilin. On the first evening we visited the famous Reed Flute Cave which is a fantasy of coloured stalagmites and stalactites and the next day cruised down the Li River. Apart from the stunning scenery, my mother was most impressed by the local fishermen who trained cormorants attached to ropes to catch fish, although she thought it rather unfair that the birds were not allowed to eat any. She also spent hours in the China Crafts shop choosing carved horses and Chinese paintings of landscapes and tigers. She loved the Chinese food we ate but I tried to keep it simple and to avoid the various endangered species on the menu, such as sun bear, slow loris or golden takin.

Returning to Hong Kong, I reflected on the character of the Chinese, both from what I had seen in China and my experience in the territory. Actually, the British and the Chinese have a lot in common. They are both products of old cultures and tend to be convinced of their own superiority. They are generally hard-working and self-reliant and the notion of social welfare is essentially alien to the Chinese. In Britain the welfare state has bred a sense of entitlement and dependency unrelated to the concept of enterprise and hard work, and is now being rolled back. Both races place great importance on good manners and public decorum. Both have a basic decency, perhaps inculcated respectively by Confucian ethics and Christian morality. Both like horse racing. Both have high respect for education and good government and Hong Kong's historical success was largely due to a productive mixture of efficient British administration and Chinese entrepreneurial flair.

The Chinese are generally a calm and level-headed race. You need only travel on Hong Kong's Mass Transit Railway at rush hour to experience their unflappable self-discipline. Anywhere else in the world (except Japan) and certainly in Europe and America such extreme overcrowding would lead very quickly to disorder and violence. Also, foreigners comment on how secure and safe they feel in Hong Kong compared to most cities overseas. It would be unthinkable to let young children travel by themselves on public transport in most European cities, nor would people elsewhere walk with unconcern in inner city areas late at night, both of which are the norm in Hong Kong. Notwithstanding the refugee origin of many of its inhabitants, one is aware of an unbroken tradition of several millennia of Chinese civilisation.

I wondered how as an Englishman I was being modified by my Chinese experience. Maybe I was harder working (the English are very fond of their leisure while the Chinese work all hours). Maybe I was more direct (English are shy of asking how much something costs or how much someone earns) and perhaps I was gradually losing my Victorian moral squint and hypocrisy.

CHAPTER FIVE

Her Majesty's Overseas Civil Service

I DECIDED TO TAKE the long way home. I say 'home' because at that time the Orient was still fairly new to me and absence does make the heart grow fonder. I was dreaming of the English countryside and some good country pubs. It was time for some intensive tourism. I went to Hawaii and San Francisco with side trips to Los Angeles, Las Vegas and the Grand Canyon before flying to New York to see the Statue of Liberty and the Empire State Building. There are really only two proper cities in the US, one on each coast, and the rest is Middle America. The last leg took me over to London. Boarding the train to Bath, I reflected on how small, provincial and run-down England looked, compared to the breathtaking sights of Asia and America. However, after a few beers in the train bar and some views of the rolling green countryside as we approached the West Country, things started to look up.

It was delightful to see my mother, and my friends did not seem to have changed at all, although I felt twenty years older having spent three years doing a serious job on the other side of the world. They took me down to the pub and started to call me 'Flashman'.

'You old rogue,' one of them said, 'Up to no good and skulduggery in Hong Kong, probably chasing the girls and caught with your pants down!'

I protested that I was serving Queen and country at great risk to my health and safety and that it was a hell of a job, but someone had to do it.

Others, who had never been further than Calais, said I was full of the proverbial and would I like another pint?

Our next-door neighbour then was a retired naval officer. He plied me with gin as he imbibed my Hong Kong stories avidly. As I left, he looked at me with tears in his eyes. 'Keep the flag flying, young man!' he said. The British Empire had only been gone for twenty or thirty years but already there was great nostalgia among the armed forces and others who had served overseas for a world that had almost disappeared. I suppose it is because Britain is physically so small that generation after generation of Brits over the last few hundred years have jumped at the opportunity to go abroad and settle in the wide open spaces of America, Asia and Africa, and here I was in the last chapter of that huge adventure!

These days it is fashionable to talk about the empire only in terms of exploitation, and there was certainly plenty of that. However, there were also countless high-minded public servants who helped to establish law and fair administration, infrastructure, education, medicine and science in the countries they served, while up until the twentieth century, those same people suffered and died prematurely of dysentery, malaria, cholera and typhoid. Today as you travel the developing world, observing tribalism and widespread political corruption, it is hard to say that people are significantly better off now than they were sixty years ago. When I voiced these sentiments to my friends, they smiled and called me 'Colonel Blimp', but I had seen it and I believed it. At the end of the day, the British bowed to the inevitable and in most cases beat a graceful retreat, unlike the French, who tried to hang on in Indochina and Algeria, with disastrous consequences.

Having lived in Hong Kong, I understood more about the Chinese restaurants in the UK. From the sixties onwards, when agriculture was in decline in the New Territories, rural residents had flocked to the UK and been assisted by the government with their air fares. Traditionally, rural Chinese had also worked in the navy and as stewards on ocean liners. In 1978, there were around 150,000 Chinese in Britain. Their restaurants had sprung up in many towns and the local Chinese 'takeaway' was already displacing the traditional fish and chip shop. There was a fair amount of racial prejudice and people were still influenced by the archetype of Fu Manchu, the sinister operator of opium dens who lured white women to a fate worse than death. Now, when I entered a 'Chinese' I would immediately ask the family in Cantonese where they came from. Most were from the New Territories: Tai Po or Sai Kung. As soon as they realised I was from Hong Kong, they would become animated.

'Ah Sir, you not enjoy our regular food. English people no idea about Chinese food! They just eat *chop suey* and things like that. Come back tomorrow and we give you some real food!'

The use of the expression 'Ah Sir' reminded me of the fact that I was now a colonial officer.

The Chinese immigrants to the UK were model citizens. Hard working, law-abiding and self-sufficient, even though most came from modest backgrounds, they built up successful businesses, bought property and sent their children to the best schools. Their only failing was a weakness for gambling so large amounts of hard-earned money would often change hands at private gambling dens in the early hours. Yet, by virtue of the British Nationality Act 1981, Hong Kong Chinese were denied full British passports, while millions were handed to immigrants from the subcontinent. Maybe that reflected political reality, especially as Hong Kong was last on the de-colonisation list, but certainly more significant Chinese immigration would have boosted Britain's GDP.

After a few agreeable weeks in the green and pleasant land visiting family and friends and enjoying country pubs – one of the great joys of returning to the UK – I boarded a flight to Bangkok. My plan for the rest of my leave was to visit some Buddhist temples and take the train up to Chiang Mai from where I could explore the Golden Triangle. In Bangkok, I visited the Grand Palace, Wat Po, the Emerald Buddha and enjoyed some rather colourful night-life. The beers were ice cold and every gyrating bar girl seemed to be dancing to either Fleetwood Mac's *Rumours* or the Bee Gee's *Saturday Night Fever.* The girls were sweet and tender and had a lovely way of pronouncing my name, 'Be-teer'. One night I went to watch the Thai boxing at a big public stadium where they sat me in a private box. The Buddhist faith is so fundamental to the

Thais that it permeates everything, including boxing. The fighters were all very young but had great respect for their trainers. They would prance into the ring, then stop to pray for a while before the bout began. Throughout the combat, rough as it was, they showed a sporting and friendly attitude to their opponents.

I continued north, to the ruins of Ayutthaya and Sukothai, and the delights of Chiang Mai and the Doi Suthep. On my way down from the famous temple, my motorbike broke down. I was sitting by the side of the road considering what to do next when a truck filled with good-looking sixth-form schoolgirls screeched to a halt.

'You need help?' asked one tall beauty with flashing white teeth.

Before I could reply, a few strong girls had jumped down and lifted both the bike and a startled Peter onto the truck. I sat down and smiled at the giggling girls, not quite believing that this could really be happening. Maybe it was good *karma* from making an offering at the temple? As it turned out, it was Valentine's Day, so upon arrival at the town I invited all the girls for dinner. We ate and drank our fill while two of the prettier girls competed for their 'English Boy'!

From Fang, in the northwest, my guide took me up through poppy fields to a remote Aka village. As we entered the village we met a group of smiling children dressed in multi-coloured, hill-tribe outfits. One of the young girls had a baby strapped to her back in a papoose. They led us to the headman's house, made of wood and thatch, with pigs and chickens happily rooting below and a ladder to the upper floors where the family lived. The old man spoke a Chinese dialect and had served in a KMT army that had settled there at the end of the war.

After an early dinner, his daughter prepared some opium pipes for us and I considered it rude to refuse, especially as this was the very substance that had led to the British acquiring Hong Kong. The guide asked if I had smoked before and I said no. He said I must not smoke more than six pipes or I would be sick. In the event, I smoked around twelve pipes with the old man, who spoke of his wartime experiences. Over the next few hours I experienced the most incredible waking dreams, peopled by the weirdest, most bizarre images imaginable. Think Hieronymus Bosch meets

Fellini's *Satyricon,* or Coleridge's *Kublai Khan.* It was not at all frightening, just totally captivating and it occurred to me that every single image we have ever seen is stored in our brain and that the mind is capable of scrambling them and putting them together again in a jigsaw of the strangest combinations.

Of course, my guide had been right. In the morning I got up and vomited off the balcony. For a second I was embarrassed, thinking I had done something rude, but within seconds the pigs and chickens had gobbled it up. Those animals must have had an interesting day! Far from feeling addicted, I thought that that was probably enough opium for one lifetime. Then, in that moment of clarity, it occurred to me that it really was about time for me to get back to Hong Kong and report for duty.

Arriving back in early 1979, I reported to the Administrative Service Division of the Government Secretariat in Lower Albert Road. Hong Kong's Administrative Service had started in 1861 with the selection of three 'cadets' by competitive examination. Although China had been conducting examinations for its officials for over a thousand years, these were only introduced by the British government in 1855 in response to the disasters of the Crimean War. Up until 1900, only another eighteen cadets were appointed. It took a further seventy years before a unified Colonial Administrative Service was introduced in 1932, excluding India, which did not come under the jurisdiction of the Colonial Office. Administrative officers (AOs) continued to be recruited for the 'Eastern Colonies', which comprised Hong Kong, Malaya and Ceylon up until the outbreak of war and then continued from 1950 to 1984. Of course, the Eastern Colonies were relatively rich compared to their counterparts in Africa and the Pacific. The first local Chinese AO was appointed in 1946 but with increasing frequency from the 1960s onwards.

Following Macmillan's 'Wind of Change' speech in 1960, global decolonisation speeded up and in the seventies quite a few mid-career officers from Africa and the Pacific, known as colonial 're-treads', were appointed as AOs. Up until then the local:expat mix had been around 50:50 but by the time I joined the target recruitment level was 2:1. Government service had never been a popular career choice for Hongkongers, but after the introduction of a nine-month training course for local officers at Oxford University in 1973, recruitment of local AOs shot up. From 1985, no further expatriate officers were recruited.

My first post as an AO was Assistant District Officer (Development) Tuen Mun, which was then a remote area on the western side of the New Territories. First mentioned in Tang dynasty reports, Tuen Mun ('Fortress Gate') sported a garrison which guarded the mouth of the Pearl River, and its harbour was the first port of call for ships travelling from Canton to Southeast Asia. In the early sixteenth century, it had been occupied briefly by the Portuguese before they withdrew to Macau. Overlooked by the towering Castle Peak (known as Green Mountain in Chinese) at the foot of which lay both a famous Buddhist temple and the colony's principal mental hospital, the sleepy area of farms and fishing villages had been selected as the site for a 'new town' with a design population of 500,000. This required extensive site formation and the construction of a multitude of urban facilities, such as roads, public housing, schools, hospitals, markets, parks, police and fire stations. The main concept of the new towns was that they should be self-contained so we also included industrial areas to provide employment. However, the established patterns of employment throughout the territory couldn't be changed quickly and most new residents of Tuen Mun continued therefore to commute to work in other districts.

My job was to facilitate development of the new town by helping to clear land and coordinate building works. This involved difficult negotiations with those occupying the land, complex compensation matters and rehousing arrangements. Another of our roles was to act as secretary to various government committees, taking concise notes summarising decisions and action to be taken and circulating to all parties concerned. In those days we used to dictate minutes and reports to our long-suffering secretaries who would take it down in shorthand and then type up a draft for our correction. My boss, the district officer, was known to locals as *Lei Man Foo* or *Foo*

Mo Gwoon, meaning 'Father-Mother Official', and he dealt with many different things, including land matters. We had all read *Myself a Mandarin* by Austin Coates about a district officer and special magistrate in the New Territories of the 1950s with its amusing stories about rural life and Chinese law and customs.

Inside our office we had a land registry with all the land deeds and titles. The New Territories had been surveyed at the turn of the century by staff brought over from India and you could still see Urdu markings on the land documents. The British had recorded details of land ownership and then leased the land back to the owners. As it happened, the ratio of agricultural land to building land was around 5:2 so this became the magic formula for the surrender of agricultural land in return for promissory notes, called Letters B, and the grant of building land in the New Towns upon payment of the difference in land value. The New Territories coming under British rule at the end of the nineteenth century had caused minimal upheaval as one set of foreign officials (Manchu magistrates) had merely been replaced by another (British DOs).

What struck me forcibly upon arrival in Tuen Mun was the difference in status and respect given to an administrative officer compared to a police inspector, reflecting perhaps our increased authority and future potential. At my lavish welcome banquet, I received over-the-top 'face' and hospitality from the District Board and Rural Committee. I was informed that some of the rural elders had been gangsters in the past but were now 'respectable'. However, having served in the police and so seen the reality of life in Hong Kong's slums and on the streets, I vowed not to let my new status go to my head. At least, I tried to remain objective although sometimes it was difficult not to succumb to the flattery of rural committee members who would try to convince you that you were the brightest of the bunch or spoke the best Cantonese.

Life was not all easy. One particularly difficult clearance involved an area called Mouse Island, which was home to a lucrative fresh fish trade. Although it was government land (as opposed to private land which needed to be resumed by statutory means) we had to establish the status of every structure. If it had a number painted in red then it was included in the Squatter Control Survey and the occupant's family was therefore eligible for public housing. If they had trees or cultivated vegetables then they could be compensated. Needless to say, before a scheduled clearance, new huts sprang up everywhere, complete with red markings, not to mention hundreds of trees and plants and other items attracting compensation. We normally paid up, except in cases of outrageous deception.

Then there was *fung shui* (wind and water), the ancient Chinese science of geomancy, dating back to the Han dynasty and a staple of Confucian classics such as the *I-Ching* and much Taoist philosophy. Essentially, the situation of all man-made structures must be considered with regard to the lie of the land and the currents of local and cosmic energy so that buildings are placed in harmony with nature. To situate them wrongly or to make mistakes with their internal layout is believed to have profound effects upon the luck and prosperity of the people who inhabit them. In layman's terms this is all part of the 'feel good' factor where we feel secure and comfortable in certain rooms and not in others. A fair amount of common sense is naturally involved: if you sit opposite a door then you will be constantly distracted when it opens; if you sit with your back to a door then you might get a nasty surprise. Wherever you sit, you may wish to have air and light and hopefully a good view.

So, whenever the government wanted to build a new road, the villagers would suck their teeth and say that unfortunately this road would cut the dragon's back, or some such thing, which would have a bad effect on their future health and prosperity, and that of their children. They really did not want to stand in the way of progress and were prepared to make a sacrifice subject, of course, to the payment of appropriate compensation. All this involved painstaking negotiation and the drinking of gallons of tea.

The status of the New Territories (NT) was anomalous. Acquired late in the colonial day in 1898, when liberal sentiment at home was beginning to turn against colonial expansion, the NT had been leased for ninety-nine years – the famous lease which was ultimately to lead to the return of the whole colony to China in 1997. At first, some villagers were unhappy with British rule and the walled city of Kam Tin rebelled and had its iron gates removed and sent by

Governor Blake to his country estate in Ireland, although they were later returned. Due to the temporary nature of the lease, the NT enjoyed certain privileges which did not apply to other areas.

The local people, some of them Hakka who had migrated centuries earlier from northern China, and others from the Tang clans who had assisted the young Sung emperor, enjoyed the protection of a local representative body called the Heung Yee Kuk and all sorts of other privileges, such as the right of male descendants to build a small house in their village with minimum regulation and to bury their dead in the hills. Later, the small house policy would become subject to massive and systematic abuse as villagers sold their traditional rights to property developers. Meanwhile, their relative freedom to use land and develop property was a source of resentment to Hong Kong residents in the urban area.

In the case of Mouse Island, the locals were particularly aggressive and we needed to resort in the end to a forced clearance with the help of the Police Tactical Unit. Despite the payment of substantial compensation, the locals screamed blue murder and threw bricks and dung at the police and advancing bulldozers. The week before, a vivid graffiti had appeared on a monolithic rock near the site, which read, *'Man Pui-dak ge fan mo'* or 'Peter Mann's grave'. I could do worse, I thought.

Back at the District Office, we arranged meetings with the engineers who were anxious to get on with building their new town. At lunchtime, we would sometimes play tennis near the hospital if it was not too hot, or go for a curry at the Dragon Inn, which was a small hotel on the Castle Peak Road with a traditional Chinese garden, popular with bosses and their secretaries. Another popular pastime was to go and look at the amazing collection of bonsai trees that were to be found at a large Taoist temple in the area, called Ching Chung Kwoon. The art of bonsai is to take many varieties of tree and constantly prune their roots so that over the years the trees take on the characteristics of miniature ancient oaks or banyans, often artfully decorated with tiny models of tea houses or bearded sages sitting in mountain pavilions. As you walked around row upon row of these delightful scenes, it was like looking down from a great height onto past landscapes of Chinese history.

The annual Tin Hau Festival was another colourful local event when fisherfolk gave thanks to the Queen of Heaven or Goddess of the Sea, who is able to forecast weather and save people from shipwrecks. In early May every year, a huge matshed theatre, constructed of the biggest bamboo poles available and seating hundreds of people, would be erected at Mouse Island for a series of traditional Chinese opera performances. The audience, composed of assorted farmers and fisherfolk: grannies in their best clothes with jade bangles, shrieking kids running around and young men puffing away at cigarettes made almost as much noise as the performers in their bright silk costumes with heavy makeup and accompanying orchestra. The performances went on for at least three hours, although European guests would normally excuse themselves after sitting politely for thirty minutes.

Up the road, in Yuen Long, was held the traditional Tin Hau procession, which wound around the streets and culminated in the stadium, where there were lion and dragon dances to the thunderous sound of drums. The goddess was offered roast suckling pigs against ill health and bad luck; joss sticks and money; oranges for immortality and a good future; persimmons for joy; pomegranates, whose seeds represent fecundity; and of course many large and beautiful *fa pau,* floral paper offerings.

The dragons, made out of a hundred feet of bright material with the dragon's head following a Buddha holding a large pearl, were carried by at least twenty dancers and the trick was to avoid getting tangled up as the dragon coiled and undulated around itself. The lions were handled by two serious *kung fu* adepts, the one in front holding the head with its expressive winking eyes. This pair needed to prance and jump in the most athletic way to the vigorous sound of drums and even perform at the top of iron poles. The lion also had to walk backwards at times lest he present his bottom to the Goddess. During the finale, a scroll bearing auspicious characters would pop out of the lion's mouth to be presented to the guest of honour.

A most curious aspect of the procession was the group of painted children – little 'gods' and 'goddesses' who were dressed in colourful silk costumes with their faces made up and carried aloft on special platforms attached to poles. These exquisite children had become the children of the goddess and were subsequently placed under her special protection.

Also near Yuen Long was the village of San Tin, which was the headquarters of the Man Clan, along with the Tangs, one of the powerful clans of the New Territories. At one reception, I met one of their senior members, William Man, who had set up a reasonably priced air link to the UK, known as Eupo Air. One day he invited me for lunch, and having discovered that my Chinese name was Man also, proclaimed that I should henceforth be an honorary member of the Man clan. However, he doubted whether this would make me eligible to build a small house.

One of our senior Chinese staff, who wore thick glasses and had a bald, round head that looked like an egg, was a practitioner of Tai Chi and would often suggest we go up on to the roof of the District Office to practise that graceful exercise, which is like a moving meditation and profoundly relaxing. I had recently taken up the sport following a visit to a remote monastery on Lantau Island where I met an American monk called Guo Yi who had come to Hong Kong after the Vietnam War. Guo Yi told me that a Tai Chi *si fu* called Kwok had recently visited the temple with the ashes of his grandfather and that if I was seriously interested in learning, he would put me in touch. When I met Kwok Si Fu, he explained that his wife's grandfather was the founder of the Wu School, and asked me if I knew any of the form. I showed him what few moves I knew and he looked rather bemused.

'Where did you learn that?' he asked.

'From a book,' I admitted.

He smiled and said, 'Tai Chi is the Taoist martial art. Its long form has 108 movements. It is based on ancient Chinese principles and meets hardness with softness and vice-versa. Each movement, which all have names such as 'Carry Tiger to Mountain' or 'Cloud Hands', represents a block, a kick or a punch. The slower the form is practised the more difficult it is. You must be completely relaxed. A lifetime is hardly long enough to learn this art.'

I subsequently went to Master Kwok for regular lessons and later learned the sword form. It was the only Chinese home in Hong

Kong which I regular visited, as most Chinese entertain in restaurants, and so I saw how it was decorated at Chinese New Year and other festivals. The old man had a gentle nature and was like a father to me. His wife was one of the best swordswomen in town and his daughters all had successful careers, although he complained to me that they had not given him any grandchildren.

I returned to see Guo Yi a few times. The stepfather of one of my friends had established a tea farm on Lantau after the war and organised an annual three-day event called the Long Long Walk for members of the judiciary and legal profession. One night we all stayed at his monastery and Guo Yi told us some fascinating stories, such as the time the monks had captured an enormous King Cobra that was terrorising the monastery. They wrapped it up in a large sack and carried it to the other side of the island, but the snake returned before the monks got back. The abbot informed them that this was no ordinary snake but a *naga* and ordered them to build a large statue of a dragon at the back of the monastery, as dragons are king of the species. Once the dragon was finished, the snake disappeared and never returned.

Guo Yi admitted that sometimes he slept with a loop of wire around his manhood. He added that when he drank milk he was prone to erotic dreams and wanted to avoid the possibility of a nocturnal emission.

'When you meditate and accumulate spiritual jewels there are ghosts who would like to take them from you,' he explained.

We all looked at each other with wide eyes. It was an interesting variation on the usual theme of going blind.

Another of my friends used to go to that monastery to meditate. However, one time he was practising transcendental meditation rather than following the instructions of the monk. He was roused by a sharp pain on his back and became aware of the manic, glittering eyes of Guo Yi staring at him. In the monk's hand was a bamboo rod he had used to strike him as a lesson in discipline. Being an American and Vietnam veteran to boot, he was rather extreme in his behaviour. My friend decided not to return there for further meditation.

Another of my district office duties was to take charge of the local public works section. Each DO had an annual budget for small local works such as footpaths, pavilions and gardens. When the rural committee had endorsed a project, we would put it out to tender and then supervise its construction. Our works inspector was nicknamed 'Blackie' Chan, doubtless because of the long hours he spent in the blazing sun. When we were required to build a footpath up a hill, I showed Blackie a picture of the lovely pathway, replete with undulating green and red dragons on either side, which graces the entrance to the Doi Suthep Temple near Chiang Mai.

'Can we build it like this?' I asked.

Blackie looked pained and said simply, 'No, ADO, we can't build it like that.'

So, for budgetary reasons, it was built in a very mundane, utilitarian way, according to Public Works Department guidelines and my artistic aspirations were frustrated. However, later in my government career I would discover ways to produce more creative projects.

There was a remote village on the other side of Castle Peak without electricity, so we acquired a generator and booked a government helicopter to airlift it in. I sat in the helicopter to assist with the operation. One bright Saturday morning, we took off with the generator slung below, flew over the mountain, gently laid the generator down, unfastened the sling and then landed nearby. As I walked up to him, the village headman had tears in his eyes.

'ADO, you are a god among men,' he declared. 'Not only are you the ADO, but you can fly a helicopter too!'

I smiled modestly and not wishing to disabuse him of my divinity, replied that it was all in a day's work.

The Secretary for the New Territories, David (later Sir David) Akers-Jones, lived in a beautiful residence set on a small island near Tai Po called Island House. The colonial mansion had a lovely garden, full of exotic trees and flowering plants, which ran down to the shore of Tolo Harbour. In front of the house was a large flagpole on top of which flew the Union Jack. A hospitable man who had previously served in Malaya, with a great love for all things Chinese and a strong empathy for the local people, he and his wife frequently invited us young ADOs over at the weekend for a few beers and a barbecue. One evening I had a few too many drinks and decided to climb to the top of the flagpole, where I stayed for a long time, resisting the entreaties of the other guests who were trying to persuade me to come down.

'If you fall off,' said the secretary reasonably, 'I shall have the trouble of finding a new ADO for your district.'

This made sense so I climbed down.

Later that year the secretary's son Simon, who was a good friend, was tragically killed in a car crash on the Castle Peak Road. Returning home late at night after a long day at work, he had fallen asleep at the wheel and hit a lamppost.

Off the coast of Castle Peak were a number of islands that came under the administration of our district. Beyond them, in the Pearl River delta rose the conical black rock of Lin Tin Island, where all the opium had been unloaded from East Indiamen and stored for subsequent delivery up the river, prior to the first Opium War. The New Territories Administration had its own launch, the *Sir Cecil Clementi,* named after a previous governor, and every few months we would plan expeditions to the outlying islands. This involved purchasing large amounts of San Miguel beer as an accompaniment to the chicken curry that was inevitably served for lunch.

We would set off early on the sparkling sea – although the waters became muddy in the delta – dock at the pier of one of the islands, go ashore for a meeting with the villagers, assisted by our liaison officer, take note of whatever issues might be raised, perhaps agriculture or fishery matters, ferry services or repairs to government facilities. We would then shake hands and repair to the *Clementi* for lunch. In the afternoon, we would visit another island or two. There are well over 200 dotted around the coast. During one of these cruises we heard the news on the radio that a woman had been elected for the first time as prime minister of the United Kingdom. Her name was Margaret Thatcher.

As expatriates, we loved to listen to the news on BBC World Service with its distinctive musical signature. Later the cut-glass tones were replaced by broad regional accents, though how local listeners were expected to understand them, I do not know. In April

1980, a group of us listened to a news broadcast about the lowering of the Union Jack in Salisbury, Rhodesia, as 'Fatty' Soames, having sorted out the white rebels, with a little help from his Commonwealth advisors and their election monitoring group, was presiding over the birth of Zimbabwe. One of our group was an old Africa hand.

'That's it then', he announced. 'We are now the last.'

'What about the Falklands and Gibraltar?' I asked.

'The last that matters,' he hissed.

Lilian seemed to have family all over Southeast Asia, so we decided to take a trip and visit some of them. We started in Penang, Malaysia, which was a lovely colonial island filled with graceful houses, rubber plantations and palm trees. We were met at the airport by the family and driven to her aunt's house near the racecourse. They had three man-eating Dobermans running around the garden and I was warned not to go out at night. That evening we were taken to a very elaborate Chinese banquet for twelve given by Lilian's ninety-year-old uncle, who owned a tin mine in Ipoh. The old boy was an amazing character with a fund of colourful stories and proceeded to drink me under the table. Meanwhile, the mother spent the evening inscrutably sizing me up. At one point she managed to get me alone for a short chat.

'You are a civil servant in Hong Kong, right?'

'Yes,' I said.

'Won't it affect your promotion prospects if you marry a Chinese girl?'

I blushed. What she said had been true up until the seventies, but I thought that Hong Kong was now becoming a more liberal place. In fact, this prohibition had been inherited from India and was originally intended to prevent the emergence of a settled colonial class which might challenge British rule, as it had done in America.

'Never mind,' she said, 'You are still young.'

A more polyglot gathering you could hardly imagine, with people speaking Thai, Malay, Hokkien, Cantonese, Mandarin and English.

In Penang's capital, Georgetown, we visited the outdoor food stalls and sampled delicious satay and seafood. We rented a beach house which at night looked out on phosphorescent surf under the tropical stars. A few days later, we flew to Kota Baru and rented a car to drive down the east coast through jungle kampongs, over muddy rivers and past beaches with views of tropical islands out to sea. At one such beach we watched huge leatherback turtles lumber up the sand to lay their eggs. Passing the Genting Highlands, we arrived In Kuala Lumpur for more family dinners. Before returning to Hong Kong, we spent a few days in clean and green Singapore which provided an interesting contrast. After enjoying a few gin slings in Raffles Hotel à la Somerset Maugham, we slipped off to Bugis Street, which was famous for its beautiful transsexuals. The Singapore authorities subsequently demolished Bugis Street but were then forced to rebuild it due to pressure from tourists. We were happy to return to Hong Kong at last.

I was now living in a comfortable flat in Broadcast Drive with Lilian. However, she had graduated from Hong Kong University and was off to the UK to do a medical internship. On the night her plane was due to leave, Typhoon Hope, the biggest storm of the decade and packing wind speeds of more than 100 knots, roared into town and caused major damage, wrecking ships and destroying the Star Ferry pier. All the plant pots were blown off our balcony and two of the windows were smashed. It seemed to mirror our high emotions. She left for London the next day. I missed her a lot, although I was also somewhat relieved as a young man of twenty-six is in no hurry to settle down. We kept in touch for a while before she eventually married a British civil servant.

A typhoon or tropical cyclone is basically a rotating mass of warm humid air with the lowest pressure near its centre. Most form between latitudes 5–20 degrees on both sides of the equator. Known as hurricanes elsewhere, they are called typhoons in the Pacific and China seas. Hong Kong is normally affected by around six typhoons per summer with one or two maybe coming close. It is a bit like ten-pin bowling with the direction of the storm subsequently affected by prevailing winds so that they might make landfall anywhere along the coast from Japan in the northeast to Vietnam in the southwest. In Hong Kong, when they come within 800 km, the standby No. 1 signal is raised. As the storm approaches, No. 3 signal (strong wind) and No. 8 signal (storm) may be raised. The No. 10 (hurricane) signal signifies a direct hit with wind speeds up to 220 km per hour. The taller buildings in Hong Kong are constructed to sway in typhoons because if they were too rigid they would snap. One of the highest residential buildings in town is rumoured to have its water tank on a track so that it can move in high winds to provide a counterweight.

Meanwhile, back in Tuen Mun, plans for the New Town were taking shape. One issue with regard to development of Hong Kong's hilly terrain is slope stability and geotechnical matters, especially during typhoons. Since the Kotewall Road collapse of a block of flats due to a landslip in 1972, the colony had adopted very high standards of slope protection. In that notorious incident, one of my friends, a young police inspector, rushed down to help upon hearing the news and dug all night for survivors with the emergency services. His efforts were rewarded when he managed to pull out a leading member of the legal profession who had been taking a bath and was saved by that cast-iron fitting.

Under the 1,800-foot-high Castle Peak lay some slopes that the planners had set aside for public housing. The geotechnical engineer warned that these slopes were not suitable for high-density development and should be rezoned. Now, administrative officers are generalists who pride themselves on their ability to grasp any subject quickly, but I was having trouble following the engineer's talk of fissile strata and hydraulic counter-movements.

'Could you put it simply?' I asked.

'Aye,' said the engineer, who was Scottish, and he held up his two hands like cups. 'When a weight is placed here (left hand down) then this area will rise (right hand up)'.

This meant that we needed to find another location for the 20,000 public housing spaces that had just disappeared.

Near this site lay one of Hong Kong's oldest temples, Castle Peak Monastery. The monastery has two treasures: one is an inscription by a Tang dynasty scholar, *'Kao shan dai yat'* ('High mountain, first in merit') and the second is a dinosaur fossil which the locals say is a dragon's bone. In a cave behind the temple, the Buddhist saint, Pui To, was reputed to have meditated for twenty years. Upon the death of the old abbot in the early seventies, the temple had been taken over by a cunning disciple who had allegedly sequestered its assets and was running a lucrative illegal burial business on nearby government land. The new abbot resisted all directions to set his house in order. A protracted court case dragged on and the pile of dusty files in the District Office that charted the vagaries of the case was a towering monument to this seemingly intractable problem.

It was at least twenty miles from Kowloon to Tuen Mun. Unfortunately, my old red Mini Cooper (with a *yin-yang* symbol on its bonnet) had given up the ghost; they are not really suitable cars for Hong Kong as it is very wet in the summer and their electrics are too close to the ground. I needed a good car to commute back and forth every day and one of my staff talked me into buying a sporty new two-door red Toyota Carina. This was a great car that served me well for ten years. On 8 December 1980, I was driving home along the Castle Peak Road listening to the radio when I heard the stunning news that John Lennon had been shot dead in New York City. I remember stopping the car and taking a deep breath. It was profoundly shocking to me that someone so associated with the cause of peace should have been killed this way.

Imagine there's no heaven
It's easy if you try
No hell below us
Above us only sky.

CHAPTER SIX

Lower Albert Road

I N EARLY 1981, I was posted to Security Branch in the Government
Secretariat on Lower Albert Road, the 'corridors of power' where
all government policy was formulated and public finances controlled.
The various branches were the equivalent of ministries (without an
elected minister) which set the policy for executive departments.
They also helped to prepare new legislation and budgetary proposals for the consideration of the Legislative Council. This set-up
had been recommended in 1972 by consulting firm McKinsey to
separate policy formulation and execution. The appointment of
management consultants had come as a shock to the 'old guard'
AOs who had expected such a sensitive job to be kept in-house. The
result was the establishment of six policy branches and two resource
branches for finance and staff matters.

My job, as an assistant secretary, was to consider policy matters
for the police, immigration and customs. Immigrants from the
Mainland had taken up a lot of police resources, although until
1980 the government operated a 'touch base' policy which gave
immigrants a sporting chance and allowed them to stay in Hong
Kong if they reached the urban area. At this time, there was a lot
of smuggling and illegal immigration around the outlying islands,
so we came up with the idea of introducing a system of port
controls. We would build pontoons in various strategic locations,
staff them with departmental officers and control the movements
of small craft. This would require new legislation and considerable
funding. In the event, after a year of hard work and in typical civil
service fashion, it was decided that the scheme was prohibitively
expensive and was shelved.

Two major initiatives were then being introduced to control illegal immigrants (IIs – pronounced aye-ayes). First, ID cards were to be issued to the entire population, which was a major administrative exercise. Second, a security fence was to be built from east (Sha Tau Kok) to west (Lok Ma Chau) across the entire border, complete with razor wire and electronic sensors that would bring Gurkha patrols to any location of II activity. This eighteen-foot-high steel fence was soon to be nicknamed the 'Bamboo Curtain' although an agile and determined II could still get over it in about twenty seconds. Another complication was that the fence needed to have gates every mile or so to allow farmers to reach their fields on either side, so they were opened under supervision every morning and evening for this purpose. We needed to make frequent trips to the border, sometimes by helicopter, to check alignments and construction progress. We also needed to test equipment, such as expensive thermal imaging nightscopes that the Gurkhas had requested.

As members of Security Branch, we were invited to join the Volunteer Officers' Mess which was just across the road in Beaconsfield House. This was a most congenial place to have lunch (always a problem in crowded Central) and you could order a cold beer in a pewter tankard and a set lunch or simple curry. They kept a wonderful condiment on their tables in a little silver bottle which was sherry with red chilli peppers, a delicious way of spicing up soups.

Many of the officers in the branch were dealing with Hong Kong's escalating Vietnamese refugee crisis. Thousands had arrived on board the ships *Clara Maersk* in 1975 and the *Huey Fong* in 1978. By 1979, the Vietcong had started a form of ethnic cleansing and ethnic Chinese found themselves vulnerable. That year 69,000 refugees sought asylum in Hong Kong, many arriving in leaky boats. Thailand, Malaysia and Singapore refused to allow the Vietnamese to land, but the UK urged Hong Kong to declare itself a 'port of first asylum'. Later that year, a rusty old freighter called the *Skyluck* arrived in local waters. The master claimed he had picked up the 2,600 refugees at sea but it was suspected to be a well-organised people smuggling enterprise. The ship spent some months in the harbour until the anchor chains were cut and she drifted onto the rocks of Lamma Island. Luckily, all the refugees managed to disembark safely.

That weekend I happened to be walking on Lamma Island when we decided to take a look at the ship, which was lying on the rocks. We climbed on board and visited the bridge and various cabins. It was truly like the *Marie Celeste*. The refugees had jumped off the ship fearing that it might sink and left behind most of their personal belongings such as clothes, cases and books, but had probably taken their gold with them.

In 1980, a further 30,000 refugees had arrived, but by then the US and Europe were starting to slow down their resettlement programmes. The government therefore decided that it had to do something to deter further arrivals. In 1982, it declared a policy of 'closed camps' and embarked on a rigorous screening process to distinguish genuine political refugees from opportunistic economic migrants, who became known as 'boat people'. Hong Kong people were generally hostile to these boat people and the huge amount of resources needed to look after them. In 1989, under the 'Comprehensive Plan of Action', the government started to repatriate all remaining boat people back to Vietnam.

At this time, given the gradual opening up of China following the reforms of Deng Xiaoping, it was considered opportune to arrange the first Security Liaison Meeting between Hong Kong and China. I was assigned to be secretary to the working group. After months of preparation and meetings between the political advisor, police, immigration and customs to agree an agenda, we departed by the Kowloon-Canton Railway for Guangzhou.

On the first evening, we were invited to a welcome banquet. It was my first experience of generous Chinese official hospitality and I could not believe how much alcohol we were expected to drink. At the side of our plates were at least three different glasses for the copious quantities of beer, wine and spirits we were encouraged to consume with the twelve dishes of the banquet. As the youngest member present, I was fair game to be set up, or *jing gwoo,* with endless toasts. Towards the end of the banquet, we drank a massive amount of Mao-tai, a fiery white liquor, around 50 per cent proof, made famous by Nixon's visit to China in 1972. With taunts about

whether the English could drink or not ringing in my ears, I
staggered to the toilet and, lest I let the side down, put my fingers
down my throat and vomited, thus clearing the way for further
intake. Our hosts were impressed as I returned to the table and
knocked back another bottle. In the tradition of *in vino veritas,* the
Chinese would not do business with anyone who had not got drunk
with them first. This is still the case today, although given the
current purge of corruption within the party and following certain
celebrated cases of people dropping dead after such binges, it may
now have been moderated.

At the first official meeting the next day, we established a bizarre
ritual for our exchanges. All the local Hong Kong officers spoke
Cantonese and so did most of the officials on the other side.
However, due to diplomatic protocol, the Hong Kong side spoke
in English which was then translated into Mandarin or Putonghua.
The Chinese side replied in Mandarin which was then laboriously
translated back into English. One of the main topics, aside from
cross-border issues of policing and simplified immigration and
customs procedures, was the establishment of a hotline across the
border through which senior officers from both sides could quickly
get in touch in an emergency, The possibility of a regular through-
train service between Hong Kong and Guangzhou, which did not
have to stop at the border, was also discussed. After more banquets
and sightseeing we were escorted back to our train and returned to
Hong Kong.

By this time, I had moved from my flat in Broadcast Drive,
which was in north Kowloon near Radio Television Hong Kong,
and into the Hermitage, a government block on Kennedy Road
providing bedsit accommodation for single government servants.
On the top floor was a restaurant and bar which enjoyed a stunning
panoramic view of the harbour. It was difficult to sleep late there,
as long before 7 a.m. the familiar sounds of a great harbour city
waking up drifted through the windows: the engines of the ferries
and ships and the roar of buses and lorries. It was a very convenient
location as I could walk down to the Secretariat in just ten minutes
through Victoria Barracks (now Hong Kong Park).

In the Ho Man Tin service flats the year before, John Mac-Lennan, an unfortunate young police inspector, had shot himself five times in the stomach. The police had set up the Special Investigation Unit tasked to look into homosexuality in the public service and this poor lad had been tipped off the day before by a well-meaning superior that he was about to be questioned. There was predictably a lively public debate on whether it was physically possible to shoot yourself five times with a revolver, but in the end the inquest delivered a verdict of suicide, which some found hard to accept.

Another duty in the branch was to microfilm many old security files dating back to before the war. The circulation lists on the memoranda were sufficient to conjure up the heyday of empire: 'Urgent and Secret. For immediate despatch to Commanders-in-Chief Gibraltar, Malta, Cyprus, India, Hong Kong, Singapore, West and East Africa, Caribbean, Dominions of Canada, Australia and New Zealand; and Flag Admirals of the Mediterranean, Atlantic and Pacific fleets.' Some of the documents were related to the visits to Hong Kong of aircraft carriers and nuclear submarines. There were also detailed contingency plans for various disasters such as radiation leaks from nuclear-powered aircraft carriers or submarines (destroy all nearby supplies of milk); or an aircraft crash at Kai Tak (mobilise the army), that all required regular updating. Confidential files were pink while secret files were orange.

One of my colleagues, who was called Leeks (we had an Onions too), gave me an invaluable piece of bureaucratic advice. Having lunch sitting outside a delicatessen owned by the Sardinian, Mauro, one of the first eateries in Lan Kwai Fong – and little did we foresee how that area would blossom into the entertainment centre of Hong Kong – he told me that I must never hold on to a file. Write something on it and move it along to someone else, 'Never forget that a moving file is a happy file,' he declared.

This was probably the best piece of bureaucratic advice I ever received. When George Nathaniel Curzon was appointed Viceroy of India in 1898, he commented on the file-shuffling tendencies of the Indian Civil Service in the following terms:

Round and round like the diurnal revolutions of the earth went
the file, stately, solemn, sure and slow: and now, in due season,
it has completed its orbit and I am invited to register the
concluding stage.

I, naturally, played my part in these stately orbits of government's
corridors with judicious solemnity, and sometimes tongue-in-
cheek.

There was a horror story told about one senior official who fell
terribly behind in his work. When he left some years later, his
replacement pulled opened a cupboard door that was wedged shut,
only to have a cascade of hidden files fall out. I suppose that was
one way of dealing with the problem, but not one you could use
in today's digital age.

There was also a lot of material relating to the Pacific War. Hong
Kong defended itself valiantly against the Japanese attack, whereas
the loss of Singapore was a fiasco. The colony had been reinforced,
just months before, by two Canadian battalions so, together with
the Volunteers, it was able to muster around 18,000 against 60,000
invading Japanese troops. Hong Kong's defences in the New Territories, the Gin Drinker's Line, were breached fairly quickly and
there is evidence that the Japanese had purchased plans of the lines
in Canton. The popular barber at the Peninsula Hotel, patronised
by many army officers, was later discovered to be a Japanese spy.
On the other hand, the British had never had a serious enemy in
Asia (apart from the Russians) so I suppose their complacency can
be understood, although it was bordering on *hubris*.

Having invaded on 8 December 1941, it took the Japanese ten
days to fight their way to Hong Kong Island. The Volunteers held
the Japanese at the North Point Power Station and fell back for a
last stand at Leighton Hill, which was defended by the Middlesex
Regiment (the 'Diehards') who beat off a number of Japanese
attacks until 23rd December. Meanwhile, the rest of the defenders
were making a last stand at Stanley. On Christmas Day, the
governor, Sir Mark Young, decided to surrender to avoid further
loss of life and so became the first British governor to surrender a
colony since the American War of Independence.

What is of particular interest was the clash of cultures between the opposing sides. The Japanese could not comprehend the concept of surrender and would frequently massacre troops who lay down their arms, but when soldiers fought bravely they would often stop the battle to honour them. There is a famous story about Japanese soldiers entering the Repulse Bay Hotel and bayoneting Allied wounded until a British matron, dressed in white, appeared and told them to stop. Thinking she was a ghost they were terrified and ran away. This cultural collision is well portrayed in the film, *Merry Christmas, Mr Lawrence.*

There are many ghost stories in Hong Kong, several of them involving the Japanese occupation. In the sixties, Japanese imperial soldiers were sighted in the area of Shouson Hill, where they had been billeted. The old Mental Hospital on High Street had been used as an interrogation centre and was reputed to be haunted. When I was in the Garrison Players, we used to rehearse our dramas in a wing of that old building and frequently heard strange noises. One day we invited a Taoist master to perform an exorcism. He had a *fung shui* compass with him and as he approached the suspect area, the compass started to revolve at high speed. Nobody stayed in that building after midnight. One tries to forgive and forget and move on but for the elderly feelings remain strong.

We can imagine life in Stanley (for civilians) and Sham Shui Po camp (for military) from Spielberg's wonderful film, *Empire of the Sun* set in a similar prisoner-of-war (POW) camp in Shanghai. It was said that the local girls wept when the Allied prisoners were marched into the camps and many came to the wire to give food and soap to their boyfriends, risking beatings from Japanese guards. The imprisoned soldiers called them the 'Angels of Wan Chai'. Some POWs did escape and joined the British Army Aid Group (BAAG), which had been set up by Colonel (later Sir) Lindsay Ride, a professor at Hong Kong University who had escaped to Chungking. Another colonial administrator, Ronnie Holmes (later Sir), a classics scholar who spoke fluent Cantonese, worked out of BAAG in Kweilin and frequently entered and left the occupied colony dressed as a Chinese peasant. He helped arrange escapes from the Sham Shui Po camp and liaised with the East River Column, communist

soldiers based in Sai Kung spearheading the anti-Japanese resistance. Scandalously, after the war the KMT refused to recognise their
contribution. Sir Ronnie was also a pillar of strength during the
1967 leftist riots, urging the administration to dig in its heels and
take a hard line against the communist agitators.

In the weeks leading up to the Japanese surrender in August 1945
and while Admiral Harcourt's squadron was on its way from
Sydney, former Colonial Secretary, Franklin Gimson (ex-Ceylon
Civil Service) with great determination, took over as officer ad-
ministering the government. Roosevelt had been keen to hand
Hong Kong over to Chiang Kai-shek but Truman saw it as a matter
of operational expediency. So when Admiral Harcourt finally
arrived on 30th August he was met by Gimson rather than the
Japanese. Also by comparison with what had taken place over the
last few years, British rule was perceived by local Chinese as more
efficient and certainly more benevolent.

Mid-1982 was also the time of Britain's last great military hurrah
– with a little help from the Americans – the Falklands War. Those
windswept islands in the South Atlantic, packed with sheep, had
ceased to have any strategic importance after the opening of the
Panama Canal in 1913. Yet, following an ill-advised Argentine
invasion, the Iron Lady had sent a task force 8,000 miles across the
world to defend Britain's honour and the rule of law. She had been
careful to seek both American and UN approval, unlike Anthony
Eden for his disastrous Suez adventure in 1956.

Although we were on the other side of the world, we followed
the campaign closely and watched some harrowing footage of the
storming of Goose Green, the sinking of the *General Belgrano* and
subsequent Exocet missile attack on HMS *Sheffield*. For a while, we
succumbed to the delusion that Britain was still a global power. During
the war there was a possibly apocryphal incident where a squad of
retreating Argentine soldiers were fleeing from some Scots Guards
when suddenly they encountered Gurkhas with their kukris drawn.
They immediately made a U-turn and surrendered to the Scots.

One of my unforgettable memories of this time is a formal mess
curry at Lei Yue Mun Barracks, on the east side of Hong Kong
Island, where a friend, John Birt, served as a major of the 7th

Gurkha Rifles. A splendid affair with full regimental silver and Gurkha bearers at attention around the room, we enjoyed succulent beef, lamb, chicken and vegetable curries served in silver tureens and drank ice-cold beer from silver tankards, while the soldiers discussed some of their famous campaigns. Those Gurkha officers sure knew how to live in style.

One of my more colourful jobs, based on marine police intelligence, was to plot Chinese gunboat incursions into Hong Kong waters on a monthly basis. My boss Bim Davies, the secretary for security, was a man of the old school. The first time I performed this task and minuted the file to him, I received a summons to his office. As I timidly crept into his august presence, he picked up the file and hurled it at me with all his strength.

'Get it bloody right next time!' he shouted.

But I had the last laugh. Working late one Saturday evening and quite alone in the impregnable office with its double locks and security gates, I entered the room of the man who made the commissioner of police and the commander, British Forces nervous. As I was about to be posted elsewhere, I decided to make a childish anti-authoritarian gesture. Under a large NO SMOKING sign, I took out a fat cigar and smoked it sitting in his padded leather chair with a foolish grin on my face. On Monday morning, the secretary was heard to remark that his office had a funny smell.

By the early eighties, the domination of big business in Hong Kong by British companies was drawing to a close. A new breed of Chinese tycoon was starting to make inroads into listed companies, starting with Sir Y.K. Pao's acquisition of the Hongkong and Kowloon Wharf and Godown Company in 1978 and Li Ka-shing's of Hutchison Whampoa in 1980 and Hongkong Electric in 1985. This trend made the Princely Hong, Jardine Matheson, nervous so in 1981 their lawyers worked out a highly complex cross-shareholding arrangement with their property subsidiary, Hongkong Land, to avoid a hostile takeover by the Chinese tycoons. Jardines had plenty of experience of sharp business practice. Back in 1866, they discovered just one day early about the collapse of London bank Overend Gurney and managed to withdraw all their gold. The next day, rival company Dent went bankrupt and was snapped up by Jardines.

In 1983, the sinking property market caused the spectacular collapse of another listed company, Carrian, whose founder, Malaysian George Tan, had boasted the year before about buying Gammon House, a commercial property in Central, for $1 billion and selling it three months later for $1.6 billion. There was also the unfortunate case of the Bank Bumiputra (Malaysia) which appeared to be owed some US$850m by Carrian. Doubtless George would have continued to be the toast of boardrooms for much longer had he not been blindsided by the market. The case threw up all sort of unpleasant incidents, such as one senior accountant who was found one morning at the bottom of his swimming pool with a block of concrete tied to his neck. This was Hong Kong's very own South Sea Bubble.

While this was happening, I had become friendly on the social scene with girls working as air hostesses in Cathay Pacific. They came from all over Asia, and especially Japan, Singapore and the Philippines. My new girlfriend was a stunning Malaysian girl of Tamil origin with ebony skin offset by huge dark eyes and perfect white teeth. There were always parties going on around town and the girls loved to dance and enjoy themselves. Many of my friends married such girls, but I was still enjoying my bachelor life.

For a few months, I took an advanced Cantonese course at the Government Language School in the Wing On Centre. One of our fellow students was Lady Pamela Youde, wife of the Governor, Sir Edward. Lady Youde was very friendly and absolutely without the airs and graces you might expect in a governor's lady. One afternoon she invited us all for tea at Government House. It was spring and the famous azaleas were blooming in a riot of red, pink, white and purple in the garden outside the French windows. We were served tea by staff wearing white livery with red piping, on tables each bearing silver cigarette boxes embossed with the initials GRI for George Rex Imperator (George VI was the last emperor of India). Tragically, Sir Edward was to die a few years later from a heart attack suffered in Beijing during negotiations on the future of Hong Kong. Such was his popularity with local people that many thousands of them queued up outside Government House to sign the book of condolence.

The principle of moving administrative officers around regularly is twofold: it gives them all-round experience for high office and it prevents corruption. My next posting was to Transport Branch where I was required to work on the extension of the Mass Transit Railway and the electrification and privatisation of the Kowloon-Canton Railway. My new boss, Alan Scott, was a jovial fellow who had held senior positions in the Pacific. It was a revelation to me to find out how very different he was from my previous chief. On my first morning on the job, I was sitting in my office with my feet up on the desk reading a copy of the *South China Morning Post* when a knock came at the door and in he walked.

'I'm sorry,' he said with evident sincerity, 'are you busy?'

Hong Kong has an extremely efficient public transport system and our job was to make it better. The Victorians had got off to a good start by introducing the Star Ferry (named after the famous Tennyson poem, 'Crossing the Bar') and the Peak Tram in 1888 and HK Tramways in 1905. To reduce street congestion and for environmental reasons, the government continued to give priority to rail networks. The Mass Transit Railway (MTR), brainchild of Sir Murray MacLehose, had just opened its first line and was recognised as one of the best underground systems in the world. It had therefore been decided to upgrade the Kowloon-Canton Railway (KCR) from diesel to electric operation and, following the example of the Thatcher government in the UK, to transform it from a government department to a private corporation.

This entailed a major civil engineering project and the drafting of a new law or bill. The government had a special law drafting division in its Legal Department and what we had to do was detail precisely what we wanted the new law to achieve. The draftsman then turned these into a bill which would one day, hopefully, become an ordinance. When it was complete, it was submitted together with the financial implications to the Legislative Council for amendment and final approval.

The MTRC had been saddled with enormous debt. It was therefore decided to give the KCRC sufficient capital to make it financially viable, not to mention generous property development rights. The KCR was an important rail corridor serving the New Territories and the new towns then under construction (e.g. Sha Tin, Tai Po and Fan Ling) so it was decided to double-track and modernise the railway and to introduce electric rolling stock. I had the pleasure of riding on the last KCR diesel service which ran in mid-1983. Through-trains were already running all the way from Kowloon to Guangzhou (Canton) and journey time had been cut to ninety minutes.

The MTR, which opened in 1979, had been a huge success. It is a tribute to the ingenuity of the corporation that it could build a railway at all under one of the busiest and most congested cities on the planet, let alone one so efficient, reliable, affordable and clean. Most of the tunnels had been built by a Japanese consortium but the rolling stock was all British (Metro Cammell). Just about the only problem that occurred upon its opening was one of comic trivia. Passengers discovered that they could make a clicking noise by flicking their plastic tickets and a new regulation had to be introduced quickly to stop it. Another unforeseen hitch was that it swiftly became popular with would-be suicides who had previously jumped from the top of high-rise buildings – it saved the climb. One of my tasks was to compile a monthly report of those who had jumped in front of trains and who mostly died. This caused service disruptions and later sliding glass doors were built on the platforms to improve safety.

After the success of the initial system in Kowloon and its subsequent extension to Central and Tsuen Wan, the Island Line was built along the north coast of Hong Kong Island. At this time, many famous people came to have a look at the MTR. In 1985, both the Queen during her official visit and former British prime minister, Edward Heath, on a private visit, rode on the MTR. A great raconteur and traveller, Heath sometimes fell asleep at dinner parties. After a gruelling trip to Beijing, where he was feted as a 'Friend of China,' having visited Mao in 1974 and 1975, Heath dozed off at a dinner party at which I was a guest. Upon awakening, a Chinese woman on his left asked him if he liked Hong Kong.

'I'm glad you asked me that question,' said the great man, 'because Hong Kong is one of the most fascinating cities in the world.' He then winked at me and said in his plummy voice, 'I always say that when I'm in Hong Kong!'

Although Hong Kong has one of the best public transport networks in the world, its middle class are greatly attached to their private cars and would no more consider taking a bus than walking down the road naked. Although private car ownership was well over a quarter of a million at this time and traffic jams were chronic, especially at rush hour near the Cross-Harbour Tunnel, they would rather sit in a traffic jam than be seen on any form of public transport. This attitude was reinforced by the influential road transport lobby and the construction companies that tendered for bountiful government road projects. Indeed pedestrians were continually put to maximum inconvenience with sub-standard pavements and few crossings lest they disrupt the slow, majestic flow of *taai-taai*s on shopping expeditions and children being taken for yet another maths tutorial. I must admit that I was also an offender, and it was only after retirement and loss of my convenient parking space that I discovered the joys of bus travel.

At that time there was only one Cross-Harbour Tunnel which had opened in 1972. Then Financial Secretary, John Cowperthwaite, the high priest of small government and positive non-interventionism, had initially suggested that the private sector bear all the costs, although he had accepted that the government must provide the road infrastructure. He brushed aside the recommendation of Transport Department to build a one-tube two-lane tunnel and with some foresight insisted that it be two-tube and four-lane. There are now three tunnels and it has taken the government a long time to harmonise the tolls so that vehicles use the nearest tunnel to their destination rather than the cheapest. Trying to get through the old tunnel at rush hour is like trying to get a herd of camels through the eye of a needle.

One of the best things about the Hong Kong civil service was the possibility of 'acting up' when your immediate boss went on leave or on a duty visit. If approved, you were able to take on the extra job as well as your own and receive a generous allowance for doing so. If your 'acting allowance' continued for a month or more, this proved to be quite a financial windfall. One of the most difficult things we had to do was write Executive Council (Exco) memoranda, which had strict deadlines, inflexible formats and required many other officers to comment or sign off before they could be issued. They could be a serious intellectual challenge. Some officers used to finish them off at home in the middle of the night and others in more unusual locations. One of my colleagues claimed to have finished an Exco paper in the Tonnochy Ballroom (a hostess club in Wan Chai) one evening as he refused to turn down a night out and his deadline was the next morning.

The time came for me to be positively vetted prior to my promotion to senior administrative officer. Positive vetting is a security procedure for any public servant who might have access to secret or sensitive information. It involves interviews with colleagues and friends to ascertain whether you have any dark secrets that could be exploited for blackmail and so become a security risk. The suspect character traits searched for included homosexuality, alcoholism and money problems. Normally one was interviewed by a retired wing commander, or the like, attached to Special Branch. Questions might go:

Q: 'Have you ever been a communist?' A: 'No, sir, can't stand them.'

Q: 'Have you ever taken drugs?' A: 'Once tried it at college, can't say I liked it, sir.'

Q: 'Have you ever had sex with a man?' A: 'No sir, apart from the usual stuff at boarding school.'

Now, two of my bachelor friends in the service and I were famous for chasing girls and having long drinking sessions in watering holes such as the Dragon Boat Bar of the Hilton Hotel. Towards the end of my vetting, the wing commander was called away to an urgent phone call. As I waited, I couldn't help but see one of the remarks written in my personal file by a local Civil Service Branch officer. It read:

Mann, C. . . and S. . . : The Three Musketeers – NOT to be trusted.

Notwithstanding that less than ringing endorsement, I managed to pass muster even though I had had two brushes with the law since joining the Administrative Service and concluded that some police officers disliked the fact that I had 'jumped ship'. The first involved a high-speed car chase pursued by off-duty police officers that resulted in a charge of dangerous driving, and the second a misunderstanding in a public car park which led to damage to the exit barrier and a charge of criminal damage. Although I was exonerated on both charges, I noted that I should be more careful and not underestimate the resentment of some former colleagues.

We were still leading a fairly wild life in true Hong Kong style. One of my AO friends had already been carpeted by the secretary for the Civil Service, who had informed him that 'his private life was a matter of public scandal.' The same officer had managed to arrive very late for an important meeting with the financial secretary (FS).

'I'm sorry I'm late,' he said, 'but my father has just died.'

'I'm very sad to hear that,' said the FS, 'Please go home.'

A few days later, the FS spotted the officer and said, 'Are you going back for the funeral?'

'No,' was the reply, 'He's better now.'

We always seemed to run out of money towards the end of each month and were reduced to eating at cheap street stalls, known as *daai pai dong*. One was run by a big Chiu Chow man who wore a jade bracelet that he claimed was a thousand years old. One day we ordered eel, which escaped on the way to the pot and he chased it down the alley with a chopper. My Malaysian girlfriend had married a German (they did that) and I was now going out with a pretty girl of Shanghainese origin who worked for a local TV station.

A typical Friday evening would see my friends start drinking at 7 p.m. in either the Foreign Correspondents' Club (FCC), the Hong Kong Club, the Dragon Boat Bar in the Hilton, or the Captain's Bar in the Mandarin Hotel. By 9 p.m. the party would become boisterous and the more sensible people would depart for dinner. By 10.30 we were in the bars and clubs of Lan Kwai Fong, either California, 1997 or Soho. By midnight, it was time to visit the late night clubs or to venture to Wan Chai for a nightcap. Marriage might have slowed down some of my friends, but not much.

The Hong Kong Club, known simply as 'The Club', was the most exclusive in Asia and home to the colonial elite. Unfortunately, the delightful old Victorian renaissance building was demolished in 1981 to make way for a rather prosaic twenty-five-storey office building. However, it still enjoys the highest standards of food and wine (it is unusual to meet a member with less than ample girth) and is an excellent place for entertaining and business networking. Chinese membership has soared over the last two decades and the *gwai lo* are now in a minority.

The FCC was a less formal watering hole and full of interesting people. During the Vietnam War it was full of journalists covering the conflict. Photographer Hugh Van Es was a regular and his famous picture of the last helicopter out of Saigon was displayed on the wall. There was also a picture of a topless girl romping in French Polynesia and when some women members complained it was decided that rather than take it down, a picture of a young Scottish soldier raising the flag with his bottom exposed by a gust of wind should be placed next to it in the interests of balance and fairness. One side of the bar was informally reserved for members of the legal profession, including some very colourful characters. It was here that one lawyer drunkenly pulled the toupee off corrupt Crown Counsel Warwick Reid's head and unceremoniously dumped it in a pint of beer. A New Zealander, Reid was arrested in 1989 but fled Hong Kong for Macau, China and the Philippines from where he was finally deported back to Hong Kong in 1990. He was sentenced to eight years in jail and made to repay $12m in ill-gotten gains. Another regular was Gary Alderdice, a top Queen's Counsel who fell in love with a Russian call girl in Macau and was murdered in Vladivostok in 1994 along with his girlfriend while trying to buy off her contract. We used to player snooker every Wednesday evening in the downstairs bar.

In the early seventies, Hong Kong's nightlife was pretty sedate and centred around a few hotels. Then in 1978, Gordon Huthart opened 'Disco Disco' in Lan Kwai Fong, which was a wild, party club which really shook up the nightlife scene. He famously said, 'A good disco is like a zoo!' Canto-pop stars such as Leslie Cheung, Anita Mui and Danny Chan frequented the dance floor. As everyone had seen the film *Saturday Night Fever,* disco became the essence of a good night out. Quickly, Kowloon caught up with Hot Gossip, Hollywood East, Canton and Rick's Café, opened by an Australian MTR construction worker who thought that the nightlife business might be more fun. Lan Kwai Fong then followed with 1997 and California. Allan Zeman would subsequently extend his reach to take over most of the area. We spent a lot of time in Club 97 and even joined their crazy party in 1986 to see Halley's Comet on board a Boeing 737. Around 200 drunken people jumped on a bus to Kai Tak and boarded the plane. The only drink they were serving on board was Brandy Alexander, which is a bit nauseous for bumpy air travel. I remember when the pilot announced, 'You can now see the comet on the right side of the plane,' we almost fell out of the sky as everyone rushed over to have a look.

Long weekends were often spent in Manila or Bangkok and there was the famous New Year's Eve party (or Blartfest as it was known) in Pattaya or Koh Samui. A gang of us from Hong Kong would take over a beachside resort and enjoy a decadent evening of alcohol, live music, fireworks and special cookies. One time we arranged a gratuitous display of female mud wrestling. Girlfriends, and later wives, would be obliged to put up with this exuberant display of self-indulgence.

Another orgy of spectacular overindulgence was the annual Rugby Sevens tournament held at the Government Stadium. Established in 1976, the Hong Kong event quickly became the premier rugby sevens event in the world, with Fiji, Australia, England and later New Zealand regularly winning the Cup. Famous for its party atmosphere, streakers, people dressing up and drinking thousands of jugs of beer, the South Stand became renowned for its party animals. Everyone agreed that it was the best Hong Kong party of the year. In 1994, the government built a new 40,000 seat stadium, although the cognoscenti preferred the less formal ambience of the old venue. These days the event has become more corporate and it is difficult to find tickets so many of the old timers prefer to watch the event on TV at home.

Another popular and nearer destination was Macau, which in those days was a sleepy little Portuguese enclave with romantic hotels like the Bela Vista and charming restaurants such as Fernando's on Hak Sha (Black Sand) beach, where you could eat African chicken and drink good Vinho Verde. There was then only one casino, the Lisboa, while now there are scores and being the only legal casinos in China, Macau's gambling revenue has grown to many times that of Las Vegas. There were also mini-moke cars you could hire to get around the enclave and visit the Ah Ma Temple, the bones of the Nagasaki martyrs or the Westin Resort in Coloane.

Talking of Macau, I must give an account of the Portuguese, our neighbours across the Pearl River Delta, the nation who really opened up East Asian trade and indeed were given a monopoly to do so by the Pope at the Treaty of Tordesillas in 1494. Following Henry the Navigator's dream of opening trade routes to the East and finding a way to attack Islam from the rear after the fall of Constantinople in 1453, the Portuguese arrived in India and took Goa after defeating the Muslim fleet at Diu in 1509. Next, they took the highly strategic port of Malacca and finally settled in Macau in 1557.

In the sixteenth century, the Portuguese enjoyed a golden age of trade. Pepper from the Moluccas, cotton and muslin from India and European goods were traded in Canton for silk, which was sold at great profit in Nagasaki. Japanese silver was then used to buy more Chinese goods (silk and porcelain) at Canton to send west to India and Europe. The Portuguese also had an enormous influence on the Chinese diet. They introduced peanut oil, sweet potatoes, pineapples, guava and papaya from Brazil; and green beans, sprouts, lettuce and shrimp paste from home. They moreover greatly improved European pork by sending Chinese pigs home for cross-breeding with the Western variety.

Unfortunately for the Portuguese, it all fell apart rather quickly. In 1578, the young King Sebastian fought a disastrous battle in North Africa in which he and his whole army were wiped out. With no heir, the throne was taken by Philip II of Spain and the Union of the Crowns was subsequently disastrous for Portuguese overseas interests. Increasing Dutch assaults on her possessions and finally the closure of Japan completed the decline. The Tokugawa Shogun had become increasingly concerned about foreign influence following missionary rivalry between the Macau-based Jesuits and the Manila-based Franciscans. Fearing the Spanish might attempt to colonise Japan or ally themselves with one of his rivals, the Shogun in 1638 ordered a massacre of all Christians in Nagasaki.

Macau, however, survived for another 400 years as an enclave on the China coast and even enjoyed a resurgence in the late eighteenth and early nineteenth century as a summer base for European companies doing business with China through Canton, prior to the founding of Hong Kong.

Apart from travelling, another great hobby of mine was amateur dramatics. Shortly after arriving I joined the Garrison Players and the Stage Club. My first big show was a review called *Roaring Trade* in which I played the Government Information Services man, who was a sort of MC. Subsequently, I appeared in Tennessee Williams' *Camino Real,* Tom Stoppard's *Jumpers,* Strindberg's *Miss Julie* and Pinter's *Betrayal,* among others, including some Shakespeare. It was great fun and I met many friends through the theatre, although I sometimes thought that it was a lot of hard work for only a few nights of performance. Finally, I turned my hand to directing Ibsen's *Ghosts* in the Shouson Theatre, which was a great success, except on the opening night the special surface we had painted on the stage was not quite dry so the actors felt as if they were walking in treacle. Also, I learnt how difficult it is to let go and release control of a project you have personally developed from scratch. From the moment the curtain goes up on the opening night, the director is essentially redundant. We had a lot of fun in these shows and I remember one particularly funny incident where an actor went on stage with a bucket on his head, but with his flies undone so then misinterpreted the audience's laughter for appreciation of his comic skills, and became more energetic and excited in his delivery.

For our rehearsals we either used the old (haunted) hospital building on High Street or rooms at the back of the Helena May, which is a lovely old colonial building on Garden Road opened in 1916 as a hostel for single ladies, and often called the Virgin's Retreat. Its doors were always closed at 10.30 p.m. to keep out any men that might have funny notions. The aspiring actresses that took part in our productions did sometimes invite us up for a drink (before the curfew).

At the beginning of September 1983, a huge typhoon called Ellen whistled in from the Philippines. I was invited to a big typhoon party, which were normally all-night affairs, but being on the government's emergency duty roster for the next day, I left early. When I awoke at 7 a.m., I realised that this was one very serious storm with howling wind and torrential rain. Foolishly, I opened a window to have a look out and the whole thing was wrenched off its hinges and blew away. My instinct was to stay put but my sense of duty prevailed. Donning a raincoat I hurried out to the car park and jumped in my car. The only other vehicles on the streets belonged to the police. At one point I ran over a large tree branch and thought I would get stuck but managed to get free and make it to the nearby Government Secretariat.

Inside the emergency centre were a number of tired colleagues. On the board was a list of incidents that had occurred during the night. Wind speeds of 134 knots had been recorded at Stanley, nine inches of rain had fallen, twenty-two ships had run aground, six people had been killed and 277 injured by collapsing structures and flying debris. I became immediately busy with reports and phone calls. At 10 a.m., the Chief Secretary, Sir Philip Haddon-Cave, arrived.

'The worst is over,' he announced. 'The storm will make landfall near Macau. We have suffered a lot of damage and casualties and I fear we may have lost as many as one million trees, especially as there was some tornado activity.'

He went on to explain that in his experience bad storms affected the sexual characteristics of trees and caused all sorts of anomalies. We thought it was a bit academic for that time of the morning but the cs was absolutely right. For the rest of the year, the trees' inner clocks went haywire and they blossomed and changed colour at totally unpredictable times.

A few weeks later, I was sitting in my office one Saturday morning (we worked alternate Saturday mornings) when the door opened and a grim-faced colleague entered.

'Have you heard the news?' he asked grimly.

'What news?' I enquired.

'The Hong Kong dollar is collapsing. It's nearly ten to the US dollar. I'm thinking of going down to the bank now to change all my savings into US dollars.'

Over the year the Hong Kong dollar had depreciated considerably as a result of recession in the US, collapse of the local property market and political uncertainty over the territory's future, and had fallen a further 15 per cent in the last two days. We had heard that the Sino-British talks on Hong Kong's future were not going well. Quite often in the lobby of the Secretariat I would see the chief secretary having hushed and earnest words with the senior unofficial member of the Executive Council, Sir S.Y. Chung. We wondered what was going on.

According to my friend, panic buying had started that morning and all the rice had been stripped from supermarket shelves. I advised him against doing anything hasty. At lunchtime, we went for a drink in the Dragon Boat Bar. There was a generally sombre mood around town and subsequently that day, 24 September 1983, was known as 'Black Saturday'. A few weeks later, the government announced that the Hong Kong dollar would be pegged to the US dollar at the rate of 7.8 to 1. Luckily, the peg held and a currency crisis was averted.

The main architect of the peg was Sir John Bremridge, who had been plucked from Swire by Sir Murray in 1981 and appointed as financial secretary. It was the first time that a businessman had been parachuted into the administration and senior civil servants were wary of Sir John's commercial style. One mandarin, who had crafted a long minute supporting a new policy was surprised to receive a very unbureaucratic reply which simply said, 'Bugger off'. Another aspiring mandarin drafted a minute which included the word 'connexions' to which Sir John replied, 'Bollox'. His minutes were written in blue or black, as only the governor was allowed to use a red pen. Now and then we saw an impressive red 'M' from Sir Murray – or Big Mac as he was known.

A few months later, just as confidence was starting to return to the markets, Jardine Matheson, the largest British *hong*, let loose a bombshell by announcing that it was moving its legal domicile from Hong Kong to Bermuda. When the Chinese government complained that such peremptory moves were not conducive to preserving the colony's stability, the government could only reply that it had no control over the commercial decisions of private companies.

Another of my transport duties was running the Student Travel Scheme. It had been decided that students should enjoy subsidised travel on public transport, although how we divided up the subsidy from the Treasury was a matter of horse-trading. I had to arrange meetings with the rail operators, ferry and bus companies. I remember my visit to one bus company whose ageing owner had once been an important man in the Legislative Council. As I arrived at the bus company headquarters, I was shown to a waiting room outside the board room. From my seat I could see into the office of the old man who had a big smile on his face and appeared to be looking at a TV screen. I asked the receptionist what the old man was watching.

'Oh,' she said, 'that is a closed circuit TV to the money counting room.'

In those days all bus fares were paid in coins and the old man enjoyed watching his staff count up the takings. A few minutes later, the boss's daughter, who was effectively running the company, unceremoniously told me to enter the board room and sit down. She then demanded a much larger student subsidy than I was prepared to offer and we had a bit of an argument.

'You are a very insolent young man,' she declared, but we finally arrived at a compromise.

In the New Year, we had another bit of excitement. My boss had been trying to introduce electronic road pricing (ERP) as a solution to Hong Kong's chronic traffic congestion. It was a fairly simple idea – all private cars would need to have an electronic sensor installed and receptors would be buried at busy road junctions. The cost of using the road would vary depending on the road's capacity and the time of day. The idea was to charge for use of congested roads, especially during the morning and evening rush hour, and so reduce non-essential traffic. In theory it was a good idea and ahead of its time. However, the policy makers had not taken into account Hongkongers' paranoia about privacy. For example, the itemised monthly ERP bill might have alerted a businessman's wife to the fact that on Friday evening he was visiting his mistress in Kowloon Tong rather than attending a board meeting in Central, so the scheme was frowned on.

While the branch was preoccupied with ERP (or ERPes as people jokingly referred to the scheme) taxi drivers took exception to a proposal to raise their licence fees and threatened a strike. My boss, in a rare lapse of judgement, decided to call their bluff. He had been assured that the taxi drivers could not afford to go on strike. However, this proved to be duff advice as most of the taxis were owned by finance companies, which were indeed prepared to sponsor a short strike. On 15th January, what started as a protest drive by hundreds of taxis, degenerated into serious rioting on Nathan Road. This was a volatile area that had seen youth riots a few years before. Rioters attacked buses, overturned vehicles and smashed shop windows. There was also a manifestation of a particular Hong Kong phenomenon – designer looting. People were observed stealing shoes and trying to match them with handbags. At the end of the day, 150 rioters were arrested and that part of Nathan Road looked like a war zone.

That was not a good day for Transport Branch and it probably cost my boss his promotion to chief secretary, although he did serve for a while as deputy CS. In any case, policy secretaries were not then politically accountable as government policy was made by the Governor in Council. However, he did leave Hong Kong shortly afterwards to become governor of the Cayman Islands. I note that the HKSAR government is once again considering the idea of road pricing but somehow I don't think they will be as sensitive to adverse public opinion as was our old-fashioned colonial administration.

CHAPTER SEVEN

The Pearl of the Orient

WEEKENDS WERE NOW MOSTLY spent at an old Hakka house I had rented with a friend in the Sai Kung Country Park in the far northeast of the New Territories, where the turquoise waters of Mirs Bay lap gently against the coast of Mainland China. Like all country parks in the territory, it had been set up not so much to preserve nature as to protect the watersheds of the reservoirs in a place where water, before supply agreements were signed with China, was in critically short supply. It had been remarkably successful in both respects. Ranges of wooded, rolling hills rose to high peaks over which black kites and sea eagles soared. Hidden in the folds of valleys were small Hakka villages, many built in traditional style with stone walls and high tiled roofs, with watchtowers and windows barred against the pirates who had once terrorised the area. The Hakka ('guest people') were an ancient folk who had migrated to South China a few hundred years earlier, having fallen out with the emperor they served in the north. The Punti ('local people') migrated to Hong Kong during the Sung dynasty (960–1127) and had spread out over the fertile plains, so when the Hakka arrived they tended to settle in more remote, hilly areas. An extraordinary people, they produced two of the greatest Chinese leaders of the twentieth century, Sun Yat-sen and Deng Xiaoping.

Most of the lush, thick forest that now covered the territory had only developed since the late 1960s following the collapse of agriculture in the New Territories caused by the import of unlimited cheap food from China, and due to the mass planting of trees to moderate water flow and prevent silting in the water catchment areas which fed the reservoirs. When the British arrived, Hong Kong had been described as 'a barren rock' due to the practices of chopping down trees for firewood and burning hillsides to provide ash for fertiliser. The only exceptions were the groves of *fung shui* trees maintained near each traditional village, and which were carefully protected.

Uk Tau Village lay underneath Cow's Ear Mountain and consisted of a few ancient houses surrounded by paddy fields and fruit orchards. The locals were at a loss to explain what the village's name meant and suggested that it had originally been called Juk Tau (or Bamboo Ridge) which had been incorrectly copied in English by some illiterate clerk. When I first chanced on the village, I was hiking past and noticed an old man and woman sitting peacefully outside their house. 'Come and drink tea,' urged the old man with the great hospitality of country people everywhere. They wore the loose-fitting black pajamas typical of their folk. As I sat with them, he informed me that they had just built a new house at the back of the village and would soon move there. I told them I would be happy to rent their old house and gave them my phone number. A few months later, I received a call asking if I was still interested. My friend and I went over to sign a lease, bringing with us a bottle of brandy and a live duck we had bought from a nearby farm to seal the deal.

The traditional two-storied Hakka country house had high stone walls with a ceramic tiled roof and was over a hundred years old. The windows were barred and the huge wooden doors had granite lintels which could be barricaded against pirates. Inside, the roof was supported by large wooden beams (the main beam had a lucky red cloth hanging from it) and the upstairs rooms were separated by shoulder-high panelling. In the kitchen were a number of antique devices for pounding grain and threshing rice. There was a huge wok under what had once been a wood fire. Next door was a Chi Tong, or ancestral hall, and the whole area was surrounded by a courtyard.

The first thing we did was build an outside barbecue and the old man insisted on supervising our every move until we 'accidentally' dropped a trowel-load of cement on his shoe and he then reluctantly moved away. Next, we installed in the courtyard two large country park picnic tables made by inmates of the Correctional Services Department which could seat around twenty people. To protect diners from the rays of the sun, we built a pergola and planted creepers such as honeysuckle and jasmine. As we sat enjoying lunch after our long country walks, we could look out on the paddy fields and rolling green hills underneath the bright, blue sky. It was a veritable paradise.

Over the years, we acquired more like-minded partners and the old house next door. Our favourite walk was out of the village and up an ancient boulder pathway that took us up into the hills. We would walk over Cow's Ear Mountain, where the old man's ancestors were buried, over a plateau where anti-Japanese guerrilla had operated during the war, past ruined houses and down a steep path called Jacob's Ladder. Or we would go in the other direction over Sharp Peak and down to Tai Long Wan, a string of fine white beaches with surf which were amongst the best in the territory. Hiking in the autumn and winter was a joy but during the high summer it was just too hot and humid. Sometimes in the summer we walked down to an almost deserted village called To Kwa Ping and swim off its small pier.

At Mid-Autumn Festival we sat outside eating star fruit and mooncakes while gazing up at the huge Harvest Moon that hung like a white dinner plate in the velvet sky. That evening all children throughout the territory carried lanterns or candles. One night we sat entranced as a shower of Leonid meteorites lit up the sky and kept us entertained for hours with a most impressive light show. At Christmas, we decorated the garden with lights and enjoyed a traditional lunch of turkey and Christmas pudding. In the evening we often sat around the fire and played charades. Winters in the countryside can be quite cold with temperatures as low as five degrees.

Each November brought a charity event called 'Trailwalker'. It was organised by Oxfam, assisted by Gurkha troops stationed in Hong Kong, and was a sponsored walk for teams of four that followed the 100 km MacLehose Trail from Sai Kung in the east of the territory to Tuen Mun in the west. Most of the walk traversed the country parks which by then covered 40 per cent of the territory and one section of the trail passed fairly close to our house.

Someone had calculated that the accumulated ascent of all the many hills en route was equivalent to climbing Mt Everest. We walked the trail for three years in a row before our knees started suffering and our best time was around twenty hours. The Gurkha team managed to run it in twelve hours. Our first attempt was a lot of fun as our support team of girlfriends and spouses dressed up and served us a candlelit dinner with fine food and wine in the middle of nowhere. Then we walked straight through the night using head-torches and as dawn broke, some of us started to have hallucinations. By the time we limped across the finish line, our blisters needed the attention of the Gurkha doctors, but we had made it in decent time and raised a fair amount of money for charity too.

The local market town of Sai Kung was a fishing village that had been expanded in the seventies to provide for the relocation of villages moved to build the nearby High Island Reservoir. There was a large public pier which catered for the many junks and pleasure boats providing swimming and fishing trips for summer visitors, and it was famous for its seafood restaurants and al fresco dining. Known as the 'back garden' of Hong Kong, the Sai Kung area had an almost Mediterranean ambiance. On our way back from a long weekend in the country, we often stopped at one of the many restaurants for a quiet dinner before we headed back to the city. The road that connected Kowloon to Sai Kung was called Hiram's Highway and had been built by British army engineers in recognition of the spirited resistance but up by local villagers against the Japanese during the war.

On our walks around the country parks we were frequently disappointed with the actions of the Agriculture and Fisheries Department, who were meant to be looking after the maintenance of the parks. Having little idea of the needs of hikers, they liked to spend their budgets on destroying ancient stone pathways and creating ugly concrete paths with handrails, all in the name of safety and convenience. They also saw no problem in putting street lights through the parks, which made developers happy, but upset conservationists who enjoyed looking at the stars and who pointed out that wildlife would not cross illuminated roads. Following an outcry, there have been no further 'improvements'.

One of the great joys of the seasons in Hong Kong is the variety of vibrantly colourful plants and trees, many of which we passed on the trail. At Christmas there are vivid red poinsettias and coral trees. Hong Kong's national flower, the bauhinia, blooms in red, purple and white until the spring. At Chinese New Year, the fruit trees flower and peach blossoms adorn every home. They are not allowed to blossom early and if they are presumptuous enough to do so before midnight on Lunar New Year's Eve, then the offending flowers are plucked off. In February, the cotton trees (sometimes known as Public Works trees as they are very basic and their flowers annoyingly arrive before their leaves) thrust forth their huge orange-red flowers, especially on Cotton Tree Drive going up to the Peak. In the autumn, large sacks of cottony hair hang from the trees and drift airborne in the wind. Spring also brings the white blossom of the May tree and the pungent odour of the Horse Chestnut.

Come the misty weather in March, the azaleas are getting ready to burst into a riot of colour. The most famous display is in the gardens of Government House where they appear in all the colours of the rainbow: purple, yellow, white and orange. By late April, the acacias are putting forth their delicate flowers which are like little yellow balls. On the roads in Sai Kung in May, a carpet of yellow emerges as they fall to the ground. The purists don't like acacias or paperbarks as they are imports from Australia. At the first hint of June, around the time of the Dragon Boat Festival, the flame trees erupt in a glory of scarlet and orange and locals know it is time to head for the beach. You may see the large red flowers of the African tulip trees and the blue haze of the occasional jacaranda. In the markets, the first succulent *lai chi* and *lung ngan* (dragon's eyes) fruit are available to enjoy. Locals also enjoy durian but, smelling as they do of rotting cheese, these are not for the faint hearted. In July, bright orange seed pods hang from the *sterculania* trees and all over town, the purple blossoms of the *ji mei* abound. Nor have I mentioned the abundant frangipani, bougainvillea and hibiscus flowering in every garden. In the countryside numerous banana, mango and papaya are ripening in the sun. Come the dry weather in autumn, the colour of the flowering creepers becomes intense, culminating in the glorious orange firecracker at the end of the year.

Hong Kong's fauna is equally diverse. In the New Territories, wild pig, monkeys and porcupine are common. Barking deer and leopard cat can still be seen but are increasingly rare. In Sai Kung and Lantau are many feral cattle descended from draught animals used before the collapse of agriculture in the sixties. There is an abundant snake population, including cobras and python which will feast on calf and other small animals. There are pangolin and in the delta swim the Chinese White Dolphin, although now seriously endangered.

The bird life is extremely rich, with over 500 species. High in the sky all over the territory, and particularly over the harbour, may be seen soaring Asian kites. Near any secluded stream hikers can glimpse kingfishers of iridescent blue and crested bulbuls which rise and dip in the bamboo groves. Sulphur-crested cockatoos, which escaped from the zoo during the Japanese occupation, are particularly raucous in town. There are sea eagles and ospreys, herons, egrets, plovers and the noisy koel, which is the harbinger of summer. In the densest parts of the city, colonies of hardy sparrows thrive. There are also 235 species of butterfly, including the glorious swallowtail, jezebel, albatross, peacock and tiger. Sometimes spread on a bush may be seen the giant Atlas moth.

The advent of summer means that people think not only of beaches but of boats. Hong Kong developed and prospered mainly because of its excellent harbour. A large part of the local population originally lived on boats as Tanka boat people and there are also Hoklo fisherfolk from the coast of Guangdong. Up until the eighties there were thousands of boat people living in the typhoon shelters and many more in the various fishing fleets. It was a common sight to spot huge Mainland junks, with not a lick of paint on them, sailing through the harbour and sometimes we would toss them cans of beer from our boats as they sailed past. Aside from all the ferries and working boats, there are thousands of pleasure craft in local waters. Yachts, speedboats and huge gin palaces owned by fat-cat tycoons fill the many marinas and the moorings of the Royal Hong Kong Yacht Club.

In the eighties, some friends and I owned a small junk called *Sandgroper* and when it was destroyed in a typhoon we bought a larger pleasure junk named *Middle Island* although everyone called it *Titanic* because things were always going wrong. One day our engine failed off the south coast of Hong Kong Island and we drifted into Chinese waters. One of the guests on board was an ex-Gurkha major. 'Surely you have a radio and emergency supplies?' he asked. We could only shake our heads. Eventually, I flagged down a Mainland trawler while ostentatiously waving some $100 notes. The trawler threw us a line and towed us to Aberdeen, where the irate major disembarked. Most Wednesday evenings we would motor over to Lamma Island for a seafood dinner and a few bottles of wine. An all-day boat trip meant a lot of booze, sun and swimming and instead of being pleasantly refreshed, you tended to return home absolutely exhausted.

Some of our friends had large sailing yachts rather than gin palaces. One friend used to race in the harbour and around the island. Another inherited a Baltic ketch called *Solitaire* from his grandfather and he sailed her all the way from Europe to Hong Kong. He frequently visited the Philippines and one summer we joined her in Puerto Galera. I remember a memorable evening with a stunning sunset streaking the sky pink and red, sitting around drinking Cuba Libres and putting the world to right. What a carefree crew we were, chatting and laughing on board or in a seaside tavern. Yet life is impermanent. Sadly, a few years later this lively friend died in a diving accident, which gave us all pause for thought. At some stage in our lives, we all have a 'wake-up' call or see an image of the Grim Reaper, which reminds us of how the unexpected can strike and gives an added urgency to do something important with our lives.

Back at work, my next posting was to Housing Department. Hong Kong has one of the largest public housing programmes in the world, and at that time about half the population of 5 million was living in subsidised housing. This was an anomaly, given Hong Kong's famous laissez-faire economy, but it helped social stability and enabled local employers to pay lower wages. My job was to help coordinate the enormous construction programme and to prepare monthly reports.

The authorities had been reluctant to build public housing lest it encourage even more refugees from China. Then there was a terrible fire on Christmas Day, 1953 in the Shek Kip Mei squatter area that left 53,000 people homeless. The government established a Resettlement Department which put up basic housing blocks with a space allowance of twenty-four square feet per adult and half that for children in families within the financial eligibility limits (up to $600 monthly income for a family of four; rising to $2,000 in 1973). One of the officials involved told me that the original blocks had been designed on the back of an envelope. Although most of the older ones have now been redeveloped, one of the early Shek Kip Mei blocks has been preserved as a historic building.

This desperate need for housing must be seen in the context of Hong Kong's rising population, which was increasing at the rate of a million per decade from 1950–1980. In 1961, eighteen estates were built under the Low Cost Housing Programme and by 1970 the blocks had reached sixteen floors with elevators. The first self-contained estate with commercial facilities was Oi Man Chuen at Ho Man Tin, built in 1975. Subsequently, Sir Murray MacLehose announced a ten-year housing programme, which required 1.5m public flats to be built in the urban area and 300,000 in the New Town Development Programme. Within this period, all squatter areas of jerry-built huts were to be cleared. In 1980, the first Home Ownership scheme was introduced, with flats about half the price of those in the private sector because government subsidised the land cost.

I found my workload at Ho Man Tin a little light, but when I complained to the other AO in the department he looked at me aghast and snarled, 'Lei m sik dim jo' (You don't know how to behave). They did, however, give me some extra duties, including taking various overseas visitors around public housing estates. One of them was the writer, Bruce Chatwin, who absolutely refused to believe that a family of four could live in 200 square feet. I explained that Hong Kong was very short of space and that local people were used to leaving in cramped conditions. He was not convinced. He also wanted to know more about the so-called 'cagemen' who were normally singletons living in cheap hostel-type accommodation. The lockable cage around the bunk was to protect their possessions, although the foreign press always liked to compare them to caged animals in a zoo.

There were few adjustment problems in Hong Kong when families moved from low to high-rise accommodation, unlike in the UK, where high-rise public housing has been a completely unsuccessful experiment. The one exception is Tin Shui Wai, which was built by the private sector without proper open space or recreational facilities, and became something of a ghetto for newly-arrived Mainland families. One of the reasons high-rise living has worked here is due to general urban density where each development is surrounded by other residential or commercial developments so there is little chance of people feeling lonely or isolated.

On the other side of the fence, one of the great things about colonial government service was long leave. Normally, after a two-and-a-half year tour of duty, you were entitled to four months leave, based on the time it took (before air travel became the norm) to return to the UK and back by ship. You could also opt for annual leave, which was six weeks. Either way, you had enough time to do some proper travelling. That year I flew to South America and spent a month in Peru and Bolivia, walking the Inca trail from Cuzco to Machu Picchu with a girl from Vancouver and spending a week on an island in the middle of Lake Titicaca. At one point we camped near a ruined village in the jungle and I walked down alone to the river to find some water. I was just thinking how strong and fit I felt when the path collapsed near a steep drop but luckily I managed to hang on to a bush and climb back up. If I had fallen, I would have broken my leg at least and, as we were miles from civilisation, I could have died. I took it as a sign for me to respect nature and not to be so cocky.

I had another reminder of my mortality in the north of Peru in a town called Huarez. The evening before we had been chewing coca leaves – which are legal – and one of the group had bought a bag of bicarbonate of soda to aid the process. I guess one of the locals must have thought it was a bag of cocaine as early the next morning there was a Wagnerian banging on my hotel door and when I opened it, two police officers were pointing their revolvers at me. It took a few hours to explain the mistake. Incidentally, the only other time that happened to me was in Saigon when a soldier pointed a Kalashnikov rifle at me when I was riding in a rickshaw with a local girl. He ordered me out and asked for $100. It is amazing how fast you pay up when you are staring down the barrel of a gun!

As we were waiting for a ferry on Lake Titicaca, I decided to take a dip in the highest lake in the world (12,000 feet). The locals threw me a lifebelt assuming I had fallen in, as no one, they reasoned, would be stupid enough to jump voluntarily into water that cold. As it turned out, I swam in both the highest and lowest lakes in the world during that leave. In Israel, we swam in the Dead Sea and my friend made the mistake of diving in and came up blinded and covered in salt rashes.

In La Paz, we met a Spanish hippie who insisted on accompanying us to an area outside the city called the Mountains of the Moon to look for San Pedro, a form of hallucinogenic cactus.

'There is a beautiful one!' said the hippie, pointing to a seven-foot cactus. 'Now we have to take a large piece.'

I reached for my penknife but the hippie grunted with shock.

'No! San Pedro is holy – cannot cut. Must use rope.'

So we used the cord from a sleeping bag and snapped off a one-foot section of cactus. Then the hippie sat down and carefully removed the spikes and skin with a knife and sliced the tender flesh into thin sections like a green mango and put them on a rock to dry in the strong sunshine. In the evening we returned to the city with our haul.

La Paz, apart from being situated at high altitude, is the exact opposite of Hong Kong. The poor people live high up on the mountain while the rich live down at the bottom. Our guesthouse was halfway up the hillside. After dinner we decided to try the San Pedro. It was very difficult to eat, with a slippery texture and a nauseous, bitter taste. Around ten minutes after swallowing it we all threw up, but it was enough. Then followed one of the most intense psychedelic experiences I have ever had. For the rest of the night we watched the intense colours of the moon on the hillside and drank tea. When we finally went inside, we heard a loud banging on the door that seemed to go on for hours as if something was trying to come in after us. We did not open it.

Psychedelic experience has often been described as a gateway to spiritual understanding. It breaks down the concept of self, reveals the sublime beauty of the universe and like the famous New York hot dog, makes us 'one with everything'. It came as no surprise to find out years later that Steve Jobs, the brilliant founder of Apple and purveyor of the iPhone, had been a regular user of psychedelics at college. For those who did not actually blow their minds it appeared to deliver a potent creative empowerment.

Upon arriving back in the UK, I arranged an extravagant dinner party for my friends. We drank many bottles of wine and had a wonderful evening, laughing and telling stories. My mother sat on one side, bemused. On the way home she looked at me sideways and finally observed, 'I must admit, you certainly know how to enjoy yourself!' Her tone was ambiguous but the statement was true. The next day an official letter arrived from the Hong Kong government. On it was scrawled, 'Welcome to the effluent society', accompanying the news that I had been posted to Health and Welfare Branch as principal assistant secretary pollution.

Back in Hong Kong, I noted that almost everywhere there was a huge amount of new construction of roads and housing estates. It is said of Hong Kong that you will know that it has changed when it stops changing. Moreover, while I was away a very disturbing event had taken place. I have said that Hong Kong is generally a very safe place. However, in April 1985, a rare and profoundly shocking interracial hate crime occurred. Two British teenagers from the Island School were revising in a section of country park near Braemar Hill when a gang of five Chinese youths passed by, whose ringleader was a junior member of a triad society. This unfortunate encounter turned into a brutal double murder when it transpired that the foreigners only had a $1 coin on them. Following a territory-wide manhunt and after a large reward was offered, the ringleader was shopped by a triad informer. Although two of the gang were juvenile, the others were adults and sentenced to life imprisonment. Throughout the trial the junior triad never showed any sign of remorse.

These were the early days of environmental protection. The EPD had just been set up and being 'green' at heart, I took to it like a duck to water. I was secretary to the Environmental Protection Committee (EPCOM) and we needed to enact a lot of new legislation: water quality regulations, a public air quality index (which lasted twenty years), regulations to control livestock waste and a new Noise Control Bill. We kept the law draftsman very busy.

As part of Hong Kong's commitment to protect the ozone layer, we needed to control the use of fluorocarbons, which were used in air conditioning and aerosol spray products. To illustrate the average Hongkonger's reaction to such measures, I intercepted a letter from an eminent professor who sat on EPCOM addressed to his commercial clients, urging them to hurry up and establish such polluting businesses before the regulations took effect. When I remonstrated with him about this, he really could not see that he had done anything wrong. To him it was just pragmatic.

Another environmental problem that was to grow exponentially in the next few decades was air pollution. Measurement of key air pollutants (particulates, SOx, NOx, CO and lead) caused by power stations, diesel vehicles, shipping and cross-border emissions were already starting to rise. This would lead to widespread smog; health problems such as asthma, allergies and respiratory disease; and economic loss to Hong Kong due to medical costs, lost productivity and decreasing tourism. By the turn of the millennium, Hong Kong University would say that air pollution was responsible for 90,000 hospital admissions and 2,800 premature deaths per year. The economic cost was estimated at $20 billion.

Around half of Hong Kong's air pollution is generated locally while half comes from Mainland sources such as factories, coal-fired power stations, vehicles and the general use of low-quality fuel. As our prevailing winds are northerly in the winter, smog is more likely at that time of the year, whereas our skies tend to be clearer in the summer due to southerly winds. The government therefore needed to start a dialogue with the Guangdong authorities to reduce cross-border emissions.

Left: Thomas Evans, my great-great-grandfather, was sent from his native Pembrokeshire to India in 1856 by the Baptist Missionary Society and met his wife in Agra Fort during the Mutiny. He died in 1906 after 50 years' service and is buried in Moradabad.

Below: Rev. Clare Boulton, my great-uncle, owned a cider works in Hereford. Having learnt to fly in the 1930s he bought a De Havilland Moth and used to land on beaches to preach to holidaymakers. He was known as 'The Flying Vicar'.

Above: David Hooper, my great-grandfather, was government botanist in Madras and subsequently curator of the Indian Museum in Calcutta. In 2012, on a visit to Calcutta, my friends and I found his portrait in a dusty corner of the museum.

Below: Oxford days – celebrating with friends in June 1974 after the last of my final exams.

Above: On the hippie trail outside the Taj Mahal in summer 1972, having travelled overland from Istanbul.

Below: My grandparents' wedding in 1916. Standing behind my grandmother is great-uncle Clare (who looks like me) and the second lady from the right is great-aunt Gwyneth, who lived to be 98.

Family portrait, around 1955. My father sits in the middle with my grandfather standing, grandmother to his right and my brother, sister and cousins sitting on the ground. I sit in my mother's lap and suck my thumb.

Above: With my father and mother in a nifty outfit, aged 3.
Right: It seems that I liked ice cream.

Above: In police summer uniform, smoking a cigar on my balcony in Kadoorie Avenue in 1978. The length of my hair indicates that I was already in CID.

Below: Mess Night at the Police Training School, Aberdeen, 1977. Such events were formal dinners with much drinking, toasts and speeches, including the Trooping of the Duck, our 'regimental' mascot.

Above: A party after 'passing out' from the Police Training School. My girlfriend, Lilian, is leaning on my shoulder.

Below: My mother, stepfather, Lilian and I enjoy a dinner out in 1978.

Above: My first trip to China in 1978. This is the old Bailey bridge across the Shenzhen River at the main border crossing, Lo Wu.

Below: PLA soldiers in the back of a lorry stare at the strange foreigners.

Above: Clowning around with Chinese children, one of whom has his mouth full of rice.

Below: With Liu Je, the urbane party secretary of Shenzhen, around 1985. We had been invited across the border that summer to sample the excellent *lai chi* harvest.

Above: Posing with the wife of a transport official, I celebrate riding on the last KCR diesel train before electrification.

Below left: Wan Chai District Office Sports Day 1990, awarding a prize to the chairman of an area committee.

Below right: As District Officer, introducing Wan Chai District Board Chairlady, Peggy Lam, to the Chief Secretary, Sir David Ford, in 1992.

Taking part in the Keep Hong Kong Clean Campaign: Miss Hong Kong is on my left and on my right is Denis Bray, senior Hong Kong civil servant and former acting Governor District Police Commander, Ian Nicholson, looks on.

Above: Chatting with the Governor, Sir David Wilson, at a spring reception in 1991 while Secretary for Home Affairs, Peter Tsao, looks on.

Below: Discussing the first direct election to the Legislative Council in 1991 with Director of Home Affairs, David Lan.

Above: The Junior Police Call Dinner, 1990. The *kaifongs* (neighbourhood associations) were great supporters of police activities.

Below: Dotting the eyes of the dragon, a duty of the guest of honour, which brings the dragon to life.

Above: The opening of the Wan Chai District Office new public enquiry counter in 1989. Peggy Lam, David Lan and Mike Prew, District Police Commander, sit behind.

Below: Tree planting in the Green Wan Chai Campaign with Dr Stuart Reid, Director of Environmental Protection. This was one of the 600 street trees we planted.

Above: Barbeque lunch at Uk Tau, Sai Kung country park, 1985. A Sunday walk followed by a picnic lunch was a Hong Kong way of life.

Below: Amateur dramatics with the Garrison Players in the 1980s. This was 'Quire's Complaint' performed at the Fringe Theatre.

Above: Zoe and I tie the knot at St Thomas à Becket Church, South Stoke, near Bath in July 1999, flanked by my mother and brother and sister's families.

Below left: Zoe and I visiting Buddhist temples in Sikkim, 2012.

Below right: Lama Kelzang, born in Bhutan, has run Buddhist centres in Hong Kong for nearly 30 years.

Above: As Chairman of the Royal Commonwealth Society, we celebrate the Queen's 90th birthday at the Helena May in April 2016.

Below: The Lion and the Dragon have been dancing together for hundreds of years (see the last chapter).

GAVIN COATES

On the welfare side of the house, there was an eccentric Chinese lady who was obsessed with *fung shui*. Whenever I entered her office it was being redecorated and reconfigured to ensure better luck. It appeared to be working as we understood that she enjoyed private wealth. One winter's day we read in the newspapers that she had been driven in a limousine to visit a group of street sleepers under a flyover and stepped out of the car dressed in a mink coat in order to reassure them that the government had their best interests at heart. She was clearly a fan of Imelda Marcos!

Another serious environmental problem was the increasing amounts of livestock waste that were being dumped into our streams and watercourses. Although most of the colony's pork came from China, local pig farmers made good money when shortages arose over the border. In the New Territories, so much pig waste was being pumped into Tolo Harbour that it was fast turning black and anaerobic due to the huge concentration of nutrients. I was asked to chair a working group to suggest how we could introduce and enforce controls. In one meeting, a rather humourless local officer asked what sort of legislation we were planning to introduce. *'Habeus Porcus,'* I replied, straight-faced. When the livestock waste control regulations were debated in the Legislative Council, the pig farmers created a minor riot and dumped a number of buckets of pig shit on the governor's Daimler (this may have been the third riot I helped to start, if you counted the hawker in the harbour in '77 and the Taxi Riots in '84).

The governor, Sir David Wilson (who had been political advisor when I was preparing my reports on Chinese gunboat incursions) summoned the secretary for health and welfare and myself to Government House the next morning at 9 a.m. sharp. In reply to his question about why the farmers had been upset, we explained that if we did not take action soon, then Tolo Harbour would become a black, stinking mess. Sir David, who was a great hiker and lover of wildlife, listened politely, nodded and dismissed us. It is most gratifying to have a boss who gives you his full support.

I was asked to arrange a meeting in Beijing between EPCOM and the Chinese central government. The Chinese agreed that a regular meeting should be set up with the Pearl River Delta authorities.

They said that as China's economy developed, they foresaw that this would become a big problem on the Mainland too, so they were considering their own legislation and control measures for environmental protection. Unfortunately, the pressure for economic growth over the next two decades was so great that environmental quality was sacrificed in the name of progress. In between meetings, we managed to visit the Forbidden City, the Temple of Heaven and the Great Wall, which makes you realise what a truly great empire China was in its heyday – and to those prescient enough, how quickly it would assume great power status once again.

Returning to the UK on leave in 1988, I was invited by an Oxford friend, John Carmichael, to visit his family in Ghana. We decided to risk Aeroflot via Moscow as another of our friends was serving in the British Embassy there. Upon arrival at Sheremetyevo Airport, we walked out into the snow and hailed a taxi. It was to be the most frightening journey of our lives. Although the roads were covered with snow and ice, the driver, who spoke no English, drove at full speed towards the city, sliding and skidding. We surmised that he must be drunk or that his wife had just left him, or both. The more we yelled, the faster he drove. After what seemed an eternity, he came to a stop. We opened our eyes and saw to our great relief that we were in front of our hotel.

Our friend showed us around the city and we dined in a restaurant near Red Square. This was still the hard-line communist days, and it was a revelation for us to see how well the diplomatic community and senior party members lived. We started with champagne and moved on to vodka and caviar. Our succulent sirloin steaks were washed down with an excellent Georgian red wine. Outside on the street, it was cold and grey and looked like the Harkonnen homeworld. Also of interest was that all the apartments had humidifiers to counteract the extreme dryness, whereas in Hong Kong we had dehumidifiers to reduce the thick humidity.

From Moscow, we flew to Accra. Before independence, Ghana had been one of the most successful countries in Africa; a thriving economy, the world's largest cocoa producer and the highest literacy rate on the continent. Nkrumah's Marxist experiment ended all that. He tried to create heavy industries and ignored agriculture.

The cocoa crop was ruined and the country sank into poverty. This was a sad story repeated in many ex-British colonies due to tribalism and corruption. Indeed, it has been said that one of the few territories that actually became economically better off after independence was Singapore, thanks to the industry of the Chinese.

Accra in the mid-eighties was like a living museum. Everything was crumbling and run down. It would have been depressing without the high spirits and vitality of the local people. My friend's father lived in a compound near the airport. He was a Scotsman who had served with the RAF during the war, training colonial pilots to fly Spitfires and Hurricanes to take part in the desert war. Sporting long white hair and a beard, and looking for all the world like an Old Testament prophet, he was a true eccentric. Having had a traditional African night out, including drinking the murderous bitters or *apotache* with two Ashanti girls called Ebony and Ivory, I was warned that breakfast was at 7 a.m. *sharp* and that the old man did not take kindly to lateness. Pulled from my bed with a raging hangover at 6.55 a.m., I stumbled into breakfast at around 7.03 a.m.

'Good morning!' I said in what I hoped was a cheery manner.

'Good afternoon!' was the reply.

Later in the day, we were on the roof admiring a beautiful creeping plant when we saw the old man emerge in his beekeeping outfit.

'Shall I bring some of these lovely flowers down for the dinner table?' I called down.

'No!' he said, glaring at me.

One day we had lunch in what had been a five-star hotel but was by then a crumbling ruin with a cracked and empty pool. Then we went to the Accra races, which was fun. My friend sponsored a very good local band called Grass Roots which played at events all over town, and later we brought them to perform in Hong Kong where they were destined to play an important role in my life. At the weekend, we went to Oburi Botanical Gardens where there were some huge trees and colourful plants. In a corner sat two very dignified local men wearing formal *kinti* robes.

'Here come some big white men!' said one of them.

'There are no big white men any more,' the other replied.

Another time we were driving through the city when we were stopped by a policeman directing traffic.

'What colour am I?' he asked.

I wanted to say he was as black as the ace of spades but luckily kept my mouth shut.

'When my hands are up, I'm red,' he continued, 'and when they're down, I'm green.'

Another expedition took us to Cape Coast Castle and El Mina, the two greatest slaving forts on the West African coast. It is estimated that the ancestors of over half the black population of the Americas came through these horrible places. As you stand on the battlements, the old cannon point out towards the thundering surf. In Takoradi, we met some Chinese businessmen who invited us back for dinner. Even in those days, the Chinese were big players in Africa. They had a factory with their own living quarters and private restaurant. My friend said that he had never before in his country tasted food as good as that served by these Chinese.

On a later trip to Ghana to celebrate the wedding of our friend, Prince George, whose father was chief of the coastal Fanti tribe, my friend, who had spent much of his life in Africa, was 'ambushed' by the villagers of Fete on the Atlantic coast and underwent various rituals to make him into a tribal chieftain. To be 'enstooled' is a great honour in recognition of services rendered to the community and with it come privileges and responsibilities. Prince Charles was also made a chief some years before. All chiefs need to have 'linguists' at their side who speak on their behalf.

On my way back to the UK, I stopped in Egypt for some sightseeing and early one morning managed to climb to the top of the Great Pyramid of Cheops. It is not strictly allowed but it is useful to know what a little baksheesh can achieve. The sight of the sun rising over Cairo is something I shall never forget. The other thing which sticks in my memory is sitting in the bazaar drinking a cup of coffee and watching a camel pass by strapped to the top of a jeep.

Back in Hong Kong, I had moved from Conduit Road to a large quarters with a garden at Mansfield Road on the Peak. Actually, it was more Magazine Gap than the Peak and a mischievous friend used to write to me at 'Mansfield Road, Almost-the-Peak, Hong Kong'. Nearby was a trail that led to a country park with excellent hiking. I was still a carefree bachelor but had recently met a Eurasian girl who had been living in California. We became fairly serious until she had to return to LA to nurse a friend who was dying of cancer.

When I moved into the Mansfield Road flat, I had a large housewarming party to which I invited my Chinese secretary. She was an eccentric girl who liked to wear colourful and romantic party frocks to work. Having arrived at the party and drunk one glass of wine, her face turned red and she decided to lie down in the middle of the floor. When I asked her if she would not rather rest in a chair, she replied that she was perfectly comfortable. My guests were then forced to walk around her sleeping figure for the rest of the evening.

As a bachelor, I did not have any of my own furniture but luckily the government had plenty. You could also apply for an 'emergency kit' which was intended for newcomers from England and consisted of basic cookware, crockery stamped with the official crest, and towels and sheets that most women would turn their nose up at. The original HK government had been an offshoot of the Indian administration and used a lot of arcane Indian terms. As you looked through the furniture list you found items such as a *charpoy* which was a woven bed and a *tallboy* which was a cabinet. There were, and still are, many other Anglo-Indian words use in Hong Kong, such as *tiffin, rickshaw, verandah, cheroot* and *bungalow.* You paid your bills to a *shroff,* a cashier, and you tried not to fall in the *nullah,* which was a small river or storm drain encased in concrete.

It was at Mansfield Road that I decided to employ a full-time maid. Prior to that, I had hired a part-time *amah* called Ah Lo, who wore the traditional uniform of black baggy trousers and a white top. Chinese *amahs,* however, refused to clean floors or windows without extra pay and expected a fat red packet at Chinese New Year. My new maid was Filipina and called Leticia, or Lety. She served me faithfully for over ten years and followed me to Clear Water Bay. Her son, Jeff (or Jep as she pronounced it) was immensely strong and would come over to do odd jobs. One day, as some unknown people had been cutting down trees, I asked him to number all the trees in a certain part of the village. When I came back I found that all the trees had Xs painted on them. I pointed out that this was not much use as you were not sure whether there were ten or twenty Xs.

'Sir,' said Lety, 'I told him so, but *Jep porgot!*'

Another time Lety said, 'Sir, I have thrown away that bottle of water in the freezer as it was too old.'

'Do you mean my special vodka, Lety?' I asked.

Then there was the time we were decorating the house and the kitchen looked like a bombsite. I walked in and called for her. Suddenly, a towel levitated spookily and underneath was Lety who had been taking a nap with the towel over her head.

I am a great dog lover and my family always had dogs when I was a child. Recently, we had taken in a black Chow called Inky who came from Middle Island. She could jump at least ten feet and no wall could keep her in. One Sunday, we went for lunch at the Frog and Toad on Lantau, a rustic pub where the owner was a Chinese *kung fu* practitioner who enjoyed drinking tequila. His dog had recently given birth to a litter of puppies and he offered me one. When I arrived home that night I put the puppy in the garden. Next morning, I was woken early by Lety.

'Sir, there is a strange dog in the garden.'

I did not reply.

'Sir, what shall we call the dog?'

As I lifted my head, a fleeting memory of the previous day's events stirred in my mind. 'Tequila,' I replied.

About a week later on her day off, Lety left a note which read:

'Sir, Killer's dinner is in the oven.'

Talking of dogs, recent research has shown that the release of the 'love hormone' oxytocin floods the bodies of both humans and dogs when they look into each other's eyes, similar to when mothers look at their babies. Evidently, over the last ten thousand years dogs have developed this ancient function and it may explain the close relationship that exists between humans and their pets. I sub-sequently had a dog called Ja Ja, who was a mix of German Shepherd, Chow and Rottweiler and was the greediest dog I had ever known, even eating fruit and vegetables; and B Lui, an intelligent and loyal Japanese Shiba who was prone to nipping strangers. When I had a party, I had to put her in a room with a sign that said, *Do not touch the yellow dog!*

When I first arrived in Hong Kong, local people were generally scared of dogs. I had wondered whether this was a guilty reaction as in the past dog meat was popular with Chinese. However, over the last two decades, there has been a huge increase in dog owner-ship among middle-class locals, although pets are still not allowed in public housing estates. One bizarre anti-dog manifestation is the horrible case of the Bowen Road dog poisoner, the nemesis of local dogs, who lays poisoned meat in the area and has been responsible for the deaths of hundreds. Despite action by the police and vigilante groups, and the offering of substantial financial rewards, this wicked person has never been caught.

In early 1989, I was appointed district officer, Wan Chai. It was meant to be a penalty posting as I had got into a bit of trouble in my environmental job. Apart from being too 'green' for the government's liking, I had made some critical comments about the slow implementation of environmental policies, which had been reported in the local press. Although we had been sent on media courses, talking to the local press was always a risk for civil servants as you could never be sure whether what was published would be an accurate summary of what you had said. That is why most public servants avoid reporters like the plague. On this occasion I had also committed the cardinal sin of recommending privatisation of some traditional civil service jobs, such as drainage services.

I was possibly too candid with the press and it sometimes got me into trouble. The main rule is never to answer specific questions but to concentrate on the information you want published. TV interviews also had their drawbacks, as the news producer could edit what you said to create a story that would stir up controversy. They could also make you look pretty stupid if they so wished. My predecessor smoked a pipe and had given an interview on the proposed livestock waste measures. When the interview appeared on TV, they focused on him cleaning his pipe and then cut to pigs rooting around in the mud. However, what was meant to be a penalty posting from the Secretariat to Wan Chai turned out to be the best job I ever had.

However, there now occurred a most terrible event. In May 1989, following the death of popular reformist Communist Party General Secretary, Hu Yaobang, and under the gaze of moderate new party leader, Zhou Ziyang, the students in Beijing had taken to the streets with demands for political reform. Criticising the corruption of the party elite and calling for government accountability and freedom of speech, they set up camp outside the Great Hall of the People in Tiananmen Square (ironically meaning the Square of Heavenly Peace). Hard-line premier Li Peng tried unsuccessfully to negotiate with the protesters whom he dubbed as 'counter-revolutionaries' and martial law was declared on 20th May when troops were mobilised in the capital. Things were getting out of hand and the authorities panicked. Unfortunately the capital did not have trained riot police or smoke grenades. There had been no civil disorder in China since the Cultural Revolution, and then it had been encouraged at the highest levels.

China's leaders had an ancient fear of chaos and were concerned that this was a counter-revolutionary rebellion that could have led to civil war, so they sent in soldiers and tanks. The famous picture of one brave student standing in front of a row of immobilised tanks quickly went around the world. The forces sent in to the square were not Beijing troops, who were unlikely to fire on their own people, but the Hubei garrison who may also have been dosed up on amphetamines. On June 4th, there was widespread bloodshed. No one knows how many died as this 'incident' is still a taboo subject in China. Estimates range from several hundred to a thousand. This is denied by the authorities to this day in a spell of collective amnesia, but sooner or later a Chinese leader is going to have to say something about the 'incident' that is known in Hong Kong simply as *luk say* or 6/4.

The reaction in Hong Kong was one of shock and horror. It appeared that the Joint Declaration on the Handover of Hong Kong in 1997 might well unravel on the strength of this carnage.

The stock market plunged and thousands of Hong Kong people queued at the American, Canadian and Australian consulates to apply for foreign passports. Many families did subsequently emigrate (at least 130,000 people left in 1990–91) and this was the origin of the 'astronaut' – a Chinese businessman whose family is in Toronto or Melbourne but who works in Hong Kong. Given the mood of uncertainty, Britain subsequently agreed to grant passports to 50,000 local families. To boost confidence, the government announced a mega project to build a new airport at a cost $200 billion, which was dubbed as the 'Rose Garden' and seen by the Mainland as a British plot to drain Hong Kong's financial reserves. People continued to walk around the city in a sombre mood shaking their heads. Although China's economy subsequently recovered and grew in a spectacular fashion following Deng Xiaoping's 'Southern Tour' in 1992, political reform in China has effectively been frozen since that sad day.

Meanwhile, the exact opposite was happening in the Soviet Union and this is one of the reasons for the hard-line reaction to events in China. Under Gorbachev's policies of *perestroika* (restructuring) and *glasnost* (opening up) a programme of political reform and liberalisation had been unleashed which led in late 1989 to the fall of the Berlin Wall and the loosening of Soviet hegemony in eastern Europe. China's fear of political reform was intensified by the subsequent dissolution of the Soviet Union, loss of power by its Communist Party and the rise of long-suppressed nationalist feelings in the former Soviet republics. All-in-all, this was a nightmare scenario for the Communist Party of China.

As a postscript to this tragic incident, Hong Kong played an important and rather subversive role in helping student leaders who had survived and were in hiding to escape through Hong Kong to reach exile in the US and Canada. The operation was called 'Yellow Bird' and various local agencies, including the police Special Branch, helped in this exercise. Hong Kong's reaction to the events of June 4th and to Mainland politics in general provoked a stern response from Jiang Zemin, who observed, 'Well water and river water should never mix.'

CHAPTER EIGHT

The Sheriff of Wan Chai

IT IS ONLY A FEW MINUTES by car or bus from the glittering towers of Hong Kong's Central business district to Wan Chai, but the difference is striking. Although high-rise buildings have gone up along the main roads and in Wan Chai North, the area still has a homely, Chinese feel to it. In Southorn Playground, office workers eat lunch boxes while watching local teams play energetic games of basketball and football. Under the Canal Road flyover, ageing female exorcists will, for a fee, beat shoes on pictures of your boss or anyone else you dislike. In hundreds of small, local restaurants, or *cha chaan teng* you can buy a decent lunch for around HK$40. On Lockhart Road, modern-day Suzie Wongs still dance in girlie bars, although these days the girls are mainly imports from the Philippines and Thailand and gone are the days when the bars were filled with American sailors on R&R from Vietnam. Wan Chai was immortalised by the 1957 publication of Richard Mason's famous book, *The World of Suzie Wong* and the subsequent film starring William Holden and Nancy Kwan. Mason had been in the RAF during the war and had been taught Japanese in order to interrogate prisoners in Burma.

Wan Chai, which means 'Little Bay', is full of historical colour. Towards Causeway Bay is the Noonday Gun, immortalised by Noel Coward in his song *Mad Dogs and Englishmen* and still fired every day by Jardines as a Victorian punishment for saluting one of their *taipan*s with a twenty-one-gun salute, regarded as a breach of protocol by the Royal Navy. On a hill to the west was the Naval Hospital (now the Ruttonjee Sanatorium) and you can still see stone markers with the RN anchor crest on Wan Chai Road. Across the road was the China Fleet Club which was one of the colony's great social centres and in early days, Government House itself was located in Spring Garden Lane. Lockhart Road was named after a famous colonial secretary who was a Chinese scholar and talented administrator. Johnston Road was named after another colonial administrator and tutor to the last Manchu emperor. Messrs Fleming, March, Stewart and Southorn were all colonial secretaries; Luard was an army commander, Tonnochy the superintendent of Victoria Gaol and Jaffe the Public Works Department engineer of Tai Tam Reservoir.

District officers (DOs) had in the nineteenth and early twentieth century administered large parts of the empire. After the Cultural Revolution spilled over into Hong Kong in 1967, causing riots and civil disorder, the government thought it advisable to extend the DO scheme from the rural areas to the city, so they could keep a finger on the pulse of the local people. Wan Chai District, traditionally conservative and pro-China, included Causeway Bay, Happy Valley and Tai Hang and had a population of around 200,000. In the absence of an official Chinese diplomatic presence in Hong Kong, the New China News Agency, or Xinhua, situated in the heart of the district, fulfilled this role. The main duties of the DO were to provide administrative backup to the District Board, a half-elected and half-appointed local representative body, and to chair the District Management Committee, whose job was to identify and solve local problems and to make district administration more efficient. The DO was also an ex-officio justice of the peace, thus giving him higher status. In fact, he was like a mayor, coordinating the work of government departments concerned with security; public transport; environmental services such as street cleaning, markets, food hygiene and hawker control; cultural facilities and planning and development.

I was not entirely unaware of the irony that twelve years earlier as a newly arrived police inspector, I had been an enthusiastic partaker in Wan Chai's colourful nightlife – and here I was as its district officer. There again, it was certainly an advantage to know the district well.

The District Board (DB) was more of a political body and its elected members behaved like politicians, so the DO could not always rely on them for support. You were never sure which way the wind would blow. Luckily, the chairman, a formidable Chinese lady who sat on the Legislative Council and many government committees, was a tower of strength. The DO also had Area Committees (ACs), whose members he appointed, and which were a more reliable source of support for government policies and initiatives as Chinese professionals were understandably wary of the hurly-burly of electoral politics. Another important duty was to provide a weekly intelligence report, consisting of public feedback on government policies or other topical issues, mainly provided by AC members. Sometimes the feedback was startling. It was only through such reports that I realised how profoundly resented was the British policy of offering political asylum to large numbers of Vietnamese refugees. True, running and policing the refugee camps was very expensive in terms of resources, which were thus diverted from the local population, and many of the refugees were regarded as economic migrants. When asked to defend the policy, I could only say that Hong Kong had its reputation to consider and that we should show compassion for these unfortunate people as one day (perhaps after 1997) we might need help ourselves.

We also had a public enquiry counter near the MTR station which stocked lots of government forms and dispensed official information. This counter was open until late in the evening and people could come in and ask about government services or make suggestions and complaints. One evening a week we had a duty lawyer scheme where the public could receive free legal advice.

Upon arrival as DO, I noticed that there was scarcely one tree in the urban area, which was basically a concrete jungle. Having been brought up among trees in England, it struck me that a street tree-planting campaign would greatly improve the district. Hence the 'Green Wan Chai' campaign was born. My first move was to seek funds from the DB for a consultancy report to identify where we might plant the trees and which species would be most suitable. The DB was dubious about this strange idea, but with help from the chairman, funds were granted. Our consultant suggested an initial scheme of 600 street trees and recommended various species with a preponderance of *Ficus Benjamina,* weeping figs from Australia, which were fastigiate – meaning they grew upwards rather than outwards, which is what you want in a street tree. Having talked to tree specialists, I quickly became an expert – in my own mind – on the subject.

For a number of days, I patrolled the streets, accompanied by various government staff, looking for suitable locations for these trees. We needed to avoid obstructing entrances and I learnt to look for manhole covers which indicated where utilities such as water and gas pipes and telephone cables were running. The city streets were also crowded with other street furniture such as lamp posts, street signs, vendors' booths and telephone boxes. It was not easy finding good locations, but when we did, I would call a halt, point at the pavement and one of the staff would paint a red X on the spot. The staff would look at me with the sort of sympathy that one reserves for the simple minded.

One major problem was that our consultant recommended tree pits of 1.5m square; whereas local government staff insisted that due to limited space they could not be larger than 1m square. We had to compromise. In fact, most government departments thought that I was crazy or *chi sin* (crossed wires). The only exception was Highways Department which was very supportive.

Indeed, my attempts to plant trees in the district were met by the same incredulity on the part of government departments that had greeted Gary Mulloy's attempts to improve Wan Chai's footpaths in 1971. They told him that it was out of the question as there were only plans for footpaths in Central District. His persistence eventually paid off and I hoped that mine would too.

I was informed that not only would my trees' roots grow down and interfere with telephone conversations and cause gas leaks, but old ladies would climb up to get blossoms for their hair and perverts or *sik long* (colour wolves) would hide behind them and flash at school girls. I am not making this up – these objections were actually made. The best of all was from Transport Department (TD). When we circulated our proposal for comment, TD objected to 80 per cent of the trees on the grounds of 'sight-lines'. By this they meant that cars turning right or left would not be able to see oncoming traffic due to trees on the pavement. This was clearly ridiculous as the young trees' trunks would only be a few inches in diameter, but TD would not budge.

I thought up a strategy and invited the traffic engineer for a site visit at 11 a.m. on a summer day. The temperature was 32 degrees Celsius with humidity of 90 per cent. This engineer was a fat Chinese gentleman who spent most of his time in an air-conditioned office. We walked down the road together to the first tree site. He looked unhappy.

'Sorry, cannot approve because of sight-line,' he said.

'But it will only be a skinny little tree and surely this will not be causing accidents!' I replied reasonably.

'Sorry – this is departmental policy.'

We repeated this pantomime about twenty times by which time he was sweating profusely and mopping his face with a handkerchief. It was true what they said, he was thinking, this DO is completely mad (or 'Upton Park' as the British say – one stop short of Barking).

'OK,' he said finally, 'Let me go back to my office and think about what you have said.'

He fled for the air-conditioning. Some days later I received a call from him.

'Would you like another site meeting?' I asked, with enthusiasm.

'No need,' says he, 'I have reconsidered.' TD was now only objecting to 10 per cent of the trees.

The other dilemma was whether we should use 'light standard trees' (young ones that would in the long-term grow better) or 'heavy standard trees' (older trees that had been in a nursery for a few years and would give a better initial impression). In the end this issue was decided by cost. Heavy standard trees were expensive. However, we did source six mature mahogany trees for Luard Road, which to this day forms a handsome avenue. Subsequently a typhoon blew down one of these magnificent trees and the government replaced it with a weedy-looking shrub. When I complained, a functionary told me that nowadays they must consider safety aspects first.

Kadoorie Farm also gave us twenty palm trees, which had to be moved for a road widening project, which created a good impression along Hennessy Road (named after the eccentric Irish Victorian colonial governor who started the Ashanti War and attacked a prominent barrister on the Peak with his umbrella because he suspected that he fancied his wife).

A further refinement of the 'Green Wan Chai' scheme was the introduction of a private tree-planting scheme. We approached all the main property developers in the district and asked if they would pay to have trees planted around their buildings. Encouragingly, they all recognised that this was a good thing and joined the scheme. As the trees appeared, they caught the imagination of the press. RED LIGHT AREA GOES GREEN was one headline. To my great satisfaction, everyone agreed that the trees made a huge difference to the urban area, making it greener and friendlier. More restaurants and bars opened and later seats were placed outside for *al fresco* drinking and dining. Most significantly, what started as an eccentric and controversial scheme became widely imitated all over the territory.

When Prince Charles visited Hong Kong in 1993, he asked for a briefing on the Green Wan Chai scheme. I explained the project to him and, as a tree connoisseur himself, he was very interested in what species we had chosen. He was particularly concerned about environmental issues such as the cutting of forests to make disposable chopsticks. Subsequently, it became fashionable for celebrities to plant trees in the district. The last governor, Chris Patten, planted one at the junction of Luard Road and Queens Road East and John Denver, country singer, planted a beauty at the junction of Wan Chai Road and Johnston Road. We then went off to a karaoke for a few beers and sang *Country Roads*. I am pleased to say that both these trees are doing magnificently.

Denver's visit was arranged by a fellow member of the Craft Club, an exclusive (we thought) dining society that met to indulge in fine food and wine in the private rooms of clubs and restaurants on the last Friday of each month. The club prided itself on its rituals, which included speeches, fines and the support of various charities. It was regarded as bad form to leave the lunch that Friday afternoon in order to return to work. The club also had annual overseas lunches in places like Manila, Saigon or Bangkok. On one occasion, one of our members was able to introduce us to the King of Sweden. Hong Kong had a number of such luncheon clubs, including one called GODS (Gentlemen's Oriental Dining Society).

As DO, I was frequently invited out for excellent lunches. I remember one time when an aged *kaifong* took me to the Derby Room at the Jockey Club, which was then the height of gourmet excellence. He insisted on ordering fresh oysters and lobster and a bottle of Chablis Premier Cru before discussing district matters and the forthcoming elections. Towards the end of the lunch, the sommelier wheeled over the liquor trolley. Ignoring my protestations of needing to get back to work, two glasses of 1888 Armagnac were duly poured. I reminded myself that it was all being consumed in the line of duty.

The Jockey Club (Royal until 1997 when it decided to drop the title, unlike the Royal Hong Kong Yacht Club which decided to keep it) was founded in 1884 and did well until a disastrous accident in 1918, when a matshed grandstand collapsed at the Chinese New Year races onto some cooked food stalls, thus causing a terrible fire which killed over 600 people. There is a memorial to the victims on the hill above the new Government Stadium, which, like so many other public facilities in Hong Kong, was paid for by the Jockey Club.

The Jockey Club tries its best to keep horse racing clean but has not always succeeded. In 1986, a major scandal hit the racing fraternity when the ICAC investigated the 'Shanghai Syndicate' which was fixing races with the connivance of owners, trainers and jockeys. The stakes were so high that it was said that up to $20m could be paid to fix a single race. In the end, the syndicate's leader, textile magnate Y.L. Yang, was given a hefty fine and a two-year suspended sentence on the grounds that he was suffering from terminal cancer. As it happened, Yang lived happily for another twenty-one years.

Monthly District Board meetings were normally rather tedious so I would always have a strong black coffee beforehand to keep me awake, although it did not always work. One afternoon, as the board discussed its master plan for a Clean Wan Chai Campaign, the door opened and my secretary entered, making a beeline for me. 'Urgent phone call from England for Mr Mann,' she announced, while the board members gasped, wondering whether this might be bad news.

'Excuse me, I'll be back in a minute.' I said, rising and leaving the conference room. Entering my office, I picked up the phone.

'Darling?' It was my mother. 'Darling, I have just seen a BBC documentary on carrots. They are very good for you, especially as you smoke and drink. It doesn't matter whether they are cooked or raw, but you must promise me to eat more carrots.'

'Mother,' I replied, 'can I call you back?'

Then I asked my secretary to pour me another strong black coffee before I returned to the meeting.

In September 1991, the first direct elections to the Legislative Council were organised. As senior DO on Hong Kong Island, I was returning officer for the Island East constituency. This involved running a voter registration campaign before the election and publicity stunts such as hiring a tram filled with pop stars and starlets to encourage voters to turn out and cast their votes. We needed to work hard as Hong Kong had traditionally been lukewarm to elections, an attitude encouraged by the British, and over the last few decades any form of politics had tended to fuel the ideological conflict between supporters of China's communist government and the Nationalist government of Taiwan. On Election Day, I visited all the polling stations and in the evening we counted the votes in the Southorn Stadium. There were many staff members involved, including observers and legal advisors. The press was out in full force as Martin Lee, the founding father of the United Democrats, was duly elected with a huge majority. It was big news and the BBC World Service and *Time* magazine were on hand. In the event, the democrats won fourteen of the eighteen seats on offer, which came as a blow to the pro-China faction which thereafter resolved to organise itself better.

The next week, the District Board chairman and I were invited to dinner in Clear Water Bay with Sir Run Run Shaw, the legendary film tycoon. Sir Run Run, a keen practitioner of *chi gung* who must then have been nearly ninety, was seated between two stunning

Taiwanese starlets. During the meal, he told a racy story about Yul Brynner, who had visited Hong Kong during the filming of *The King and I*.

'I tried to introduce him to some lovely actresses,' he revealed, 'but he preferred streetwalkers. He certainly liked them rough!'

There was silence and my chairman froze with a prawn half way up to her mouth.

Sir Run Run passed away in 2014 at the ripe old age of 106, having donated billions of dollars to educational projects in China.

Another aspect of my work was making recommendations on older buildings in the district which were worthy of conservation. This was a thankless job as in practice the government could not afford to compensate the owners of private buildings due to their huge redevelopment potential. Most of the older buildings which could be conserved as heritage were government buildings such as police stations (the Wan Chai police station was a prime candidate), markets and courthouses. Another building that had heritage value was the old Methodist Church at the junction of Hennessy Road and Johnston Road. Built in 1930s Chinese Renaissance style red brick by Reverend Arthur Bray (Denis Bray's father) it was a landmark that had survived being bombed by the Japanese. When I discovered that the Methodists had redevelopment plans, I asked them if they could at least preserve the façade. They replied that only the British wanted to retain old buildings and stand in the way of progress. Although the architects were rather unhappy, they did come up with a compromise for the new Methodist Centre which preserved the spirit of the old church, including the charming turret at its western end. When asked about preserving the Bauhaus-style Wan Chai market, I replied that it might be historically interesting if not very aesthetically pleasing. We are, I think, one of the few places in the world to have a municipal building named after the Duke of Windsor, the eponymous Social Services Building next to Asian House.

I had by then opted for annual leave and decided that it was time to visit somewhere new. A friend, Ian Howard, who had been in government service in the Pacific introduced me to the New Hebrides, which is absolutely charming, and New Caledonia, which is very French. One night we dined on terrine of coconut crab and fruit bat and immediately afterwards were introduced to live specimens of what we had just eaten. Another day we went sailing and caught a huge sailfish. We spent New Year in Fiji, where they certainly know how to party.

Then we toured the Caribbean, where two of our ex-colleagues from Hong Kong were governors respectively of Montserrat (before it blew up) and the Cayman Islands. In the former, I had the pleasure of sleeping in Princess Anne's honeymoon bed, and in the latter diving in a famous spot called Stingray City. My friend almost got into serious trouble in Antigua. Having toured Nelson's Harbour and had a pleasant dinner in a restaurant to the accompaniment of tree frogs, we went to a nightclub for a drink. The club was run by a muscular quadroon named Lennox, who seemed very friendly. Bored, I left early but later when my friend tried to leave he found the door locked. Giving it a good kick, it flew open and struck Lennox, who was on his way back, in the face. He was no longer friendly and grabbed my friend by the throat. Luckily he had on him the card of the island's most prominent lawyer, so in the end things were settled amicably. Perhaps most interesting of all was our side trip to the Dominican Republic, where we had such a good time that we missed our flight back to Miami.

We returned to Hong Kong via the UK, where a silly thing happened. Having been out for dinner and returning home, we were stopped at a police checkpoint because one of the car lights was not working properly. I had only drunk a couple of glasses of wine but after years in Hong Kong my UK street wisdom was low and I obviously said the wrong thing. The officer asked me to step out of the car and blow into a breathalyser. My friend quickly disappeared. The result was marginal but the officer informed me that I would have to accompany him to the police station. 'You can't do this to me,' I spluttered, 'I'm a justice of the peace.' 'That's right,' the officer replied, 'and I'm King George! Now come quietly!' I ended up spending the night in a police cell and so learned a lesson in humility.

Back in Wan Chai district, another innovation was the introduction of an annual carnival and music festival. We managed to persuade the police to close a few blocks of Lockhart Road to traffic one Sunday so that a stage and stalls could be set up and the whole area turned into a pedestrian precinct. The first Wan Chai Festival was opened by a troupe of Brazilian samba dancers, which certainly caught the attention of the male *kaifongs* (community figures). We also made the chairman of the Liquor Licensing Board lie in a barber's chair and have a hefty slug of liquor poured down his throat. The local bars and restaurants loved it as they could set up stalls and advertise their products. This led to the establishment of the Wan Chai Tenants' Association, which represented and promoted the district's F&B industry.

Another performer at the festival was the Grass Roots Band from Ghana. I had persuaded a friend who owned a nightclub in Lan Kwai Fong to fly them out to Hong Kong for a few weeks and they were a great hit. Their authentic African rhythm and drumming and their 'highlife' style of music had never been heard in town before. There were also two attractive Ghanaian girls whose gyrations entranced the older *kaifongs*. There was yet another surprise in store for me. Helping to organise the event was a young Chinese girl called Zoe, who was cute and had freckles. She was later to become my wife.

My staff thought I was sailing too close to the wind by helping the private sector. Chinese civil servants tend to be very conservative. You can imagine their anxiety when one day a group of Chinese businessmen, adorned with gold Rolex watches and jade rings, walked into the District Office and asked to see me. My ADO advised me to pretend to be out.

'Why?' I asked. 'Where are they from?' He turned a deep shade of red.

'They are from the bars.'

'Which bars?' A pause followed.

'Um, the girlie bars.'

'But those bars are not illegal.'

'Yes, but. . . .' He looked at me helplessly.

'Show them in!' I said.

The point of the girlie bars was that if you bought the girls a drink, they would sit with you and chat. It appealed to lonely men away from home. Of course, some of the men made arrangements for hanky-panky outside the bar. It transpired that as most of the girls were now from the Philippines and Thailand, they needed a six-month work visa to come to Hong Kong. The police even made regulations on what sort of outfits they could wear. However, the Immigration Department, perhaps under pressure from some quarters, was now refusing to renew visas. I listened politely and said that if their bars were operated fairly and within the law, I would take up the matter with Immigration. The businessmen were very grateful and left. As they did, I could see my staff looking at me with that 'What sort of trouble is he going to get us into now?' look.

I wrote a letter to Immigration Department asking them to explain their policy. I received no reply. When I called, no one was available to speak to me. Eventually, I had to call the director himself to request that a representative be sent to a meeting in our office. Most reluctantly, they did send representatives and, in the absence of any good reason to the contrary, agreed that they would continue to process the work visas as before.

However, shortly after this, complaints were received about another of the bars which had recently moved over from the tourist area in Tsim Sha Tsui. It appeared they were cheating Mainland customers by charging exorbitant prices for drinks and threatening the customer if they did not pay up. The Mainlanders, unsure of their rights, had paid up. I went straight to the Liquor Licensing Board and demanded that their licence be revoked. It was, although the bar did reopen shortly afterwards under a different name.

At this time, Wan Chai was famous for being the fastest growing commercial district in Asia. Sometimes the DO was required to help with such developments, as was the case with Times Square. With the help of a retired administrative officer, Wharf had managed to get permission to redevelop the old tram depot. They intended to build a huge shopping mall with over one million square feet of retail space. However, the old and narrow road network was manifestly incapable of handling the future pedestrian and vehicular traffic. So we had to sit down with the police and Transport Department to work out how to avoid massive congestion.

Another duty of the DO was to organise an annual governor's visit to the district. This is the equivalent of a royal visit in the UK and takes months of planning and rehearsals. The DO must send a draft programme to Government House well in advance to ensure that the components of the visit are acceptable. A typical example might run as follows:

> 2.30 p.m.: His Excellency (HE) arrives by limousine at St Christopher's Home for the Aged. HE meets the Director and members of the Board and tours the home. 3 p.m.: HE visits new Government Market on Lockhart Road. Meets Director of Food and Environmental Hygiene and tours market. 3.30 p.m.: HE proceeds to Central Plaza 70/F for panoramic view of the district and briefing on future developments. 4 p.m.: HE visits the District Board and meets the Chairman and Board Members. 4.45 p.m.: HE meets the press. 5 p.m.: Visit ends.

As I was DO for nearly five years, I organised a number of such visits. What was interesting was the difference in style between different governors. Sir David Wilson was a diplomat and familiar with government service. He appreciated the work civil servants did and asked some searching questions, often as you were sitting in the jump seat of his enormous official Daimler as it toured the district. Chris Patten was a consummate politician, did not really have much interest in the details of government, but was brilliant at interacting with the public and identifying good photo opportunities. He loved egg tarts and would always find an opportunity to stuff one into his mouth while the flashbulbs went off. His nickname was *Fei Pang* or Fat Pang.

We had seen his theatrical style from the start. In July 1992, all senior government officers were required to go down to Queen's Pier to meet the new governor. It was a tradition that governors always arrived on Hong Kong Island by sea, even though there was a perfectly good road tunnel from the airport in Kowloon. Ostentatiously wearing a business suit, as opposed to the colonial white uniform and ostrich-plumed hat worn by the previous twenty-seven governors, Patten hammed it up for the press and made an irreverent and witty speech. He made it very clear that he was something quite new. He certainly made an impact on the colonial establishment, appointing the first local chief secretary (Anson Chan) and financial secretary (Donald Tsang) and introducing Governor's Question Time in Legco, based on best practice in the House of Commons.

Now, the number of social occasions that a DO needed to attend was large, perhaps having as many as five dinner parties in one week. A typical evening would go as follows: At 7 p.m. you would arrive in a restaurant to be greeted by a line of office bearers from whatever district organisation or clansmen's association was hosting the dinner. You would then sign a special book and everyone would exclaim 'Wah!' as you signed your name in Chinese. You would then be led to a table at which only senior members could sit to drink tea, or maybe beer as you were a foreigner, and make small talk while the other noisy tables finished their *mahjong* games which they had been playing, and gambling on, for hours. The host would then come and politely escort you to your place of honour.

The dining tables are always round; very convenient as everyone can talk to each other, and usually have twelve places, but for really grand events can have twenty-four. There is always an MC who first introduces the host who goes to the stage and makes a speech. There may be five or six speeches which everyone politely applauds. There is no concept of keeping quiet for speeches or other performances and normally all the guests are speaking loudly so that you can hardly hear what is said above the din. However, as soon as you are introduced, there is suddenly complete silence; not as a mark of respect, but because they are curious to see how many mistakes you will make in your Chinese speech. You use the same formula every time: *'Gok wai, ga ban. Ngoh ho go hing chut jik. . . .'* or 'Ladies and Gentlemen, Honoured Guests, I am very pleased to attend this evening's dinner'. When you have finished, they clap politely and as you resume your seat, the host will say 'DO speaks very good Cantonese', notwithstanding the fact that you have just butchered their language.

Then the interminable courses of the banquet are served: bar-becued pork and roast duck with fruit sauce, prawns and broccoli, shark's fin soup (now politically incorrect), whole steamed fish, roast chicken, vegetables such as *choi sam* and *bak choi,* abalone, noodles, fried rice and mango pudding. You may be served beer or wine but most of the locals drink tea. There are toasts as each dish arrives. Towards the end of the meal, there are more speeches and souvenirs are presented. Then comes the karaoke. This art form, which means 'empty orchestra' was invented by the Japanese, has become very popular and locals jump up enthusiastically to sing their favourite songs in Chinese or English. My turn comes and I have to rise and deliver a plausible rendition of *Country Roads* or *House of the Rising Sun* to rapturous applause. At about 10.30 p.m., if you are lucky, you may get to take leave of your hosts and go home.

As an official justice of the peace (or 'peaceful old gentleman' as it translates in Chinese) we were sometimes asked to witness declarations or other legal documents by people who wished to avoid paying lawyers' fees. Every month or so, together with an unofficial JP, who has been given the title as an honour, we had to carry out a JP visit. According to the law, institutions such as prisons, correctional institutions and subsidised hospitals need to be visited by JPs every month. If the institution was far away, we were taken there and back by government helicopter.

If we were visiting a prison, we would first go in and have a chat with the superintendent and then tour the facility. As we arrived at every cell, the staff would bark out, *'Yau mo tau so?'* or 'Do you have any complaints?' It was quite comical to watch the inmate's faces as they all did, but would certainly suffer if they opened their mouths. We got to meet some famous murderers and triads who always looked strangely innocent in jail. We would sometimes make suggestions regarding the running of the facility in our report but I must say that overall conditions were a lot better than in other parts of the world. Occasionally we were treated to entertainment, such as at the Tai Tam Young Girl's Correctional Institution, where the girls' pipe band paraded and performed in full Scottish uniform with kilts. By contrast, some visits were intensely disturbing, such as those to facilities for the severely mentally handicapped, who were pathetic creatures in a state of great confusion.

Other events we needed to attend included the Clean Hong Kong Campaign, where, together with Miss Hong Kong, we were expected to put on white gloves and to shovel up some symbolic (and very clean) rubbish that had been scattered near us. Sometimes an unfortunate extra in a sticky costume dressed as *Lap Sap Chung* (Litter Monster) would prance about and drop rubbish – to the delight of the children. Then there was the Fight Crime Campaign where we hobnobbed with the police and gave out crime prevention notices. Finally there was the Care for the Old Campaign where centenarians were presented with gold bracelets and sacks of rice.

Another role of the DO was to make recommendations for local worthies to receive something in the New Year's Honour List. Known as 'gongs' to us and 'bottle tops' to the Chinese, these could be British awards such as the OBE and MBE (known irreverently as 'Other Buggers' Effort' and 'My Bloody Effort') and local gongs such as the Badge of Honour or an 'unofficial' justice of the peace. These have now been replaced by Gold and Silver Bauhinia Medals. If any of your board or committee members managed to receive an honour, it was huge 'face' for the recipient, who would throw an extravagant party. However, you had to be careful that the person you were pushing for an OBE was not suddenly implicated in a scandal or your own credibility would be called into question.

Although it was entirely lawful for a district officer to accept entertainment (it was OK if you could eat it or drink it on the premises) local businessmen knew better than to offer gifts to administrative officers. Most expatriate AOs were solid, middle-class people who had been to public school and Oxbridge. We enjoyed good salaries and comfortable government quarters. The grade had strong *esprit de corps* and was a service of gentlemen (and gentlewomen). It would have been unthinkable to accept an advantage.

Once a year, we would be invited to the New China News Agency, China's unofficial presence in Hong Kong, for an afternoon of friendly chatting and ping-pong. I was not bad at table tennis but I could not handle the very tricky spin serves of the Chinese players. We had a ping-pong table in the District Office and I would frequently play with our *kaifongs* in the afternoon. I remember being called to the phone one tea-time by a harassed colleague working in the Treasury. 'What are you doing at the moment?' he asked. When I told him I was playing ping-pong with the *kaifongs* he became very angry and said that it was outrageous. I replied that it was a hell of a job, but someone had to do it.

Taking advantage of the government's home purchase scheme, I bought a small village house near Mang Kung Uk in the Clear Water Bay area, a peninsula with green hills and white beaches situated to the east of Kowloon. The Clear Water Bay Road had originally been built as an access to a gun emplacement on the tip of the peninsula intended to protect the eastern approaches to Victoria Harbour. There was excellent walking in the area and it was quite a fast drive through the new Junk Bay tunnel and Eastern Harbour tunnel to the Island, as long as you left before the morning rush hour. In order to find a good day to move into the new house, my *kaifongs* insisted on consulting the *Tung Sing,* the classic almanac which contains auspicious dates for moving house, starting a business, marriage, travel, and so on. They would not have dreamt of doing anything important without consulting this ancient reference book. Once a good date had been chosen, one of my advisors came to see the small house and garden. It was very important, he confided, to raise the height of the garden wall to block the hostile energy of the village road.

In the early nineties, many engineers and technicians visited Hong Kong, some working for the Anglo-French project to build China's first nuclear power station at Daya Bay. This project, 70 per cent owned by Hong Kong interests, opened in 1993. These technicians and other tourists would often insist on a visit to the Kowloon Walled City, which was soon to be demolished. The Walled City had been an ancient fort and when the British took over Kowloon, the Chinese claimed they retained sovereignty there. The Walled City therefore had an ambiguous status and the British were reluctant to enforce the law inside the enclave. During the war, the

Japanese had demolished the city walls and used the stone to extend Kai Tak runway. Subsequently, the population had risen to 30,000 on just six acres and the area had become a haven for crime, drugs and trades like unlicensed dentists. It was unwise to enter without an escort, but I had a contact in the District Office who could arrange tours.

It was indeed an exciting place to visit. The ten-storey buildings were crammed in impossibly close to each other and the dark alleyways lacked drainage and carried clusters of electric wires snaking in all directions. Only an experienced guide could navigate its labyrinth of passages. In the middle stood the ancient fort or *yamen* with a well in which swam a large white carp. We were told that this was the walled city's 'protector'.

In the Joint Declaration it was agreed that the enclave should be demolished, and in 1993, after suitable compensation and rehousing arrangements had been implemented, it was. The whole area was turned into the Walled City Park, which opened in 1995. The original *yamen* has been preserved in its centre, surrounded by the delightful flowering plants and sculptured rocks of a traditional Chinese garden. It is not known what happened to the white carp.

I was starting to think that my unusually long tour as 'Sheriff' of Wan Chai was too good to be true. Sure enough, the secretary for home affairs paid me a visit one day and was shocked to learn that I had been in post for nearly five years. As a result, it was decided that I was to be posted to Housing Branch. In order to bid me farewell, all the district organisations organised a huge banquet in my honour. There were the usual speeches and I was presented with a lovely painting of a tall pine tree in a forest to celebrate the tree-planting campaign and also, they said, to show that I was an upright official. I also received a beautiful piece of calligraphy, whose meaning was 'Leadership sets us free'. This message, displayed proudly on my wall, would in future make my Chinese wife feel uneasy.

The *kaifongs* had bought a special bottle of brandy for the occasion, an expensive Louis XIII, which was much superior to your normal XO cognac. As there were nearly a hundred tables at the dinner, I went around to toast the *kaifongs* and say goodbye. A waiter at my side kept refilling the glass. Normally, when performing this ritual, they use tea and I was about to discover why. By the time I returned shakily to my seat, the bottle was empty and I was well out of it. Luckily the dessert was being served so people could soon leave. I slumped in to my chair and proceeded to start snoring loudly. 'DO a little tired, work very hard,' explained my ADO.

Although I was unconscious, my enterprising staff worked out how to get me out. They lifted my chair, with me on it, onto a trolley and wheeled me to the lift. Downstairs, my burly driver lifted me into the AM car (all government cars had AM number plates) and drove me home. Upon arrival, I regained consciousness and thanked the driver. In the morning, I woke up lying on the dining room floor, still clad in my suit, with my two dogs sleeping happily on either side.

CHAPTER NINE

Twilight of the Brits

It was a nasty shock in 1995 to leave behind Chinese banquets and ping pong matches with the *kaifongs*. My new job was public housing policy which is one of the busiest and most controversial jobs in the government. Whatever you do is wrong, and is bound to annoy the left wing, who think that everyone should live in free housing paid for by the taxpayer, or the right, who think that too many rich people lived in subsidised housing and that most of them should be kicked out.

As part of the Handover negotiations with China, it had been agreed that in the last decade of British rule, only fifty hectares of land per year should be disposed of annually, with sale proceeds shared equally between the HK government and the future SAR government. Given the subsequent shortage of new land, there was considerable competition for sites for housing development. Property prices were peaking and the private sector felt that too much land had been earmarked for public housing. They thought that the government should manage its existing stock better and evict tenants whose income was over the eligibility threshold, but that was easier said than done. However, it was true that many public housing tenants tended to have higher disposable income as their rents were so much lower than those in the private sector. You only had to look at the numbers of Mercedes Benz cars parked in estate car parks.

My boss was diminutive Chinese officer, Dominic Wong, whose ironic nickname was 'Rambo'. Although a sound administrator, he had a reputation for being a very difficult character. His male staff, I was told, had to wear vests under their shirts as he had previously been offended by an expatriate officer with body odour, while another theory was that he was offended by the sight of nipples. I was once summoned to his office to discuss a difficult Legislative Council (Legco) question. Rambo was wearing a small pair of white gloves, but whether this was to prevent his hands from soiling the files or vice versa, I was unsure. He was also a stickler for the rules. As we were discussing the methodology for assessing public housing tenants' income, he started to stare at the pencil in my hand.

'That is a blue pencil,' he eventually said. 'Your rank is ineligible to use that sort of pencil. You should be using a brown one.' He took it away and gave me a cheaper brown one.

My workload was heavy and tedious and I was unhappy. Worse, every Saturday morning I had to attend a working group in the Housing Authority on whether rich tenants should be asked to pay higher rent. The democrats said most public housing tenants were poor, hardworking citizens and the pro-establishment and pro-China politicians (including a future chief executive) roundly abused them. One time I attended Legco with a colleague to hear a debate on housing regulations. Staying awake in a Legco debate is difficult at the best of times, but the night before I had been to a party. Although I tried manfully to look interested, I soon fell asleep and started snoring.

An outraged colleague, Fanny Law, jabbed me in the ribs and hissed, 'Peter, you *cannot* sleep in Legco!'

Luckily, Andrew Wells, one of my friends, was then posted as my immediate boss, and sensing my misery, was kind enough to recommend me for a special Chinese course that was being organised. So, with great relief, my public housing days were drawing to a close. Later he went off to take up a post as chief secretary and acting governor of St Helena, the last resting place of the Emperor Napoleon, a remote island in the South Atlantic whose imperial *raison d'être* had passed with the opening of the Suez Canal.

That Christmas, my mother, together with a friend, paid her last visit to Hong Kong. The first time she came, in 1977, she managed to leave her wedding ring on her breakfast tray at the Excelsior Hotel and it was never seen again. Subsequently, she had visited a few times en route to Australia, China and Japan, and had always enjoyed the city's bustle and pace and its exceptional hotels and restaurants. One of her favourite places was the Eagle's Nest on the top floor of the Hilton Hotel. Not only was the food and service superb, but she could dance to her heart's content to a live band, which reminded her of her youth. One year, aged well over seventy, she walked for miles over the mountains to Tai Long Wan in Sai Kung and then returned to dance the night away in the Hilton.

This time we decided to visit Jiangmen and Xinhui in Guangdong province. We took a ferry to Zhongshan as the huge suspension bridge crossing the Pearl River at Humen was not yet finished. Then we took a bus across the many branches of the West River which flows into the Pearl Delta. Chinese driving is stressful at the best of times, but my mother appeared not to notice the dramatic swerving and changing of lanes as she watched the countryside through the bus window. She also noticed a number of lorries filled with ducks and pigs heading in the other direction to Hong Kong's markets and felt very sorry for them. 'Poor creatures,' she observed.

We stayed at the West Lake Hotel and walked up Gui Feng Mountain, part of a national park, which has two exceptionally fine temples, one Buddhist and one Taoist. Xinhui is famous for its *chenpi*, dried mandarin orange skins, which are used extensively in cooking, and its fine Imperial Examination Hall and Confucian Temple. Nearby is the Bird Paradise where thousands of egrets live on an island near an ancient village with a Ming dynasty pagoda, which is the birthplace of Liang Qichau, famous scholar and late Qing reformer.

Margaret was always nervous about Chinese food, especially on the Mainland. One evening when they served snake soup, I got away with telling her that it was chicken. However, while having dinner in Zhongshan the night before, we were served two very dubious looking dishes. I summoned the waiter and discreetly enquired what they were.

'That's our local speciality,' he said. 'Rats' embryos and rice maggot pie.'

'Thanks,' I replied, 'but we'll do without starters today.'

'Would you like *sam luk*?' (Literally 'three six', as nine, *gau*, is a homonym for dog.)

'No!' I said emphatically. 'Do you have any fried rice?'

The next day we had indigestion. Luckily, just down the road there was a wonderful Chinese *leung cha* or cooling tea shop. The locals insist that all food and drink is either heating or cooling, although I could never understand which was which. I did know that beer was known as *'gwai lo* cooling tea'. This shop had about twenty different pots, each catering for a different ailment, such as colds and flu; sore throats; *yit hei* or hot air; stomach ache; uncomfortable gut; constipation and so on. We dutifully drank the right tea and felt much better.

That evening, we went for a walk in the huge open space at the foot of Gui Feng Mountain. On one side were a group of people dressed in traditional outfits practising Tai Chi and we were impressed by their graceful and exceedingly slow movements. On the other side, around 100 people, mainly women, performed a complicated dance routine to loud modern music, which looked like a good work-out. In the sky was a perfect half-moon. Nearby, some children were riding bikes and skating. One of the younger boys was playing with a parachute toy which he threw into the air and watched as it floated down. I was suddenly transported back to playing a similar game with my grandmother when I was around seven. I had a toy soldier on a parachute that I would catapult into the sky in her large garden. One day, my aim was off and I shot the soldier into a tree where it became stuck, which made me cry. A month later, she wrote to me at prep school telling me that my soldier had finally come down.

Next day we visited the Overseas Chinese Museum in Jiangmen. To look at the lush wide expanses of the Pearl River Delta today, it is difficult to believe that in the late eighteenth century it was highly overpopulated, leading to second and subsequent sons needing to emigrate in order to find employment. There was therefore a diaspora of young Chinese men to America, Australia, South Africa and Malaya to work in gold and tin mines, to build roads and lay railway tracks. In the Jiangmen area, more than half the young men needed to find work abroad. After they had saved enough money, they started restaurants, laundries, pharmacies or trading companies. They kept in close touch with their mother country and in order to show their new wealth, they built thousands of 'fortress' buildings or *diu lau* in the delta, especially in towns like Kaifeng. These buildings are constructed in fantastical architectural styles and have strange ornaments on their walls and pagodas on their roofs. They are strongly fortified and provided secure protection from bandits during lawless times. There is in the museum a fascinating dictionary for emigrants to America with common English words rendered in 'sounds like' Chinese characters. The suggested pronunciation for the word 'four' is the Chinese character for 'fire' (*foh*), alphabet is *'ah fu bit'* and racecourse is *'lei si goh si!'*

Upon her return to the UK, Margaret decided that it was time to resume her writing career. So she began to write books for teenagers about magic, mysticism and time travel. Her first and best book was called *The Merlin Set-Up,* which was about time travel in her beloved City of Bath. From Merlin's HQ in the Royal Crescent, the children travelled to Roman, medieval and Victorian times. The books were a family affair; I bought her a computer and helped with editing, my sister, Jenny, drew beautiful illustrations and my brother, Christopher, made recordings.

She subsequently wrote another three books to complete the Merlin Quartet. The titles were: *Under the Merlin Spell,* set in Ireland; *Merlin's Island,* set in Wales; and *Moving On with the Merlinauts,* which was her last book. Merlin, master of time and space, was the central figure who represented the union of science and mysticism. Filled with references to Teilhard de Chardin (Jesuit priest and palaeontologist), William Blake and the Arthurian legends, the books attempted to break through the cynicism and negativity of modern life and encourage teenagers to develop their imagination and personal talents. She had a passionate faith in the future of mankind. The books sold well and are still available online.

For my part, it was nearly time for me to embark on the much anticipated language course. In the old days, administrative cadets were sent to Canton to learn Cantonese. This is because very little English is spoken there and so you have 'total immersion' and also because their Cantonese is much purer than in Hong Kong where they speak 'Chinglish' with many English words thrown in. The

Hong Kong government had decided to sponsor a course on China's government and political system for expatriate officers in Cantonese rather than Putonghua, which is what most of the local officers were learning. The course started with two months of intense Cantonese training at the University of Science and Technology, which has an attractive campus in Clear Water Bay overlooking the sea. Then we were sent to Zhongshan University in Guangzhou for a month, where we attended the old Ling Nam College, which also has a lovely garden campus with shaded paths, trees and statues, all set beside the majestic Pearl River.

Our professors were decent, tolerant fellows who did their best to teach us in Cantonese and to answer our often politically incorrect questions. On the first day, after lunch, we were informed that there would be half-an-hour's reading. However, when they drew the curtains and turned off the lights, we understood that this was actually a siesta. Quite Mediterranean and civilised, I thought. At weekends we wandered around the city, which had some interesting historic buildings such as old Buddhist pagodas and the ornate mansions of the Chan Clan. We also went on tours of the Pearl River Delta region, including Zhongshan, where Sun Yat-sen, the father of modern China was born, and Shunde, Panyu and Dongguan. At Humen, we were taken to the new Opium War Museum where we were made to feel guilty about our ancestors' disgraceful behaviour. We were also shown the stunning half-built suspension bridge which was to span the Pearl River's mouth at the Bogue. The mayors we met briefed us on developments in the region and hinted at a lively nightlife, which unfortunately we were not allowed to sample as we were whisked away after our meetings. However, our professors did take us for karaoke, which was a popular entertainment. For every Chinese ballad they sang, we replied with a British song, and as we had Welsh and Scottish officers on the course, our replies were colourful and varied.

The Pearl River Delta region is famous for its game dishes. The local saying 'creature with their back to the sun', means edible; that is, any animal at all. A visit to the storerooms behind delta restaurants reveals a veritable menagerie, including deer, monkey, wild pigs, raccoons, snakes, dogs and cats, pangolins, turtles and other exotic species. This is definitely not a place for Buddhists, vegetarians or conservationists. The restaurant manager will often suggest that he has some endangered species on the menu, perhaps hinting that you may be lucky enough to eat the last one. They are very fond of cooked insects, and fried water beetles or grasshoppers make a good starter. I found they went down well with a cold Tsingtao beer.

One day we had lunch with the Mayor of Shunde. He made the mistake of raising the subject of snake wine.

'We have a special snake wine here,' he intoned gravely, 'but of course you foreigners do not drink that.'

'I'm very fond of snake wine,' I offered.

'Beer will be just fine,' hissed the leader of our group, who was a nervous fellow.

'Don't worry.' I whispered, 'You don't have to drink it, just keep a count.'

One of the mayor's flunkeys was then sent off and returned some time later with a huge pot of wine containing three colourful snakes entwined in the bottle. Thus we started on a drinking bout, which reminded me of the time I had defended English honour at the border security talks some years earlier. We played the usual games that apply to competitive drinking: you spill as much as you can and you keep finding new friends to introduce to your opponent, who must then drink with them. Then they introduce you to their friends and you in turn must drink. After about an hour of this, the mayor grew bored and announced, 'Time for beer now!' I turned to my colleague and asked, 'How many?' 'Sixteen glasses,' was the reply. Subsequently, I was merry for at least twelve hours. After lunch, we visited the famous statue of Kwan Yin, the Goddess of Mercy, at Panyu. It started to pour, but when you are full of snake wine, you really do not care. As the rest of the group sheltered under umbrellas, I danced in the rain.

Before we received our certificates for this course, we each had to give a speech, in formal Cantonese, on a subject of our choice. I chose the trees of China and talked about the banyans of Foochow and the pines of Or Mei Shan. At our farewell dinner, I was sitting next to a lady official and ill-advisedly raised the subject of how

China was firing missiles at Taiwan to discourage people voting for Lee Teng-hui. I suggested this was not the way to win friends and influence people. She looked at me askance. 'Maybe you drink too much wine,' she observed. We returned to our lonely hotel rooms. I say lonely, although we heard that there were some enterprising girls who staked out a hotel and indulged in *'luen da'* or random dialling of rooms, until they found a taker.

Taking the train back through Dongguan, which was full of smoky factories, it was pleasure to return to clear skies. After a trip to the Mainland, you really appreciated the wonderful *fung shui* of Hong Kong's mountains, harbour and dazzling seascapes. No wonder it was called the 'Pearl of the Orient'.

Upon return, I was angling for a job as district officer, Sai Kung. However, a local officer told me that times had changed and that expatriates really could not be posted as DOs any more. However, if I was interested, there was a post in the Central Policy Unit helping to draft Governor Patten's last policy address to be delivered in October 1996, some nine months before the Handover. Naturally, I jumped at it.

The Central Policy Unit is the government's think tank and helps coordinate the governor's annual policy address. It also helps the various departments to devise new policy initiatives and to benchmark their progress. The head of the unit was the brilliant academic Leo Goodstadt, whose nickname was the Mad Monk. He was a devout Catholic, along with other senior officials such as the governor, chief secretary and financial secretary. He had once shocked people at Government House by genuflecting dramatically and kissing the ring of a visiting cardinal. He was someone against whom you could not win an argument. He was also very successful at negotiating with the Mainland Chinese because he could quote back at them every single speech ever made by China's top leaders. The Mad Monk was a great democrat and supporter of Chris Patten, who had brought to Hong Kong the new public management concepts that the Conservatives had espoused and terms such as 'stakeholders' and 'serving the people', the latter a notion quite alien to China's mandarin class.

The governor's last policy address focused on the development of democracy and the promotion of confidence in Hong Kong's future under Chinese rule. I had some lively discussions with Chris Patten on the subject of democracy. Having dealt with many politicians, I thought it was overrated as a panacea and quoted H.L. Mencken's famous maxim that 'Democracy was a religion of sorts; the worship of jackals by jackasses'. He rebutted with Churchill's comment that 'Democracy was the worst possible form of government, except every other sort that had ever been tried.'

The heads of departments hated the new policy commitments that we forced them to subscribe to every year because they looked bad if they failed to deliver. The whole concept of concrete benchmarks was alien to the administration. As there was an annual progress report, it was difficult for them to disguise their failure to meet a target. The government disliked this and the first thing it did after 1997 – apart from building a high wall around its HQ – was to ditch the policy commitments.

As part of the pre-Handover preparations, we organised a briefing by some senior politicians. When asked who ran China, prominent right-wing politician T.S. Lo replied that it was obviously the People's Liberation Army. An equally famous left-wing politician, Tsang Yok-sing, admitted that he feared that the British would never really leave Hong Kong, and if they did, then they would be sure to leave behind some sort of Trojan Horse.

One day, I was beavering away late at night when the Mad Monk walked into my office. 'Working late?' he noted, 'I like my staff to show enthusiasm. But what's this?' he asked, pointing to a bottle of vodka I kept in my cupboard for emergencies. 'V for Vodka? No, I don't think so, Peter,' he grumbled, walking away with the bottle. 'I'm sure your reports will be much clearer now'.

The Civil Service Branch had encouraged all expatriate administrative officers to retire in 1997 and to take the generous compensation offered for doing so. However, a small group of us was determined to stay on. We loved Hong Kong, had made our life there, spoke Chinese and had, so we thought, had a lot to offer. However, the boot would soon be on the other foot, as it were, and the expatriates were usually more independent and less willing to *kowtow* to authority than the Chinese, for whom the boss is *always* right. Generally speaking, we were not flavour of the month.

My next job was an attachment to the Chief Secretary's Office (the CS was Dame Anson Chan) to conduct a review of the legal aid system. This was a political request from the legal community and the government had to be seen to be responsive. I reported to the Legal Aid Service Council, which was a quango supervising the administration of legal aid. My first job was to find out exactly how legal aid worked in other common law jurisdictions, so together with other members of the council, we flew to the UK, Canada, Australia and New Zealand to meet the administrators of legal aid there and to find out as much as we could.

Being a civil servant can be tedious at times, but some good 'duty travel' sure livens things up. At the end of this exercise, I wrote a long report making recommendations for improvement. This was debated by the council and at one point, our one non-legal member, Mrs Elsie Tu, asked, 'Yes, these changes are all very well, but what benefit will they bring to ordinary people?' A good question, I thought, but the lawyers around the table, who obviously had an interest in extending the scheme, looked at her as if she was completely mad. When Elsie, who was famous as a social activist and defender of the poor, passed away in 2015 at the ripe old age of 103 she was given the singular honour of having all three post-Handover chief executives as her pall bearers.

The Handover itself was an event quite unprecedented in (non-wartime) history. A major world city would, at the stroke of midnight, not become independent, but be handed by one country to another. Of course the Chinese, who referred to the event as 'reunification', were fond of pointing out that Hong Kong had only temporarily been under British administration, due to the 'unequal treaties' forced upon China during the Opium Wars. Even so, 156 years is quite a long time.

Frankly, it was lucky that it had suited China to allow Hong Kong to continue under British administration long after most other European colonies had been abandoned. This was because Hong Kong provided valuable foreign exchange and Western expertise that was most useful to the mother country.

The Chinese had signalled in 1972 that they were unlikely to accept a continuation of British sovereignty. However, in 1979, under pressure from banks worried about mortgages on leases that would expire after 1997, Sir Murray MacLehose had ventured to Beijing to ask whether the New Territories lease could be extended. This was contrary to the advice of the old China hands who thought that the lease problem could best be solved by simple recognition of Chinese sovereignty over the whole territory. Deng Xiaoping, who could not understand why the legalistic British did not just let sleeping dogs lie, said no, thus shocking the colony and sending the stock market into a tailspin. Although Deng had said that Hong Kong people should 'put their hearts at ease', there was profound concern.

In September 1982, official talks on Hong Kong's future kicked off with Margaret Thatcher's visit to Beijing. On her way up the steps of the Great Hall of the People, she famously stumbled, which was not seen as a good omen. Also, having just fought a neo-colonial war over the Falkland Islands, which made her overconfident and the Chinese contemptuous, it clearly was not a good time to start negotiations with the rising world power China. The Iron Lady started the talks by banging on about British rights under the same treaties which the Chinese had made very clear they did not recognise. This was a position endorsed by the United Nations, which had removed Hong Kong from its list of colonies. Deng is reputed to have used some bad language and to have hissed, 'I can't talk to this woman; she is utterly unreasonable!' Thatcher also reminded Deng that the British had saved Father of the Nation, Sun Yat-sen, when he was kidnapped by Qing agents in London, although that did not seem to cut much ice either.

Subsequently, the British dropped their claim to sovereignty and adopted the Twenty Point Plan which China had all along hinted was the way forward. At the last minute, Sir Geoffrey Howe had a clause inserted stating that the post-97 Legco would be constituted by elections. The Joint Declaration, expertly finessed and polished by Sir Edward Youde, was finally signed on 26 September 1984. China would resume sovereignty over Hong Kong in 1997, which would be given a high degree of autonomy similar to the 'extraterritoriality' of the treaty ports in the nineteenth century. Existing legal, judicial and economic systems would be retained and there was a guarantee of fifty years without change in the shape of a special administrative region (one country, two systems). However, Deng had promised that there would still be horse racing and dancing and Hong Kong had another thirteen years to prepare itself. Although profound shock waves were generated by the events of June 1989, by 1997 everyone was pretty much resigned to the inevitable.

With just a few weeks to go before the big day, I was still working in the Chief Secretary's Office finishing my review of legal aid. We expatriate AOs had been asked to consider taking early retirement, and one argument used was that we might block promotion opportunities for local officers if we stayed on. In my case, I thought of Hong Kong as my home and wanted to continue serving in the government. My brother, Christopher, was the producer of the BBC's popular *Songs of Praise,* which had never visited Hong Kong and as the clock ticked relentlessly on they realised that they had better hurry up. I arranged for the crew to film panoramic shots of the city and harbour from the roof of the Government Secretariat and in St John's Cathedral next door. As usual the congregation wanted to look their best for the cameras and the ladies had taken trouble with their dress and makeup. St John's has ceiling fans on long poles that keep the faithful cool in summer. Unfortunately, when recording the hymns, they needed to be switched off as they made too much noise. The subsequent heat was sweltering and caused the ladies' makeup to run down their faces as it melted. Indeed, it seemed to some that the whole colony was melting.

As the end of June 1997 grew closer, the sight of all those fluttering Union Jacks around town became poignant and I tried to visualise how it would look when they had all been replaced by China's national flag of red with one large and four smaller yellow stars in its upper corner. The predictable influx of friends from around the world had started. They were not about to miss this historic event, nor the many parties that accompanied it. Indeed, many of us were now referring to the event as 'The Hangover'. My house in Clear Water Bay was full – people were even sleeping on the floor. Guests hailed from all over, including England, America and South Africa.

An ominous event took place a few days before the Great Day. A big English mastiff in our village had for years been spoiling for a fight with my two smaller Chinese dogs. Taking advantage of the confusion of guests arriving, the mastiff saw her chance and attacked the smaller local dogs. A vicious fight ensued. With the two Chinese dogs working as a team, one engaged the mastiff while the other went round the back and sank his fangs into her rump. In the pandemonium, I looked for something close at hand with which to whack the big dog. I picked up what turned out to be a full vacuum cleaner bag which split open showering me with debris, causing my maid, Lety, to laugh out loud. I stood there angrily, looking like a scarecrow and my American guest, who had just arrived, asked, 'You aren't having a sense of humour failure, are you?' By now, the fight was over and the mastiff limped off for extensive veterinary treatment. We hoped this was not a portent of bad Sino-British blood.

It was true that relations were at low ebb, thanks to what the Mainland saw as Chris Patten's strong support for the Democrats and his provocations and political posturing. His electoral proposals, particularly with regard to widening the franchise of the functional constituencies, were ingenious but ultimately doomed to failure, given the Chinese position. They were also seen as contrary to what had been agreed in the Joint Declaration and subsequent under-standings contained in letters exchanged between the British and Chinese foreign ministers. As a result, Patten was called a host of rude names, such as 'Sinner of a Thousand Years', 'Tango Dancer' and 'Whore who builds a Monument to her own Chastity'. It also meant there would be no 'through-train' as the Legislative Council elected with the new rules would be dissolved on 1 July and replaced with a newly appointed one, which would surely be a Pyrrhic victory. The Chinese had already set up a shadow government. The old China hands deplored what they perceived as Patten's anti-China machinations and would have preferred the last governor had been a harmless British aristocrat, instead of a dangerous politician.

Patten may have been convinced that he was safeguarding Hong Kong's future interests, although the old China hands believed that Hong Kong's future was assured by the fact that the 'one country, two systems' doctrine had originally been devised for Taiwan and that until Taiwan was back in the Mainland fold, China could not afford to upset Hong Kong. As a result of frosty relations between the two sides, and the fact that the Chinese felt hoodwinked, there would be no friendly joint Handover ceremony and businessmen feared that British commercial interests in China would be damaged for many years to come – which they were – and China anyhow had the last laugh as direct elections to the Legislative Council were subsequently delayed till 2020. However, it must be conceded that sometimes in negotiations it pays to be firm and the calculation was presumably that China would not allow anything to disrupt the glorious reunification of the wayward colony with its true mother. However, the stakes for such a gamble were frighteningly high.

On 28 June, some friends and I held a big Handover party at the Aero Club at Kai Tak, a venue popular with the staff of Cathay Pacific. The dress code was Chinese, and I had bought a black silk Chinese outfit from Shanghai Tang for the occasion. The ladies looked stunning in their colourful silk cheongsams, slit up the side and revealing a lot of thigh. There was a live band for dancing and plenty of food and drink. We had also arranged an entertainment. One of my Eurasian friends and I put on a skit that shocked many people present, in which I behaved like the worst sort of arrogant colonial pig and he like a craven running dog. Perhaps the guests were not all aware that it was satire.

The next day, 29 June, saw another major party at the country house we shared. The invitation had included a cartoon of Colonel Blimp, complete with pith helmet and monocle, being booted into the sea by a Chinese coolie. Fearful of rain, we had asked local workmen to build a matshed shelter of bamboo covered in tarpaulin in the garden. The dress code was British colonial or Chinese, so guests arrived in safari suits and pith helmets, and others in PLA uniforms with Mao caps. A number of large flags were on display, including the Union Jack and Chinese national flag; the old colonial Hong Kong flag with the lion receiving the Pearl of the Orient from the dragon and the new Hong Kong flag, which was red with a white five-petalled bauhinia flower. Many of the guests had served in other colonies in Africa and the Pacific so were familiar with 'Independence' parties. Needless to say, Hong Kong was not getting independence; it was swapping one sovereign for another. There were plenty of toasts and noisy firecrackers, which are illegal but tolerated in the New Territories. We had had the foresight to order a good few cases of 'Red Dawn' lager.

The next day, 30th June 1997, was the last day of British rule in Hong Kong. Our guests enjoyed a cooked breakfast and then ate an early lunch. My American friend, who liked his drink and was known affectionately as 'The Exorcist', because when he left there were no spirits left in your house, had ordered a large vodka and few glasses of wine with lunch. He then asked for a beer and when it was pointed out that he already had two other drinks, he said, 'I know, but I'm thirsty!'

As we left the house it started to rain. The summer of 1997 was one of the wettest on record, probably due to a monster El Nino in the South Pacific, and Hong Kong was to be inundated with nearly two metres of rain. I was attending the British ceremony in HMS *Tamar* and the others would take the car elsewhere. At 4.30 p.m. the flag was lowered at Government House as a lone bugler played the *Last Post* and then it was presented, folded, to an emotional Chris Patten as Lavender and their three pretty daughters, sharing an umbrella, looked on. The family then boarded the governor's Rolls-Royce and drove around the forecourt a few times to the strains of *Auld Lang Syne* played by the police pipers before driving away.

Upon arrival at Tamar we queued for our seats. We were given bright blue and yellow umbrellas but these were to prove of little use as protection against the deluge. At 5 p.m., Prince Charles and his entourage arrived to the sound of fanfares and naval salutes. There were artistic shows, dancing and singing, and lion and dragon dances. Then Colour Guards of the Black Watch and the Royal Navy marched in accompanied by the massed bands of the Scots Guards, the Gurkhas and the Royal Marines. Although by this stage it was raining cats and dogs, as hard a rain as I have ever seen, their drill was flawless. It reminded me of the Beating of the Retreat I had seen twenty years earlier at the Police Training School. Behind was moored the Royal Yacht, *Britannia,* and her escort, the frigate HMS *Chatham.* Chris Patten was sitting next to Prince Charles and on the other side was Tony Blair, newly elected British prime minister. Famously, Patten observed, 'This is not a day for sadness but a day for celebration.'

When it was time for Prince Charles to give his speech, he stood up and carried on with *sang froid,* even though the rain was torrential and pouring in streams off his naval cap. The rain, apart from being quintessentially English, is lucky for the Chinese as water has the same meaning as money. How the microphones and sound systems worked, I do not know. I have never been so wet in my life. As we filed out, I discovered that the rain had completely soaked my wallet in an inner pocket and that the banknotes themselves were sodden.

Next we went to the Foreign Correspondent's Club to meet guests and dry out. After a few drinks and an early dinner, we walked along Lower Albert Road past the Government Secretariat. Workmen were already taking down the old colonial crest (with the lion holding the pearl of the Orient and facing the dragon) and preparing to put up the new Chinese one. Another thing they did the next day was to start building a high security fence around the government buildings. This was something the British had never considered necessary.

Meanwhile in the Convention and Exhibition Centre, the formal joint Handover ceremony was taking place. Outside, the police were drowning out noisy anti-Beijing protests by playing the dramatic parts of Beethoven's *Fifth Symphony* through their loud-speakers. On one side of the hall was Prince Charles, representing the Queen; with Tony Blair, Robin Cook and Sir Charles Guthrie, Chief of Defence Staff. On the other side was Chinese President, Jiang Zemin; with Premier Li Peng and Foreign Minister Qian Qichen. Prince Charles delivered a moving speech in which he noted that this was a moment both of change and continuity, that Hong Kong was being restored to China after over 150 years of

British administration, but that Hong Kong would continue to have its own government and institutions. He paid tribute to those who had turned the concept of 'one country, two systems' into the Joint Declaration (Margaret Thatcher was also present) and finally brought about its realisation. He also paid tribute to Hong Kong people's triumphant success, their dynamism and stability, and their strong economy which was the envy of the world, and how they had shown how East and West could work together as a flourishing cultural crossroads. He added that the United Kingdom was proud and privileged to have had responsibility for the people of Hong Kong and to have provided a framework of opportunity in which Hong Kong had so conspicuously succeeded, and pledged unwavering support for the Joint Declaration.

He concluded, 'On behalf of Her Majesty and the entire British people, I would like to express our thanks, affection and goodwill to all those who have been our good friends over many generations. We will not forget you and will watch with close interest as you embark on this new era of your remarkable history.'

After this heartfelt statement, both sides stood watching as the two honour guards did their work. The Union Flag was brought down to the sound of *God Save the Queen.* Then the Chinese flag was raised to the Chinese national anthem. A gust of artificial wind set it fluttering.

By this time, we were all seated in the revolving restaurant on the top floor of the Furama Hotel. We had booked a table with a panoramic view of the harbour and there were also TV screens so we could see everything that was going on. At around 11 p.m. Chris Patten and his family boarded *Britannia,* clutching the Union Jack from Government House. Prince Charles was already on board, talking to Tony Blair. Looking down on the harbour, we saw *Britannia* and HMS *Chatham* preparing to cast off. Before the convoy sailed into the night, the guns of HMS *Chatham* gave a mighty salute which echoed off the mountains on either side.

As this was taking place everyone was choked with emotion. It was such a moving moment that almost all present, including the toughest men, had tears in their eyes. It was not only the British. My future wife and many other Chinese were similarly affected.

The Lion and the Dragon had been dancing together for so long that everyone found themselves at that moment in an ecstasy of nostalgia for what had passed and with profound uncertainty about the future. Certainly, it was a night never to be forgotten.

There was a postscript to this historic spectacle. Chris Patten had sailed to Manila on *Britannia* and then taken a British Airways flight to Heathrow, where he found himself, together with the *hoi polloi,* in a slow-moving queue. The Last Governor's imperial adventure thus ended in a taxi queue at Heathrow Airport.

The next morning all those red flags were fluttering in the breeze. At exactly 6.00 a.m. on 1 July, a convoy of the People's Liberation Army crossed into the New Territories and drove south. It was a symbolic act to prove that sovereignty had really changed hands. The Chinese do not talk about a 'Handover'; they speak of 'Reunification'. My American friend stumbled down to breakfast that morning with a serious hangover.

'I had a bad dream last night,' he said, 'I dreamt that the Chinese had taken over Hong Kong'.

'Would you like a drink?' I asked.

CHAPTER TEN

Back in the Motherland

WHAT, THEN, WAS THE LEGACY of British administration in Hong Kong? First, proper separation of executive, legislative and judicial powers; although some may argue that Hong Kong's governance was always executive-led and that Legco was merely a rubber stamp. Next, rule of law, a free press and clean government, all of which were shining models for the Mainland to adopt when the time was right (if it ever would be). Also, the breathtaking scale of new physical infrastructure such as Chek Lap Kok Airport and the Tsing Ma Bridge, although the cynics pointed out that most of the work went to British firms.

British governors had skilfully managed to keep Hong Kong's capitalist economy rattling along during decades of post-war socialist government in the UK. Also, when British governors or civil servants were presented with a conflict of interest between what the UK government wanted them to do and what was clearly in the territory's best interests, I believe that the majority of them were loyal to Hong Kong first and foremost. A good example is the dilemma of Sir Alexander Grantham in 1950 when London insisted that he give the planes used by the Flying Tigers in the Second World War, parked in Hong Kong, to the Americans rather than to the communist government in China – the legal owners under Hong Kong law. Fearing the animosity of the PRC, Grantham argued that he must treat the KMT and communists equally and argued strongly against the British position until he was finally overruled and surrendered to the dictates of realpolitik.

True, Hong Kong was not a full democracy, but the Basic Law stipulated that there would be direct elections for the chief executive in 2017 and for the Legislative Council in 2020. Firmly in place was a prudent fiscal policy that had generated huge foreign exchange reserves that Chris Patten had described as being larger than the dowry of Cleopatra. Finally, Hong Kong was a vibrant world city with a complex civil society and unique East/West characteristics formed during the century-and-a-half embrace of the British lion and Chinese dragon.

However, things did not proceed entirely smoothly. Almost immediately after the Handover came news of a financial meltdown. Hot money had been pouring into the 'Asian Tiger' economies for years. In Thailand, a real-estate bubble had developed and there was a speculative attack on the overvalued baht, which soon collapsed. The crisis swiftly spread to the whole region and became known as the Asian Financial Crisis. South Korea was badly affected and in Indonesia rioting broke out, caused by devaluation of the currency and price increases, causing President Suharto to step down after thirty years in power. Hong Kong's stock and property markets, which had been ramped up by both sides to display confidence in the transfer of sovereignty, crashed. It was a time of doom and despondency.

Hong Kong's Financial Secretary, Donald Tsang, acted with great determination. It cost US$1 billion to defend the currency and a further US$15 billion of government money to buy shares in the stock market. It was a major game of poker with the speculators. The government ended up as a large shareholder in Hong Kong Inc. and also made a killing when share prices started to rise. This was good luck as it could have gone the other way. At the same time, the IMF stepped in with a $40 billion loan to the region, so by the end of 1998 the worst was over.

I had at last finished my review of the legal aid system. After much heated discussion and in true civil service fashion, the report was shelved and no significant changes were made. Part of the problem was that the cost of extending and revamping the system was considered prohibitive. The government had gone through the motions to satisfy the legal profession but now the political situation had changed. I heard the echoes of the Port Control Scheme in Security Branch, twenty years earlier.

Moreover, it seemed that my bachelor days were numbered. No spring chicken, I had made a solemn promise to my mother that I would get married 'this century' and it was already mid-1999. My long-suffering girlfriend Zoe and I were married in a civil ceremony in Hong Kong followed by a party at the Lifeguard's Club in Repulse Bay. We all wore Chinese dress and the bride looked stunning in her red silk outfit. She had told me that I must arrive at the party by sea, so a bemused boatman took me offshore and waited for a signal from the bride. She kept me waiting for a long time and I was quite green upon arrival. Zoe's extended family arrived and endless pictures were taken. One of my friends caught my eye. 'Dignity, Peter,' he said, 'show dignity!'

Shortly after, we flew to England for a second wedding in a small Norman church in the village of South Stoke outside Bath. My mother wept tears of joy that after a long bachelor run, she had finally seen her youngest son married off. We left by horse and carriage and proceeded to the village hall where we threw a large reception with lots of food, wine and a live band. There was also a good pub next door called the Packhorse for those who wanted a pint and a chat. Friends and family from all over the world had converged on Bath for the occasion. My best man gave a speech in which he mentioned that my wife had worked in a bar, but catching the expression on my face, added, 'in an administrative capacity, of course.'

For our honeymoon we went to the Swiss Alps and Portofino. In the Alps, an extraordinary thing happened. On the first day of our walking holiday we climbed to the snowline and, as Zoe had never seen snow before, she joyfully played with it and threw a few snowballs. Then she realised with horror that her wedding ring had fallen off her finger. We searched for around thirty minutes but could not find it. Saddened by this bad augury, we marked the spot and resumed our walk. In the late afternoon, having done a glacier walk, we returned. I told Zoe that if we managed to find the ring then I promised to accomplish something important for the benefit of others (although I did not know at the time what it would be).

Happily, by then the sun had melted the snow sufficiently for the ring to appear on the surface.

This reminded me of a similar incident when my sister lost her wedding ring while cleaning out her daughter's stable in Ireland. Having searched the place many times she gave up, but some months later she noticed a glint in a pile of horse manure only to discover her ring. She then realised that the horse had probably swallowed it while being fed some carrots. It appeared that miraculous recovery of wedding rings ran in our family.

Back in Hong Kong, the first Chief Executive, Tung Chee-hwa, was muddling along. Well-meaning but inexperienced in government, he later broke the power of the Administrative Grade by introducing a ministerial system under which appointees on contracts were given the top government jobs and AOs could at best become a permanent secretary. This was introduced under the guise of maintaining the political neutrality of civil servants and promoting ministerial responsibility, although very few appointed 'ministers' ever took responsibility for anything. The one exception to this rule was Financial Secretary, 'Lexus' Leung, who was surprised to find out that it was not considered cricket to jack up the taxes on new cars after buying one yourself at the old rate.

The third millennium was fast approaching and we were told that all our computers would crash on 1/1/2000 (Y2K) if they were not fixed by specialists charging a high fee. This must have been the biggest cyber-con in history as most of the computers were only a few years old and I could not conceivable that the problem had not been foreseen earlier. On a more positive note, Zoe and I watched the dawn of 1st January 2000 break on an empty beach in Koh Samui where we solemnly made our New Millennial resolutions.

A new element in my life was my Chinese in-laws, who always showed me the greatest friendship and support and helped me learn new things about a culture I thought I knew well. Chinese families always do things *en masse,* and as my wife had three brothers and two sisters and their respective children (not to mention uncles, aunties and cousins) family events tended to be lively. Dinners were held in her parents' flat and they had a special six-foot-diameter metal disc that, placed on a small table, created dining space for twelve to sixteen people. Ah Ma was an excellent cook and would produce impressive banquets out of her small kitchen.

Various special dishes need to be served at different festivals: for example, at Chinese New Year you must eat *faat choi,* a vegetable whose name sounds like 'make money'. After dinner, Ah Ba would smoke his pipe and the others would watch TV, which is *de rigueur* during Chinese banquets. Those who wanted to talk could do so, and those that did not could watch TV without embarrassment. Ah Ma would then unpack her jade collection and give me select pieces which my wife would later confiscate. Before I met Ah Ma, she asked her daughter whether I had green eyes and red hair, which is the Chinese stereotype of a *gwai lo.* She was relieved to find out that I had neither.

Another unforgettable experience was the frequent visits to the temple to pay respect to ancestors. If you are required to pay a visit during a Chinese festival, such as Ching Ming, then you must do battle with thousands of other worshippers bearing fistfuls of joss sticks and burning paper money, clothes, cars, and even servants for use in the afterlife. The smoke is suffocating and makes tears run down your cheeks. The family will bring a cooked chicken and suckling pig and a bottle of Chinese wine. Taking up their place in front of the urn, which normally bears the deceased relative's picture, the family lights incense and lays out the food offerings. In strict order of seniority, family members pay their respects by bowing three times, placing joss sticks in a bowl and pouring the wine, thrice, onto the ground. After the ceremony, the family finds a pleasant spot and picnics on the food, chatting and exchanging news. Chinese families are generally closer than Western ones and meet up frequently for meals and events. There may also be more social pressure to attend family outings.

At Chinese New Year, the family meets for a meal on New Year's Eve to eat traditional dishes and it is regarded as lucky to stay up late playing *mahjong.* At midnight, you may wish people *'Gung hei fat choy!'* ('Congratulations and get rich!') or *'San tai gin hong!'* (Good health!) or *'Maan si yue yi!'* (May all your dreams come true!) or *'Lung ma jing san!'* (Dragon and horse spirits!). There are certain things that you absolutely must not do, like cutting your hair or sweeping the kitchen which causes you to lose your good luck. After dinner you may visit a flower market to pick up some flowers – the later the hour the lower the price. Late the next morning, the family meets for *yam cha,* where you eat many sorts of *dim sum* ('little bits of heart') and drink gallons of tea. Every married family member must now give *lai see* (red packets containing banknotes – normally two) to all the children and those married members of the family who are junior to your spouse (such as her younger brother or sister). It is all very complicated, and can be expensive.

As a family member, I was happy to help with the children's education and they were sometimes sent over to our house for the weekend to learn English and to experience foreign customs. This included taking them out for meals and teaching them the proper use of knives and forks.

Hong Kong's schoolchildren have a huge amount of homework and extra tutorials so have little time for sport or leisure. Their education is much too exam-based and tends not to produce creative minds. Although they all learn English and Putonghua, their use of vernacular Cantonese is so prevalent that they have very little practice in speaking other languages while good jobs increasingly require fluent English and Putonghua. They also lack confidence when it comes to speaking to foreigners and the teacher's first task is to encourage them to speak up and look you in the eye. Another local peculiarity is their reluctance to ask questions. In Western education, the asking of questions is a sign of intelligence but it is discouraged in the East as challenging the teacher's authority or showing the ignorance of the person asking. One conspiracy theory holds that the tycoons who run Hong Kong like the education system to produce wage slaves who will not display too much competitiveness or originality.

My last civil service job was in the Tourism Commission (TC) organising major events. My boss was the irrepressible Mike Rowse (or Mickey Mouse as he was affectionately known for his efforts in establishing Hong Kong Disneyland). We were looking at possible international sporting events to complement the immensely popular Rugby Sevens and were planning to hold a Powerboat Grand Prix in Victoria Harbour. We did most of the planning work, and the

Marine Police were very cooperative, but unfortunately the main sponsor pulled out at the last minute. Subsequently, the chairman of the Austrian Chamber of Commerce asked the chief secretary whether Hong Kong could stage an annual Christmas Fair similar to the Christkindlmarts which were so popular in Europe. The CS agreed and tasked the TC with the job. My boss was a gung-ho Englishman, who enjoyed getting things done, as opposed to some civil servants who, especially after 1997, preferred not to do things as they wanted to avoid making mistakes which might jeopardise their careers. It was put to me thus: if you do ten things in a post, you might have nine successes and one failure. However, your enemies will never forget that one failure. So it was safer not to engage in new policies.

I was fine as long as I had a 'doer' as a boss. For me, achievement was everything and without it there was not much point in getting out of bed. The first thing we needed for our new event was sponsorship and with the CS's support we managed to raise HK$30m, which was not bad going. The biggest sponsor was PCCW, Hong Kong's largest telecom company. We hired an event manager and flew to Europe just before Christmas to see the real thing in Stockholm, Nuremberg, Munich, Salzburg and Vienna. We called the event 'Hong Kong's EuroChristmas' and it was held for a week in December 2000 on the seafront promenade of the HK Convention and Exhibition Centre in Wan Chai North.

It was a huge and ambitious project. With the support of the European diplomatic community and the chambers of commerce, we brought cultural acts such as orchestras, dancers, circus acts and jazz bands from all over Europe and vendors selling handcrafted Christmas artefacts from Germany, Austria, Sweden and Russia. We built theatrical sets in English, German and Scandinavian architectural styles to house the vendors and a big stage for the cultural acts. We also brought in a funfair, complete with Big Wheel. Inside the Convention Centre was an attraction called Winter Magic with real snow. The City of Vienna gave us a fifty-foot Christmas tree and promised us one annually. The event was opened by Olivia Newton-John, who also sang a few songs with local star, Jacky Cheung. EuroChristmas was a great success and was visited by over one million people.

The event was never held again. Notwithstanding the fact that we had arranged our first working committee at 9.09 a.m. on 9/9/99 which according to Chinese numerology should have ensured it lasting a thousand years, it was not a Chinese event and therefore politically incorrect according to the new regime. It also highlighted the rivalry between the Tourism Commission, which set tourism policy, and the Tourism Board, which promoted Hong Kong internationally as a tourist destination. A huge amount of European goodwill was lost and the event finally morphed into a tacky travesty held annually in Central, complete with a plastic Christmas tree. The funfair concept, however, survived and is still held most winters.

It was now 2001 and I had watched Hong Kong grow into a stunning world city over the last twenty-five years and seen her returned to her rightful owner, China. To be honest, I was too much of a free spirit to feel comfortable under the new civil-service regime. Also, the authority of the Administrative Grade was about to be undermined by the new political appointees. So, after much soul-searching, and the offer of a golden handshake, I decided to take early retirement. I could expect a decent pension after my long service and there were many other things I wanted to do.

I was very much aware that mine was the last British generation to be able to enjoy a colonial lifestyle, one that had disappeared from other parts of the world many years before.

When I told a friend that I intended to retire from the service, he told me not to look glum as there was life outside the HK government. The most immediate loss was my super-efficient secretary and my convenient car parking space in the centre of town. The first thing I did was set up a consulting company, having sought the government's permission, as required. The last thing I wanted was a full-time job and a boss to keep happy – a wife fulfils this role – and there is a Cantonese expression, *'Pa lo poh jau faat daat'* (if you are scared of your wife you will be prosperous). As a consultant, I wrote reports, organised training courses and events, and sometimes advised people on how to interact with the government, although I came to avoid that kind of work.

As I seemed to have developed some expertise in tourism matters, I toyed with the idea of setting up resorts in Thailand and Sri Lanka and went as far as buying some land. Luckily, the majority of my pension was paid monthly as I quickly discovered how easy it is to lose capital. I really should have listened to my wife, who expressed grave doubts about my entrepreneurial ability. After all, I had spent my whole career in the public sector and knew very little about business. I should have known that my heart was too soft to be a successful businessman.

My biggest loss was in Sri Lanka. Of course, it is a beautiful country and a paradise for tourism. It is just not suitable for foreigners trying to do business there. My partner in this enterprise was an Irishman who had lived in Thailand for many years and who had successful resorts there. Our deal was that he would handle the construction while I took care of government matters. Too late I realised I had drawn the short straw.

Our first mistake was choosing a location for the resort by a lake in the so-called 'cultural triangle' in the centre of the country. Dambulla was a beautiful location and made sense from a tourism perspective. Unfortunately, as it was an area of outstanding natural beauty, all the land was owned by the government. This meant that we could not own the land but had to apply for a government lease.

Our second mistake was not having a trusted local partner. Although I had extensive government experience, I had absolutely none in dealing with the endemic corruption that exists in countries like India and Sri Lanka. My dealings with local government offices were like something from a Kafka novel. You would have long meetings with government officials who would then write a letter to the other departments involved. Later, you would visit the other departments, who would deny that they had ever received any such letter. Growing wise to this game, I kept my own file with copies of all letters so people could not deny that the correspondence existed.

Next, a land lease in Sri Lanka has to be signed by the president personally. As he happened to be fighting a vicious war against the Tamil Tigers at the time, the signing of our lease was hardly a top priority. As nothing is straightforward or works efficiently in that country, you must employ a 'fixer' to get things done. Needless to say, such a person does not come cheap. They become parasites who find ways continually to suck your blood. Even when you get your lease, you are subject to any number of outrageous demands from local officials who always have their hands out. We had actually started to build the resort, but were haemorrhaging so much money in under-the-table expenses that in the end we decided to sell the project, at a loss, to a local businessman. After all, it was only money and you cannot put a price on peace of mind.

'Told you so!' said my wife.

While this saga was going on, Hong Kong experienced its darkest year for many decades. The first major problem of 2003 was the arrival from south China of a mysterious virus. One of my friends returned from a business trip to Guangzhou in January and said he had heard rumours of 'something very nasty up there'. It soon took on the characteristics of a Hollywood thriller. A Chinese doctor suffering from the virus checked into a hotel in Kowloon and infected sixteen of his fellow guests, who then took the virus to Canada, Singapore, Taiwan and Vietnam. The first recorded case had been in Guangdong in November 2002, but the Chinese authorities only made a report to the World Health Organisation in February 2003.

Between February and April, 1,755 people were infected in Hong Kong, with 299 fatalities, the majority in Amoy Gardens, where the virus spread quickly due to defects in the drainage system. Subsequent research showed that the coronavirus had crossed the species barrier from host animals (possibly palm civets or bats) to humans via other animals in food markets in Guangdong. It was a very depressing few months in Hong Kong. The mystery virus was named SARS (Severe Acute Respiratory Syndrome) which was rather too suggestive of (the Hong Kong) SAR (Special Administrative Region).

We had become the pariahs of the world. I remember calling up my brother and suggesting that I come to visit him in the summer.

There was a long pause. 'I don't think so,' he replied with finality.

It was like living in a plague city. People wore face masks in public, even at that Mecca of fun, the annual Rugby Sevens event. It did produce one good effect. Hong Kong people were advised to get out and take more fresh air. As a result, more locals (whose traditional leisure pastime was sitting at home playing *mahjong*), started to go out to the New Territories and discover the joys of walking in the country parks. On 28 April, I held my fiftieth birthday party in the Foreign Correspondents Club. The staff asked us to wear masks but I absolutely refused on pain of cancelling the party. In my mind, that night marked the end of SARS. However, you can still see its effects in town today in terms of increased medical readiness and improved sanitary conditions and the heat cameras that check your temperature every time you arrive at the airport.

No sooner had the spectre of SARS been laid to rest when another monster raised its ugly head. In late 2002, the government had published details of a proposed new national security law. This was basically an amendment to existing Hong Kong laws to give substance to the requirements of Article 23 of the Basic Law, which stated that 'the HKSAR shall enact laws on its own to prohibit any act of treason, secession, sedition or subversion against the Chinese People's Government, or theft of state secrets, to prohibit foreign political organisations or bodies from conducting political activities in the region, or from establishing ties with foreign political organisations or bodies'.

Local lawyers and democrats started to focus on what effect such laws would have on Hong Kong's treasured freedom of speech and they were particularly concerned about proposed police enforcement powers such as entering private property without a warrant. The official ordered to get this law enacted was Regina Ip, the secretary for security. She downplayed the public's concern about living in a police state and pointed out that every country had national security regulations. When asked why there would be no public consultation, she said that ordinary people would not be able to understand the legal language.

The 1 July holiday, 'Reunification Day', has been a focus for anti-government protest since it began in 1997. On that day in 2003, around 500,000 people converged on Victoria Park and during the course of the day marched the few miles to Central Government Offices bearing banners and chanting slogans. The chief complaints were the proposed Article 23 regulations, the government's inept handling of the SARS epidemic and the generally weak economy. The main focus of protest was the unfortunate triumvirate of Chief Executive Tung Chee-hwa, who was perceived as ineffectual and indecisive, Financial Secretary Antony Leung, who had caused public outrage by buying a Lexus shortly before he raised the tax on private cars, and of course Regina Ip. Never had such a massive protest been seen in Hong Kong. The forces of opposition had come together and agreed their future common aim: to campaign for the introduction of universal suffrage. The leaders in Beijing sat up and took notice. Some observers say that the pace of 'Mainlandisation' speeded up from that time onwards.

The effect was immediate and decisive. The next day, two prominent Executive Council members resigned and the government decided to shelve the Article 23 regulations after realising that it did not have the support to get them through the Legislative Council. On 16 July, Regina Ip resigned, citing 'personal reasons'. The same day, Antony Leung also stepped down. Although Tung Chee-hwa held on for another eighteen months, he had been gravely weakened and resigned before the end of his second term. While perceived as a straightforward and honest man, he was out of his depth and seen as Beijing's man after his family business, Orient Overseas Container Line, had been bailed out by the Mainland in the eighties.

After all this bad news, the government cast around for something impressive to show that Hong Kong had successfully thrown off SARS and was once again open for business. They came up with an event called Harbour Fest, which was a high-profile series of concerts by international performers on a spectacular harbour-front site next to Tamar. Not since Woodstock had such a stellar cast of international bands been assembled in one place. The Rolling Stones, Santana, Neil Young, Prince, Air Supply and the Gypsy Kings were the main performers. In addition to the concerts, a prime-time TV show in the US, showing highlights of the event, was broadcast. Organised at short notice by InvestHK and the American Chamber of Commerce, the intimate outdoor setting of the old Tamar site was perfect and the performances were an unforgettable experience for all who attended.

Although the concerts were a huge success and played to capacity crowds, Hong Kong's fractious politics once again generated controversy. Some politicians claimed that the event was a waste of public money; that the musical taste was too expatriate in style (although local acts also took part) and that too many tickets had been given away while some acts had been overpaid. The *South China Morning Post* branded the event a 'fiasco', although the government working group had agreed to sponsor the event and had never, until the last minute, asked for full cost recovery. It was also felt that as the economy had revived, the *raison d'être* of the event had been lost.

A witch-hunt was called for and the ideal scapegoat was Mike Rowse, then director general (DG) of InvestHK, who was not only a *gwai lo* but British to boot. There were two public enquiries, one independent and one by the Public Accounts Committee. The ministers responsible for the event disgracefully washed their hands of it, and one famously deleted the minutes of a meeting in which he said that the DG had not acted improperly and that it had been a complex event organised in a short time span. The government said that the DG had not scrutinised the budget properly and fined him one month's salary. As a point of principle he appealed and subsequently sought a judicial review, at considerable personal expense, which vindicated him and overturned the government's decision.

This 'fiasco' illustrated a lack of accountability at the top of the government. In 2002, Tung Chee-hwa, had introduced the Principal Official Accountability Scheme in response to public dissatisfaction with the performance of his government. Starting with the flawed opening of the new airport at Chek Lap Kok and then the short-piling scandal in which Home Ownership Scheme flats had been found to be constructed using substandard materials, he sought a way to preserve the political neutrality of the civil service by adding a new ministerial layer of political appointees. The cynics said he did this to increase his own influence by breaking the power of the Administrative Grade. However, very few ministers ever took responsibility for their mistakes, unless the pressure to step down was irresistible, as in the case of Antony Leung. Ministerial resignations do not seem to be part of local culture.

Meanwhile, I was enjoying my retirement. There are quite a few expatriates who have stayed on in Hong Kong after retiring from government service. It could be the poor weather or tax levels in the UK or it could be the fact that after a lifetime of working for the local community they have no wish to leave these shores. The retired civil servants sit on various boards and charities and meet for curry lunches now and again to comment on the direction that the city is taking. The retired police officers are the backbone of their neighbourhood watch committees, write letters to the newspapers on various issues and pursue their hobbies with enjoyment.

To give some examples of the lifestyles of these retirees: one retired senior police officer, having divorced his British wife and whose sons are grown up, decided to renovate an old Hakka house, including an ancestor hall, in the remote countryside. He created a small estate comprising the main house filled with antiques; outhouses, garden, aviary, fishpond, and a museum of Hakka porcelain and farming implements. He cooks excellent curries and entertains his friends on a sunny terrace overlooking the fishpond, with an old cannon standing guard for good measure.

Another retired police officer, with a Thai wife and two children, also lives in the countryside and spends his days gardening and his evenings reading. His other hobby is luxury cars and he owns a beautiful model of one of the last British-made Bentleys. A third has a HK Chinese wife, two daughters and grandchildren. He is the organiser of the local Hash House Harriers (a drinking club with a running problem) and is a great dog-lover.

As for the retired civil servants, one spends the winter in his Wan Chai flat while making a few trips around the region. In the summer he migrates to the South of France where he has another home. Another is still labouring for a local property development company in order to be able to afford to send his daughter (his wife is Mainland Chinese) to a private university in the UK.

All these people are socially active in Hong Kong, have many local and expatriate friends, are involved to some extent in charitable activities and take a keen interest in public affairs. They all consider themselves Hongkongers and prefer this part of the world to anywhere else.

In 2005, we sold our house in Clear Water Bay and moved to Hoi Ha, which is a charming little village in the heart of the Sai Kung country park. It is one of the most isolated places in the territory and is surrounded by spectacular scenery. The cove has been declared a marine park and beyond its white beaches there is a thriving coral community. The bird and butterfly life in the area is particularly rich and many starfish live in the bay, together with leaping silver mullet.

Unfortunately, the villagers have now sold most of their land to property developers and, like other village enclaves in the country parks, the environment is under threat from cynical abuse of the small house policy. No one complains about building houses for villagers' children but the majority are built by small developers with maximum ecological damage and are sold to rich outsiders. The villagers' desire for financial gain is understandable whereas the SAR government's shameful collusion in what is essentially an illegal practice is not.

As we had no children of our own, Zoe and I decided to join the local foster child programme. In late 2006, we were asked if we could take a four-year old Chinese boy called Donald, whose mother had given him to Mother's Choice for fostering at birth. He was a very confident little boy and the first time I met him in a McDonald's café, he took me by the hand and showed me exactly what small gift he wanted. He loved the beach at Hoi Ha and for the first few weeks I spoke to him in Cantonese and subsequently in English while my wife talked to him in Chinese. When he turned five, he went to a kindergarten called Leapfrog near the park entrance attended by many expatriates and his English language skills developed quickly. I taught him to play Monopoly and chess and after a short while he regularly beat me. At seven he attended True Light Primary School in Kowloon Tong and as the round trip to Hoi Ha was then too far, we rented a flat in Kowloon.

Maidstone Road was a quiet residential thoroughfare between To Kwa Wan and Ho Man Tin set back from busy Ma Tau Wai Road and not far from King George V School. Actually, it was quiet then but is no longer so as an MTR line is now under construction. A district of five-storey walk-up blocks which were mainly occupied by Chinese civil servants, it was a friendly area with a local neighbourhood feel to it. *Gwai lo* were unusual there, especially those speaking Cantonese, so within a few months I had made many friends in the local shops and restaurants. At the back was a park with steps up to a service reservoir where I liked to walk the dog. There was also a basketball court where Donald could play, while I enjoyed a fine view of Lion Rock.

When he reached the age of eight, Social Welfare Department decided that Donald should return to live with his father. Although we had been psychologically prepared for this moment, we naturally missed him a lot, but more importantly he seemed to be happy in his new home with the added bonus of a brother and sister to play with. A year later he came back to visit us with his father's blessing and since then has become a regular visitor. He is doing well at school and we are very proud of our godson.

In 2008, I was diagnosed with prostate cancer, which was a shock. I took it quite seriously as that is the disease that killed my father. Luckily, I put myself in the capable hands of the marvellous doctors and staff of the Prince of Wales Hospital, who could not have provided better treatment. Nearly ten years after my surgery I seem to be doing fine, so far.

It was while we were looking for a primary school for Donald that some of the heads asked me if I would be interested in teaching English. The idea appealed to me, so I began to teach part-time in a few primary and secondary schools, and subsequently in a tutorial centre. Having spent so long in Hong Kong, I believed I knew what these young Chinese needed; they all learned English but had little chance to practise it, especially with an English person. They also needed their confidence and self-esteem boosted to help them speak up and look you in the eye. It is profoundly satisfying to see students start to catch on and improve, and as they approach their teens you can become less of a language teacher and more of a mentor who encourages them to discuss history, politics and philosophy, their lives and possible career options.

Having enjoyed returning to academic life, I applied to teach at university. I taught a course in Business English at Baptist University and then became a part-time lecturer in Government and Public Administration at City University. We had a number of Mainland students doing a Masters course and it was interesting to watch them flexing their intellectual muscles in an environment of greater political freedom. Their written English was also better than the locals' due to the unfortunate post-97 policy of favouring mother-tongue education.

It was not long before I was approached by another institution to run courses to prepare local graduates for interviews to enter the government as administrative and executive officers. This course was a mixture of basic interview technique and political discussion of current government policies. This highlighted one of the problems of teaching in Hong Kong. Most instruction relies on feedback from students and the creation of a dialogue, whereas Hong Kong students are most reluctant to ask questions. In any venue, they are like sponges soaking up knowledge, but it is very difficult to get them to give voluntary feedback unless they have spent time overseas. This trait can make teaching in Hong Kong very challenging.

Much has been said about so-called Chinese 'Tiger Mothers'. The educational system in Hong Kong (and China too) is so competitive that students have little time for leisure or play. Many times I have asked them if they have planned anything fun over the weekend. They reply that there is no chance as they always have extra tutorials and homework. Many of them play musical instruments and reach high proficiency but do not seem to enjoy it very much: it is another certificate for their portfolio. I met a lady the other day who had just taken her daughter for an interview for pre-kindergarten school. Her little girl is not yet two years old.

I also teach English a few times a week at a language school in Wan Chai run by an English lady who specialises in speech classes and whose students always seem to win prizes. This is enjoyable, relaxing work although I prefer to teach older children as trying to get younger children to settle down and concentrate on their work is exhausting. Also, I have noticed that girls are easier to teach than boys. Girls just get on quietly with their work, while boys tend to have shorter attention spans and you frequently need to help them refocus on their work. However, the great thing about teaching is that you really feel you are making a positive contribution and can encourage young people to be more imaginative, liberal and open-minded.

Another activity that I have enjoyed in my retirement is serving on the Council of the Royal Commonwealth Society, Hong Kong Branch, and since 2015 as its chairman. The Commonwealth is made up of fifty-three independent countries that share a common heritage of parliamentary democracy, rule of law, tolerance and inclusiveness. It has a population of 2.2 billion, 60 per cent of whom are under the age of thirty. In Hong Kong we have received great support from the Australian, Canadian, Indian, New Zealand, Nigerian and South African consuls-general who attend our monthly speaker lunches and help with activities such as our annual charity ball. As an organisation the Commonwealth is a valuable counterweight to other world bodies such as the United Nations, and has great future potential.

Another society I have been involved with is the Friends of Sai Kung, which tries to preserve this beautiful area as the back garden of Hong Kong. We keep a close eye on illegal developments in the country-park village enclaves and try to keep the government on its toes in the conservation of wildlife and biodiversity. We believe strongly that the country parks and their flora and fauna are a precious resource which must be preserved for our children and grandchildren and that they cannot be sacrificed for short-term profit or political expediency. I hope we will prevail but am not sure in a society where money really talks.

CHAPTER ELEVEN

A Buddhist Interlude

ALTHOUGH I WAS BROUGHT UP a Christian, and certainly have spiritual inclinations, for most of my life I was really a hedonist with scarce a thought for the morrow. The main motivation in my private life was the enjoyment of pleasure and I chose my friends accordingly. Yet as I grew older I underwent a transformation where I no longer saw the pursuit of pleasure as the key to happiness but more as a form of addictive bondage, and the time came when I thought that surely there was more to life than that. I had always been interested in Buddhism and upon arrival in the East made a point of visiting as many temples as possible in China (including Tibet), Thailand, Sri Lanka and Japan, where I always felt a strong sense of peace. Later I travelled to other holy sites in Burma, Vietnam, Cambodia and Laos.

It was the sudden death of a friend in a diving accident in 2006 which led me to want to know more about Buddhist philosophy, so I joined a centre and found a guru (a Bhutanese lama) who taught me about meditation and dharma practice. I found that this spiritual training helped me achieve a calmer perspective on life, making me more conscious of my emotional 'weather' and habitual reactions to life's daily challenges. After a while, I became a mellower, calmer person – less selfish and more concerned with others' wellbeing. The Buddhist emphasis on impermanence and non-attachment does not stop us from loving our family, friends and possessions. It just means that we must recognise their transience.

Meditation helps us to relax in the here and now. Asked by a student how long he should meditate, a Zen Master replied that twenty minutes was enough unless he was really busy – then one hour! I began to realise how I tended to see the world simplistically as a snapshot, whereas it is actually a movie. Everything is constantly changing like the seasons of the year or the flow of a river. While we have memories of the past and thoughts of the future, all we really have is the present moment. The body may die but the mind is immortal, and what we call space and time are actually products of consciousness.

A number of friends have asked me what attracts me to Buddhism rather than Christianity. I believe that all spiritual traditions are essentially the same, albeit with different historical and cultural backgrounds. The teaching of Buddha and Jesus are strikingly similar, although their pure message has been distorted by the prism of organised religion. However, there is little proselytising in Buddhism, as opposed to the embarrassing behaviour of the evangelical Christian Church. Buddhism is also inclusive and tolerant and does not require faith in a creator God, allowing followers to judge matters through their own experience. Last, Vajrayana (Tibetan) Buddhism encourages the regular practice of liturgy and meditation and puts emphasis on the spiritual teacher or guru who can give personal advice and guidance. If you had to summarise the Buddhist perspective, you might say it was an appreciation of the concept of 'emptiness' with a liberal sprinkling of compassion: May all beings be happy!

What does this actually mean in practice? Here is 'A Day in the Life' of a Buddhist practitioner:

7 a.m.: I wake up. Well, as there is no 'I' (only a continuum of constantly changing mental and physical attributes), Peter wakes up and says 'Om mani padme hum' as usual. Another twenty-four brand new hours to attempt to live fully in each moment and to look at all beings with compassion! Peter uses the toilet – immaculate or defiled? The concept exists only in our mind. Our panoramic intelligence is hijacked by duality. He washes his body (is it his?) and tries to cleanse his heart at the same time. He looks in the mirror – the same person as yesterday, maybe, but how different from twenty years ago. Older and wiser, he hopes. His mind creates a

continuum but ultimately emptiness is the agent of causality and change. Without emptiness there would be no change; like the vampire child who can never grow into adulthood. Without change we would still be selfish brats who never developed wisdom and maturity. Without the knowledge that we will soon be dry bones how could we enjoy the sweetness of the morning?

8 a.m.: Peter runs for the bus and narrowly misses it. Anger swells in his breast and a curse begins to form but luckily his spiritual practice transforms the curse into '*Om mani padme hum*'. So he takes the opportunity to relax and check the news. He has tried to transform the energy of anger into wisdom. He has tried to smile and not show a long face to the other passengers waiting at the bus stop. Then an attractive young woman joins the queue. He finds himself grasping the sensuality of her young body before he catches his desire and recalibrates his perception from sex object to sister. He smiles an avuncular smile. He is now a *bodhisattva* rather than a lustful monster. He has tried to transform the energy of desire into wisdom. After all, it really is all in the mind.

9 a.m.: The rituals of office life unfold. The smell of fresh coffee produces a myriad of memories of similar mornings. Once Peter walked into another office where the smell of floor wax immediately transported him back to his first day of school as a child. Such is the power of conditioning. If we seek the wisdom of emptiness, we must try to unlearn all our preconceived notions on the nature of reality. We should not leap to conclusions as all forms and concepts are illusionary. Life is but a dream. You can't have the movie without the projector. However, the sudden appearance of the boss does not appear to be a dream, very possibly a nightmare. For the hundredth time, Peter tells himself that his dislike (is hatred too strong a word?) for this man is his own problem, that there is really no difference between ourselves and others, that this is a problem for his illusory and delusive ego. We all have prejudices, likes and dislikes, but the important thing is to be aware of them. Beware the person who does not recognise his prejudices. He finds that when this feeling of dislike manifests itself strongly, the only way to stop it festering in his heart is to engage positively. A beatific

smile crosses his face, 'Good morning! How are you today?' he says. The negativity of hatred has been changed to benevolence.

12 noon: It is nearly time for lunch, that blessed hiatus in the busy office workers' tedious routine. Hurrying down the road, Peter finds another nemesis standing before him, a leer on his face and a begging bowl proffered. The phenomenon of fake monks begging for money is particularly galling because it gives Buddhism a bad name. Normally, Peter frowns at them with disapproval and rushes past, but this time infused with a spirit of *metta,* he decides to try something new. 'All right,' he says, 'You've got me this time. You are dressed like a monk, do you know any mantras?' The fellow looks blank. '*Om mani padme hum*' is the mantra of compassion. Say it a hundred times and you will receive a dollar per mantra.' The 'monk' is delighted and complies. Does this action contain wisdom? Is this a pure gift? Are the giver and receiver one in this transaction? The mantra is powerful and might have some positive effect. An understanding has been reached. There is at all times a right way to do things (what the Cantonese call '*sik dim jo*') and it always involves a positive attitude. The great challenge is to apply wisdom to every action, and it is of course a challenge and a progression.

1 p.m.: Lunch has started. Aside from quietly saying grace, which is the simple expression of gratitude that we have good food when so many do not, there is the thorny issue of eating meat. We know we should not, because it destroys the seed of compassion, because it involves cruelty to animals, and because it is often unhealthy and environmentally unfriendly. Yet, there is the question of taste (crispy bacon has not been replicated in the vegetable world yet) and the question of social acceptability. If we are guests, we do not want to cause trouble. Yet if more of us stood up for vegetarian ideals then the livestock and restaurant industries would need to take notice and change their practices. Where does wisdom lie in this issue? Certainly in mindfulness while being fully aware of what we are doing and perhaps thanking or blessing the animal or fish that we are eating. Certainly in not being attached to strong 'views' which override other considerations, nor in having negative aversions to certain types of food. We need food to survive (although

Milarepa managed on green nettles) but let's have the wisdom to eat moderately and mindfully, and to be grateful for what we receive.

7 p.m.: It is close to the end of the working day in a city which combines the Protestant work ethic of the British with the 'no-choice but to work all hours' refugee mentality of the Cantonese in Hong Kong. A beautiful Indonesian helper comes to clean the office. What past *karma* has led her to be sweeping the floor instead of sweeping out of a limousine as some rich businessman's *taai-taai* wife? And would she be any happier in the latter scenario? Probably not. She looks up as if she can read these thoughts. It is said that the act of measuring or observing something changes its parameters. It is true that consciousness shapes reality. It seems as if the last hour has passed very slowly but can time exist without a perceiver? Can 'reality' out there exist without our five senses? What is the standard of beauty for a blind man?

8 p.m.: Dinner with the wife and family. We try not to be attached to the things we love: our family, friends and possessions. Yet it is so hard not to grasp them. Impermanence is really a very difficult concept to accept although it is the source of all development, transformation and positive change. 'If winter comes, can spring be far behind?' Every time we encounter death, a very natural occurrence, we are surprised and shocked. We hang on to life so tenaciously, experiencing real fear in a bumpy aeroplane landing or fast taxi ride. At these times, we tend to recite mantras to protect ourselves (well, our bodies anyway) from harm. We also try to protect our loved ones by grasping them and making them accept our views. Note the use of the word 'our', apart from being a linguistic convention, we do feel some 'ownership' of our friends and family, related to the delusion of self. If emptiness is the agent of causality and change, then it is also the agent of relativity. When does a new friend become an old friend? When does a small child become a big child?

10 p.m.: Time for meditation. Mind is a process and it must be trained. We try to turn off that spotlight of consciousness that lights up various thoughts for just a hundredth of a second. Perhaps emptiness is the space between the thoughts (like the space between

heaven and earth – the Chinese translate emptiness as 'sky' which is clear until the clouds of thoughts drift across it). Emptiness is also the non-difference between perceived opposites such as good and bad, life and death, dark and light. The awareness of the meditator merges with the object of meditation; like listening to great music where the listener becomes one with the music. The insight is that the ocean (awareness) and waves (thoughts) are essentially of the same nature. In reaching a state of personal and phenomenal identitylessness, the practitioner may see the clear light of the innate mind. Another way of expressing this is that we try to promote a 'solipsism syndrome' which is the feeling experienced by astronauts that Planet Earth is not external to their minds.

Midnight: Time for bed. A beneficial exercise before falling asleep is to review the events of the day and try to recall those lapses of wisdom where we have succumbed to anger, desire or delusion. Although life is ultimately a mirage, the *karma* created by our action, and the intention behind the action, is real and trying to develop compassion for all living beings is the highest calling of Buddhism.

Aside from that, the Diamond Sutra concludes by describing this fleeting world thus:

> *A star at dawn, a bubble in a stream*
> *A flash of lightning in a summer cloud*
> *A flickering lamp, a phantom, a dream.*

Zoe's and my interest in Buddhism was increasing and in December 2009, we travelled to Bodhgaya in northern India for the annual Kagyu Monlam prayers for world peace led by His Holiness the Karmapa, spiritual head of the Kagyu order of Tibetan Buddhism. Bodhgaya is the place where Buddha was enlightened 2,500 years ago and a huge temple complex has been built around the sacred Bo Tree under which he sat. The villages and farms around the town have not changed much over the millennia. Together with thousands of monks we said prayers in the main temple and in the evening made clockwise circumambulations, *koras*, of the central tower. Sometimes we volunteered to help clean the temple complex. In addition to the huge Mahabodhi Temple, almost every Buddhist country in the world has built a temple in the town whose dusty streets are filled with hundreds of beggars who come especially for the festival and the charity of the pilgrims.

The Karmapa escaped from Tibet in 2000 by crossing the Himalayas into Nepal, and is regarded by his followers as a living Buddha. His humility is disarming and when teaching he admits that he is not as devout as his parents and that he sometimes used to put the clock forward so that his tutors would think it was time for his lessons to finish. I offer two small stories to demonstrate his wisdom: one day, I was helping to clean the grounds of the main temple and was kneeling to remove some orange peel from the path when I heard in my head a very clear voice say in English, 'Sorry, sorry, sorry!' and I looked up to see the distant Karmapa approaching at speed with full entourage, and felt that he had sent me a personal message to step out of the way. On another occasion, we had an audience and I had brought in my bag two prayer beads (mala) for him to bless but had forgotten all about them. Just as I remembered them, he turned around, asked for the beads and blessed them.

One of the highlights of the Monlam is the parade of monks with their begging bowls and it is auspicious for crowds of onlookers to fill them with biscuits and confections. Volunteers are stationed along the route to pick up all the sweets that had been dropped and keep them in bags for orderly distribution to the local children. It was my job to guard these bags but a huge gang of street children had decided that they were going to have them, come what may. They descended on me like a swarm of locusts and I had no option but to give them up. The children gave a great cry and grabbed what they could.

That year the Dalai Lama also came to teach and I had applied for an audience. However, it was not to be. On New Year's Day, I received a call from my sister saying that my mother, who was nearly ninety, had suffered a heart attack and that I should come home as fast as possible. That was easier said than done given peak holiday travel. One of the Rinpoche (precious masters) kindly took me to get a blessing from the Karmapa before my departure and I offered a white prayer scarf (*khata*) which he put around my neck. I then rushed to the airport and persuaded Thai Airlines to fly me to Bangkok.

Unfortunately, I was not so lucky there with British Airways who, despite my regular custom and begging, refused to give me a seat on their next flight to London. Instead, I managed to get on an Emirates flight to Manchester via Dubai. I arrived just after my mother had slipped away but was able to sit with my brother and sister for a while by her bed in the hospital. It was Epiphany Sunday. Outside it was bitterly cold and the snow lay thick on the ground. At her funeral the week after, surrounded by family and flowers, I told the story of how the year before she had been riding in a taxi when her driver had got into an argument with another driver.

'Look!' he said, 'I've got an old lady in the back here.'

'Where?' said Margaret, looking around in surprise.

She was always young at heart. As she requested, we uploaded all her books, the Merlin Quartet, on to the Scribd website so that people could read them for free. The last time I checked, she would have been delighted to discover that they had all been read many thousands of times.

Upon returning to Hong Kong, I decided to take a break and spend a month at a monastery in Sikkim. I flew to Bagdogra, near Darjeeling, and then took a jeep up the steep road which loops around the fast-flowing River Tista to Gangtok, the capital. I visited Rumtek, the seat of the Karmapa, and then went on to Ralang, seat of another great Kagyu master who gives teaching every spring. The monastery has a panoramic view of Kanchenjunga, the third-highest mountain in the world. Outside lay a typical Himalayan rural community in the foothills of the mountains, surrounded by alpine meadows. There were a few hundred monks at the monastery including many young ones. A few times a week I taught English to the young monks. The rest of the time I listened to the teaching and did some practice.

Sikkim had originally been an independent kingdom like Nepal and Bhutan, ruled by a Chogyal, but due to its ethnic Nepalese majority and following a referendum in 1975, it had become part of India. There are some spectacular spiritual sites in the area such as Yuksom and Tashi Ding, where ancient temples and stupas can be found and also many caves where Guru Rinpoche (Padmasambhava) is said to have meditated. Although distances are short, it takes a long time to get around due to the extremely hilly terrain. It is inadvisable for the traveller to look down at the terrifyingly steep drops by the side of the road, unless philosophical about the shortness of life.

I went for long walks through alpine meadows dotted with yaks and woods filled with orchids and rhododendrons. A few other foreigners had come along to hear the teaching and on my birthday I invited them to drink beer at a remote tavern I had discovered. Upon our return to the monastery that evening, we were greeted by an amazing sight. All around the lotus pond outside the main gate in the silvery glow of the full moon were hundreds of amorous frogs copulating like there was no tomorrow! I suppose the celibate monks were philosophical about this occurrence. I reflected that in our modern, busy lives it is important to get away to somewhere completely different every now and again for a complete break or retreat.

I spent a few nights in Calcutta on the way back to Hong Kong. My great-grandfather had lived there at the turn of the last century and I was looking forward to the visit. Arriving at Chandra Bose Airport, an exciting journey into town in an ancient Standard taxi was enlivened by innumerable near-collisions. I was staying at the Fairlawn with some friends, an old converted Bengal merchant's house run by an indomitable Armenian lady right opposite the Indian Museum where my forbear had served as curator. That morning, a cooked breakfast appeared and despite the fact that I had lived on vegetarian food for a month, the crispy bacon proved irresistible. The afternoon was spent at the museum, a beautiful white colonial building filled with curious exhibits on the inside and numerous ancient Buddhist statues in the courtyard. Upon arrival, we asked the staff if there was a portrait of David Hooper, botanist and quinologist, and was informed that indeed there was. We were taken to the room where the portrait hung and the sari-clad staff member was happy to snap a picture of us standing in front of the eminent Victorian gentleman.

As Calcutta, once known as the City of Palaces and second city of empire, has been run by a communist local government for the last half-century, there has been very little redevelopment and most of the old colonial buildings are still standing, including Writers' Building, the old East India Company Headquarters, with St Andrew's Kirk next door. I knew where Hooper had lived because I had a postcard sent to him by his daughter (my grandmother) in 1906. Off Chowringhee is a broad boulevard called Elgin Road and it was there that I found the white Victorian house, now owned by the church, which he had called home. On the other side of the huge maidan, you could see the white dome of the Victoria Memorial, that astonishing monument in white marble which had taken the British twenty years to build and which was meant to be the Raj's answer to the Taj Mahal.

We also boarded a boat for a trip up the muddy Hooghly River (as that part of the Ganges is called). An unforgettable experience is getting off to walk over the impressive Howrah Bridge, a kind of box-girder-suspension bridge hybrid built during the war to transport resources from India into Burma and across to Chiang Kai-shek in Chungking. They say that over half a million people cross the huge bridge every day and there are thronging crowds carrying all manner of goods and a warm wind blowing off the river. I thought Calcutta (or Kolkata as we must now call it) was a wonderful city and that its reputation for poverty and squalor was largely unjustified, especially as those traits are common throughout India and all Asia for that matter.

Upon my return to Hong Kong, I found that my guru had a new dharma project. Years earlier, he had visited the Milarepa Tower in Tibet and decided to build a similar one in his home country, Bhutan. Milarepa was a famous Tibetan saint who had learnt black magic to take revenge on enemies but later became a disciple of the great Marpa, who had brought many Buddhist texts back from India. Knowing that his new student had accumulated bad *karma,* Marpa treated him harshly and asked him to build a nine-storey tower with his bare hands. When it was nearly finished he told him to move it to another location. This happened a few times until Milarepa had worked off his bad *karma.* Later, he went off to meditate in mountain caves and eventually became enlightened. Milarepa is regarded as a shining example of the virtues of renunciation, diligent practice and devotion to his guru.

An official application was duly made to the Bhutanese government to build the tower and to everyone's surprise, as new temples are generally not allowed, it was approved. Given my government experience, I was invited to help with the project. It had always been my dream to visit Bhutan, that medieval Himalayan kingdom that preserves its unique culture by severely restricting tourism. In April 2011, I visited Sikkim again and on my way back took a jeep to Phuntsokling, which is one of the border towns between India and Bhutan. I was met by the lama's brother and taken to the tower site, which is on a hill not far from the border. Surrounded by mountains to the north and the Indian plain to the south, it was a magnificent location. That night we had dinner with the engineer to discuss plans.

The next morning we drove on vertiginous roads past waterfalls and impossibly steep drops to the capital, Thimphu, where we visited the temples and the Dzong, which is a combination of fortress and administrative centre. A number of meetings were arranged with local officials to discuss the tower project: the speaker of Parliament, the home minister and the director of culture. I wore a suit and assured them that adequate funds for the project would be forthcoming from Hong Kong. The local people were very polite and all wore national costume, which is a sort of kilted dress with boots.

The day after, we went to Punaka, an ancient wooden fortress and temple complex built on a salient at the junction of two rivers. I needed to get back to our hotel early to find a TV to watch the Royal Wedding of Prince William and Kate Middleton. The lama very politely watched with me, although I'm not sure what he made of the English pomp and ceremony. Given that there is a strong monarchy in Bhutan, it was possibly not so unusual for him.

Early in the morning we continued our journey to Bumthang, which is the spiritual heart of Bhutan in a spectacular valley filled with ancient temples. Everywhere there are prayer-wheels driven by streams. Surprisingly, there are also paintings of enormous phalluses on the houses as a symbol of fertility. In the valley, there is one temple where you can run around the dim passages wearing a heavy chain mail coat in order to remove bad *karma*. At another there is a statue of Maitreya (the future Buddha) up to which you must throw a white prayer scarf, and where it lands indicates your future luck. There is also a famous temple with the body-print of Padmasambhava on the wall.

High on a pine-clad mountain is Padselling Monastery, where the monks in special costumes were training for a forthcoming festival by practising their lama dances. Here we were shown a very special *purba* (ritual dagger) that had been used a few hundred years before to despatch a zombie in Tibet. *Purbas* are normally used to kill the ego. The hotel where we stayed was like a Swiss alpine lodge with a wooden roof and roaring open fire. We dined on yak meat washed down with local *arrack,* a fiery clear liquor. Next morning we had an eight-hour drive back to Thimphu and then on to Paro to walk up to the famous Tiger's Nest, a spectacular temple built precariously on the side of a cliff at 10,000 feet, which is a must-see for every visitor to Bhutan. Legend has it that Padmasambhava flew there from Tibet on a tiger. The walk up is not for the faint-hearted or those who suffer from vertigo.

A few months later, the ground-breaking ceremony for the Milarepa Tower was conducted by the Je Khenpo (the spiritual head in Bhutan and second only to the king) and attended by hundreds of guests. Sponsored by benefactors in Hong Kong, the nine-storey tower is the tallest building in the country, which otherwise has a height limit of five storeys, and together with the shrine hall is now undergoing internal decoration. When completed, the tower and monastery will be a great spiritual centre, home to hundreds of monks and a tourist attraction.

In 2015, the construction of the tower was completed and we invited the Bhutanese home minister to officiate at the installation of the golden pinnacle or *sertok* which is filled with treasures: mantras, Tibetan medicine and banknotes from different countries. I had not seen the tower since the completion of its foundation the year before and was excited to see the structure which just a few years before had been a sketch on the back of an envelope. At exactly the chosen time, we fixed the golden *sertok* in its place standing at the top of a rickety scaffold while the monks chanted and far below many locals gazed up at us. Suddenly, like a flash of lightning, I wondered whether *this* was the important project I had promised to undertake when hoping to find my wife's new wedding ring in the Swiss Alps sixteen years earlier!

The year before, I had decided to study for a Masters in Buddhist Studies at Hong Kong University, which boasts one of the best centres in the world with professors from all over Asia: China, Japan, India, Taiwan and Sri Lanka. I took courses in Mahayana and early Buddhism, Chinese and Tibetan Buddhism, Buddhist ethics and psychology, emptiness and Buddhist art of the Silk Road. It is quite a challenge to return to academic studies later in life and not to be distracted by the young women walking around the campus in their tight shorts (a most un-Buddhist thought!) I often sat by the fishpond at the back of the Centennial Campus reading Buddhist texts and watching the colourful carp darting about in the sunlight.

So, how is the former party boy these days? I feel happier, filled with positive energy and satisfied with life. I no longer feel the need for constant entertainment (like TV and background music) and am comfortable with my own company and in silent places. I still enjoy a glass or two of good red wine. I am aware that in every one of life's situations we have the choice either to be negative and selfish, or to be positive and generous with our time and resources. In the words of the Mahayana Buddhist song:

> *When I'm happy, may my joy flow to others and fill the sky*
> *When, I'm sad, may the sorrow of all beings be mine alone.*

CHAPTER TWELVE

Pride of Lions, Blaze of Dragons

T HE LION HAS ALWAYS BEEN a symbol of courage, strength and royalty, so is known as the king of beasts. In the twelfth century, Richard the Lionheart adopted three lions passant as his royal coat of arms and over 800 years later this is still one of the most identifiable national symbols of England. The lion as protector also appears in the coat of arms of many other European countries. In Asia, the lion capital of Emperor Asoka forms the national emblem of India. Lions were introduced into China from central Asia in the Han dynasty and their statues may be seen guarding imperial palaces, tombs and temples. The male lion leans his paw on a ball which signifies supremacy over the world, while the female lion protects a cub, representing nurture. The snow lion is a symbol of Tibet and in Hong Kong, lions guard the headquarters of both the Hongkong and Shanghai Bank and the Bank of China. The collective noun for lions is a *pride*.

The dragon is a very old symbol and may represent a memory of the Nile crocodile that sometimes managed to swim across from North Africa. They represent wisdom and longevity. Dragon legends were common in Greece and the Middle East and may be found in early European literature (the Epic of Gilgamesh, Beowulf and the Bible's Leviathan). The national symbol of Wales is a red dragon. They are often the keepers of treasure or maidens in distress. In India, and subsequent Buddhist literature, they were huge water serpents known as *naga*s. In China, they are the highest ranking animal in the zodiac, so were associated with the emperor and became a national symbol. Some scholars think the Chinese name *lung* represents the sound of thunder. Indeed, the national

symbol of Bhutan is *Druk*, the thunder dragon. The collective noun
for dragons is a *blaze*.

In China, the Proud Lion and the Blazing Dragon have been
dancing together for nearly 400 years. Although their relations
turned hostile during the Opium Wars, they became allies during
the Second World War in order to fight their common enemy,
Japan. Britain was subsequently one of the first Western govern-
ments to recognise the People's Republic of China, on 6 January
1950. Although they fought against each other in the Korean War
and were often on opposing sides during the Cold War, they
managed to negotiate the successful return of Hong Kong in 1997,
and since then the two powers have formed a strategic partnership.

The first direct contact between Britain and China occurred in
1637 when Captain John Wendell sailed a squadron of four armed
ships into Macau. The expedition was a private enterprise and did
not enjoy the official backing of the East India Company, although
it was rumoured that King Charles I had invested £10,000 of his
own money in the venture. The Portuguese were hostile to the
undertaking as they enjoyed a monopoly on the China trade in
Macau and the British were likely to jeopardise their position. The
ships sailed up the Pearl River where, acting like pirates, they
captured a fort on the Bogue. After some skirmishes and limited
success, however, the ships sailed away. The Chinese authorities
subsequently demanded a large sum of money from Macau as a
fine for this rude intrusion.

In 1793, Lord Macartney, former envoy to the court of Catherine
the Great and ex-governor of Madras, led his famously unsuccessful
mission to the Qing court and was effectively snubbed by the Emperor
Qianlong, who delivered one of the most famous put-downs in history
in a letter to King George III, which stated, 'Our celestial empire
possesses all things in prolific abundance and lacks no product within
its borders. There is, therefore, no need to import the manufactures
of outside barbarians in exchange for our own produce.' The British
were anyway preoccupied with the Napoleonic wars until 1815. But
by the 1830s the sale of Indian opium out of Canton had increased
exponentially and led directly to First Opium War in which Hong
Kong was ceded. Fifteen years later the shameful Second Opium War,

manufactured on a pretext to wring more commercial concessions, led to the ceding of Kowloon after an Anglo-French expeditionary force had sacked and destroyed the Summer Palace in Beijing.

During the following years, Britain tried to normalise its relations with the Qing court and offered advice on administrative matters. From 1863 to his retirement in 1907, Sir Robert Hart acted as inspector-general of China's maritime customs, which provided useful revenue for the Qing government. In 1877, the first Chinese Legation was set up in London and it was from there, twenty years later, that the Foreign Office secured the release of Chinese revolutionary, Sun Yat-sen, after his kidnapping by Qing agents. In 1898, the British secured a ninety-nine-year lease on the New Territories and the same year leased a naval base at Weihaiwei on the Shandong peninsula in order to counter Russian naval activity at Port Arthur.

Not only were the British active in the treaty ports on China's coast but they also ruled India from the mid-eighteenth century, which bordered with Tibet, in the Chinese sphere of influence. In 1888, Britain fought the Tibetans and annexed Sikkim, where British sovereignty was subsequently recognised by the Imperial Court. However, Francis Younghusband's unauthorised 1904 expedition to Lhasa to settle the border with Sikkim and look for non-existent Russians (one of Britain's last imperial adventures) alerted China to the fact that there was an open back door into their empire, which really ought to be closed. China and Britain consequently signed a convention in 1906 under which Britain agreed neither to annex Tibetan territory nor to interfere in its administration. However, the priorities of the British Indian government and the Home government were quite different. While Calcutta was mainly interested in the protection of India's northern frontier, London was more concerned with Russian expansion in central and east Asia. Accordingly, Britain and Russia signed a convention in 1907 in which both sides recognised the 'suzerainty' of China over Tibet. It was almost as if Britain baulked at the prospect of taking on another colonial project. London was content to recognise Chinese suzerainty, if this precluded Russian influence. 'Suzerainty' means that a region is tributary to a more powerful entity, which controls its foreign affairs but allows some domestic autonomy.

China, disturbed by the success of the Russians in Mongolia and the prospect of Britain opening direct relations with Tibet, reluctantly agreed to three-way negotiations at Simla in 1914. The Tibetans, for their part, wanted an acknowledgement of their independence, having evicted all Chinese troops and officials, while the Chinese claim of sovereignty rested on the conquest of Tibet in the thirteenth century by Genghis Khan (whose grandson, Kublai, placed his grandfather on the imperial records as *taizu* or official founder of the Yuan dynasty) and the appointment of Chinese representatives, known as *amban*s, in the reign of the Emperor Kangxi.

The British plenipotentiary, Sir Henry MacMahon, who is famous for determining the borders in the Himalayan region, assumed the position of mediator, trying to find a compromise between the two conflicting positions. Although the British government was not prepared to support Tibet's claim of absolute independence, it wished it to maintain its autonomy. MacMahon proposed a distinction between Outer Tibet (Tibet proper, west of the Yangtze, over which the Tibetan government had for many centuries exercised complete jurisdiction) and which was the main object of British concern, and Inner Tibet (east of the Yangtze, up to the borders of Sichuan and Gansu, where the population was mainly Tibetan by race and religion). Britain and China were to respect the autonomy of Outer Tibet, whereas China could appoint officials and station troops in Inner Tibet. Unfortunately for Tibet, China initialled but refused to sign the 1914 convention due to disagreements on the location of the Sino-Tibetan frontier.

As a postscript to this matter, when Chinese troops 'liberated' Tibet in 1950, Tibet's appeal to the United Nations (and subsequent appeal in 1959) was ignored by the British government and the government of India, who had since 1914 been dealing with Tibet as a country enjoying *de facto* independence. Perfidious Albion! Of course, the global balance of power had changed, and China's historical relationship with Tibet was exceedingly complex. In the past, it had been based on the ancient bond between patron and priest (emperor and Dalai Lama) and the fact that the latter exerted a peaceful influence on the warlike Mongol tribes which occasionally menaced China. Moreover, China's claim to Tibet was probably inevitable given its geographical and strategic importance and the fact that the region is the source of nearly all of Asia's water.

It is interesting to note that Britain's official position in recognising only Chinese suzerainty over Tibet was given up as late as 2008 by former British Foreign Secretary, David Miliband, who confirmed, according to the dictates of *realpolitik,* that Britain would henceforth recognise Tibet as an integral part of the People's Republic of China.

Towards the end of the Qing dynasty, the British system of constitutional monarchy was looked at as a possible model for China's government, but with the fall of the Qing in 1912, and notwithstanding Yuan Shikai's ill-starred attempt to found a new dynasty, republican sentiments inspired the Nationalist Party or KMT's attempt to subdue the warlords and unite the country. Meanwhile, in Shanghai, British modern products such as cars, gramophones, electrical fittings and cinemas were increasingly popular, at least before the Japanese occupation.

British prestige in China took a hit during the opening years of the Second World War. The mid-1940 closure under Japanese pressure of the Burma Road, which had been supplying the KMT regime in Chongqing, angered Chiang Kai-shek. Subsequently the loss of Burma and the Fall of Singapore in early 1942 lowered Britain's military standing in the Far East. With China tying down a large proportion of the Japanese army, Chiang was invited to attend the Cairo Conference in December 1943 with Roosevelt and Churchill. However, he was not invited to the conference of victors at Yalta in February 1945. Also, he was too preoccupied with trying to outmanoeuvre the communist forces to prevent the British from regaining control of Hong Kong. Over the next few years, even though the KMT held most Chinese cities, the balance of power turned decisively in favour of the communists.

In April 1949, towards the end of the civil war, a British ship, HMS *Amethyst,* steaming up the Yangtze from Shanghai to evacuate personnel in Nanjing, was fired upon by batteries of the People's Liberation Army and trapped on the river for three months. With the assistance of other Royal Navy ships, she eventually escaped. Hong Kong's future governor, Sir Edward Youde, was at the time a junior diplomat involved in the incident, and requested to speak to Mao personally. A few months later, upon the establishment of the People's Republic of China, Britain had to swallow the nationalisation of £300m worth of Mainland investments, mainly in Shanghai. Nevertheless, Britain (unlike its ally, America) decided to recognise the PRC. Unfortunately, hostilities under the Korean War continued between 1950–53, with Britain being part of the UN contingent and suffering heavy losses.

In 1967, during the Cultural Revolution, the British consulate in Shanghai and the embassy in Beijing came under attack. At the same time, it is reported that the commander of the Guangzhou military region suggested invading Hong Kong, but the plan was vetoed by Premier Zhou Enlai. Nonetheless, five Hong Kong policemen were killed at Sha Tau Kok when Chinese militia opened fire with machine guns.

In 1982, Margaret Thatcher opened negotiations with Deng Xiaoping on the future of Hong Kong. When she appeared to be stubborn in seeking continued British rule, Deng evidently told her, 'We can simply invade Hong Kong.' Finally, the Joint Declaration was signed in 1984. After the successful handover of Hong Kong in 1997, Britain and China formed a strategic partnership, although many businessmen felt that British trade had been seriously harmed by Chris Patten's confrontational attitude.

These days, relations are occasionally ruffled by perceived support for democrats in Hong Kong and British insensitivity, such as wearing poppies during a trade mission to Beijing in 2010, or the willingness of British prime ministers to meet the Dalai Lama, which David Cameron did in 2012 and was for a year or two unwelcome in China. However, the Chancellor of the Exchequer, George Osborne, enjoyed successful visits to Beijing in 2013 and 2014 and signed a number of lucrative business contracts. Much to the chagrin of the Americans, David Cameron in 2015 agreed that Britain would be the first European nation to join China's new Asian Infrastructure Investment Bank.

All these overtures climaxed in Xi Jinping's state visit to Britain in October 2015. Xi, who has been described as the strongest Chinese leader since Deng Xiaoping, was welcomed with a twenty-one-gun salute, stayed at Buckingham Palace and enjoyed a ride down the Mall in a golden state coach with the Queen. In a visit arranged more by the Treasury than the Foreign Office, and in a dramatic reversal of roles from the nineteenth century, he signed contracts for a US$18 billion high-speed rail link from London to the Midlands and the North, and a US$37 billion nuclear power station at Hinkley Point in Somerset. The raising of issues such as Tibet, Hong Kong and human rights was strictly discouraged. It was heralded in the press as a new 'golden era' in Sino-British relations, although critics pointed out that Cameron had performed what Lord Macartney had refused to do 200 years earlier – the full *kowtow*. However, the warm welcome and 'face' Xi was given in Britain was highly appreciated in China as opposed to what was perceived as a lukewarm reception in America a few months earlier. How this new 'golden era' will be affected by Brexit and a new British government remains to be seen.

It has been said that over the last century, America has sacrificed its republican ideals on the altar of empire. With a military budget that exceeds that of the rest of the world combined and a thousand global bases, 'gangster for capitalism' Uncle Sam has been almost continually at war for the last half-century. It looks as though Britain has decided that given the mess the US has made of its foreign policy over the last few decades, especially in the Middle East (helped by Britain, alas, in the disastrous second invasion of Iraq in 2002), perhaps it is time for the old Lion to distance himself a little from Uncle Sam across the Atlantic and reposition himself more in the direction of the Blazing Dragon and the emerging Pacific. As Palmerston famously said, 'We have no eternal allies and perpetual enemies; our interests are eternal and perpetual.'

What of China? At the spectacular 2008 Olympics, she very visibly reclaimed her place as a great world power, and it is perfectly understandable that she had a strong desire to rise up again from the humiliation and chaos she experienced in the nineteenth and early twentieth century. In 1970, American GDP was twenty times that of China, whereas it is now less than four times. Although at present the second largest economy in the world, there are obviously questions about political reform, frozen for the past few decades, and personal freedom. It is often said that a Faustian bargain has been made with the citizens of China: they are free to make money and enjoy a higher standard of living, provided they do not ask awkward questions about political transparency, censorship, the weakness of the press or the partiality of the courts. Admittedly, the awful state of politics in America is not a good advertisement for political reform. However, the 'Great Fire Wall' that censors China's Internet can hardly encourage commercial innovation or academic excellence. Nor can China expect the RMB to become a full international reserve currency without complete economic and fiscal transparency. The same is true for the stock markets in Shanghai and Shenzhen which crashed spectacularly during the summer of 2015, wiping a trillion dollars from their value.

However, China still boasts foreign exchange reserves in excess of US$3 trillion and has launched a new and exciting strategy for overseas economic expansion and the development of soft power called the New Silk Road. On land, this route stretches west from Xian to Urumqi, Almaty, Tehran, Istanbul, Prague, Rotterdam and Venice, where it joins the Maritime Silk Road. This concept harks back to the heyday of the Silk Road along which diverse cultures, religions and lifestyles could communicate and trade, while China over the last half-century has gained increasing credibility in the developing world. Although details are sketchy about how the new route would function, it ambitiously links China with central Asia and Europe in what could be a new chapter in the Great Game. As China's own infrastructure is well developed, future economic expansion could take the form of road, airport, railway, and gas and oil pipeline projects in central Asia and eastern Europe, together with Chinese steel for construction. Oil pipelines are also planned from Pakistan and Myanmar into the interior of western China, thus avoiding the choke-point of the Straits of Malacca, where 75 per cent of her oil passes at present. Of course, economic opportunity and political reality might not correspond. China is obviously anxious that these ambitious plans should not be affected by the current problems with radical Islam.

The maritime route, known as a 'String of Pearls', extends from Venice to Athens, through the Suez Canal to Nairobi and then to Colombo, Kolkata, Kuala Lumpur, Haikou, Guangzhou to Quanzhou in Fujian (opposite Taiwan), ambitiously linking three continents. Again, it is not clear how such a route would operate in practice and whether it could link up meaningfully with the land route to produce new economic opportunities for both China and the rest of the world. China says it is interested in friendship and economic opportunities rather than military expansion. Some believe this and hope it is true but others look at developments in the South China Sea that appear to contradict this rosy assumption, with China reverting to its pre-Opium War treatment of smaller Southeast Asian countries as tributary states.

In the past, Zhou Enlai claimed, 'Even when our economy is developed we will not consider ourselves a superpower' and Deng advised his colleagues to 'Hide our capacities and bide our time.' Even Jiang had talked about a 'peaceful rise'. So does expansion into the South China Sea represent a fundamental change of policy or are the resource and strategic implications overwhelming?

In his book, *When China Rules the World*, Martin Jacques advances the argument that China will never become a Western-style nation due to its size, long history of splendid isolation and the fact that China's ruling class has never needed to share power or be accountable. It must be acknowledged that the CCP did succeed in reunifying China, and has now largely restored the Middle Kingdom's power and status. Moreover, no one can deny that the global balance of power is shifting from an America that dominated the twentieth century to a China that could dominate the twenty-first and so transform the world. However, if China accomplishes this without paying at least lip service to Western norms such as rule of law and representative government, then there is bound to be friction. Given its rising fiscal deficit, the question is whether America can afford to maintain its military edge in Asia and if not, then China is likely to flex its military muscles.

Meanwhile, China has embarked on a major push of soft power diplomacy and trade links with the rest of the world and has made a constructive contribution to the Paris climate change conference. Moreover, China's brand of non-judgemental foreign policy is often better received than America's continued emphasis on human rights. While crackdowns on dissent and the Internet continue, non-political civil society in China is generally stable, relatively unrestricted and functions more smoothly then many democratic countries (e.g. India).

A loss of moral compass in many aspects of Chinese life is unfortunately a direct legacy of the Cultural Revolution. With the Red Guards' destruction of religion and moral values, greed was unrestrained. That is why some people can sell tainted milk powder which kills children and recycled gutter oil which causes serious health problems. However, we can hope for a moral revival. China's new and powerful leader, Xi Jinping (too powerful some say) has instituted a major crackdown on corruption at senior party levels, and although cynics interpret this as a way of removing rivals, such policies may improve standards of government for the majority. At the same time, the 'Tigers and Flies' Campaign has created a lot of fear among cadres and an atmosphere similar to the Cultural Revolution where no one trusts anybody. However, the main guarantees against corruption in any society must be a free press and political plurality, which are unlikely to appear in a one-party state. The Great Internet Firewall of China is as strong as ever (no Facebook, YouTube or Google for a start) and people worry about further restrictions on freedom of information and a possible return, domestically, to the closed isolation of former times.

Now that China's economy is slowing down after decades of rapid growth and given falling stock prices, external enemies or 'foreign hostile forces' are more than ever needed to divert attention from the possible failings of China's leadership. Japan is the usual favourite, especially with its present right-wing leadership. The huge military parade in Beijing on 3 September 2015 to celebrate the end of the 'War of Resistance against Japanese Aggression' was an effective diversion, although it may have scared some of China's neighbours. The other favourite enemy is of course the US, which is seen as stirring up trouble and encircling the motherland by encouraging Japanese rearmament, South Korean war games, the Philippines' international legal case against China's occupation of various coral atolls in the South China Sea and forging a military alliance with Vietnam. Conspiracy theories are floated accusing the US of a role in the slowing down of China's economy and stock market collapse.

Despite the profound changes in China over the last few decades, Hong Kong people still hold a rather negative view of Mainlanders. It is true that some of the millions who flock to the SAR for shopping are loud and rough and in some tourist destinations (like Thailand) they have built segregated hotels for Mainlanders so they don't annoy other tourists. On the other hand, I have met some highly-educated and sophisticated people on my travels in China, who still retain the traditional qualities of Chinese gentlefolk, who can discuss philosophy over cups of fine tea, play melodious pieces on their *gujang* and with quiet enjoyment study collections of exquisite Tang dynasty paintings. In short, it seems that the scholars, mandarins and literati that Lee Kuan Yew mentioned to Deng Xiaoping in 1978 are still flourishing. So, let us not throw out the baby with the bathwater.

For Hong Kong's part, its leaders seem to be in awe of China's rise and their performance has been distinctly lacklustre. It seems that they have merely swapped one colonial master for another and are incapable of standing up for themselves. Although it has not been easy for them to adapt to new political circumstances, one might at least expect them to put Hong Kong's interests first rather than always deferring to the perceived wishes of their masters in the north. The hubris of building a grand new government HQ in a prime harbourfront location, the emphasis on expensive 'national' projects, such as the Macau–Zhuhai Bridge and the High-Speed Railway, the ham-fisted handling of youth discontent that manifested as Occupy Central, are all signs of this malaise. The undesirable side of 'Mainlandisation' is that some senior officials begin to forget that they are actually public servants.

In many areas of government endeavour, such as land administration, education and environmental quality, there seems to be
an underwhelming result. People wonder what has happened to
Hong Kong's 'get up and go' spirit. As one cartoonist put it, 'It got
up and went'. Poor air quality; the non-enforcement of laws on
idling engines and parking for the rich; proposals to site housing
development in our precious country parks; exam-based education
that does not produce creative or innovative graduates, have not
been addressed. There is generally a loss of confidence in the
government – a lot of 'gas' and not much 'go'.

As a consequence, civil society has become more active and
critical of the government's performance. Young people, the 'post-
eighties generation', are prone to protest and complaint, which is
exactly what they did in Occupy Central, provoked by Beijing's
apparent lack of understanding about what makes Hong Kong tick.
A highly sophisticated city-state was treated in 2014 like a small
child instead of a responsible young adult by the Standing Committee of the National People's Congress over the question of basic
democratic reform and the bitter political reaction was entirely
predictable. The students also complained, with some justification,
about the shortage of good jobs for graduates and the impossibility
of being able to afford to buy their own flats. There is a general
perception that the chief executive is focused on Beijing's interests
rather than Hong Kong's and widespread dismay at the low calibre
of ministerial appointments.

During Chinese New Year 2016, an ill-conceived government
clearance of illegal hawkers led to the worst rioting in Hong Kong
since the dark days of the Cultural Revolution. A radical 'localist'
group called Hong Kong Indigenous engaged in a vicious pitched
battle with the police, throwing paving stones and attacking wounded
officers on the ground, leading to warning shots being fired. It was
noted that the Occupy or Umbrella movement, which was largely
peaceful, had failed to achieve any tangible results. Many young
people feel cheated by the government and do not foresee a good
future. In a by-election soon after the riot, the leader of the 'HK
Independence' group, despite his lack of historical knowledge and
unrealistic political views, received 66,000 votes, although confirmed

localists were disqualified from running in the September Legco election. Mainland hardliners see subversive foreign influence in the pro-independence movement and have been heard to remark provocatively that the PLA garrison in Hong Kong will know how to deal with these misguided young people. The old respect for government authority now seems to have evaporated. There appears to be a lack of consensus, on all sides of the political spectrum, on the best way forward.

Unfortunately, Hong Kong's new rulers have continued the colonial government's high land-price policy and its alliance with property developers. Due to Hong Kong's narrow tax base, and opposition to the concept of a goods and services tax, the Treasury derives a large proportion of its revenue from land sales, stamp duty and profits tax on property development companies, and due to fiscal rules all income from land must be spent on capital rather than recurrent expenditure. At the moment it is being spent on 'national' projects, while our elderly receive no proper old-age pension.

Expensive land, wealthy Mainland buyers and low interest rates have seen property prices reach new heights and young people cannot afford to get on the ladder. This has a knock-on effect on residential and commercial rents and retail prices, making the city a very expensive place to live. Hong Kong is a low-tax zone, but its high property prices mean there is a *de facto* land tax which more than compensates for low salaries tax. Government apologists point out that they are building more public housing, some for sale to sitting tenants, and that they have stood up to some of the more extreme manoeuvres of Hong Kong's voracious property developers.

Inequality and income disparity are worrying trends. Hong Kong's Gini coefficient, which measures income inequality, has risen dramatically in the last few years and is now higher than China's. It is an increasingly common sight to see old people scavenging in rubbish bins, which is surely unacceptable in a city that has trillions of dollars in reserves. There exists a deeply flawed Mandatory Provident Fund scheme which largely benefits the banks that administer it. In the old days, people were not resentful of ostentatious wealth – a tycoon stepping out of a Bentley – because it was believed everyone had the chance to get rich. This attitude has disappeared because there is no longer the same level of opportunity.

I met a student recently who said he had decided not to enter the 'rat race'. He would not become a wage slave and pay half his income as a mortgage, but apply for public housing and enjoy his life; maybe have *yam cha* every morning and read the newspapers and go for a walk in the afternoon. If this attitude becomes prevalent and our young people lose their ambition and motivation, then Hong Kong is in trouble. The energy, initiative and vibrant work ethic which defined Hong Kong in the past needs to be fostered and sustained.

As Hong Kong's population ages, its birth rate has sunk to its lowest level ever as young people feel that children are just too expensive to raise and educate in this city. It is sad that so many will be denied the joys of parenthood. On the other hand, a million one-way permit holders, without any qualification except that they have relatives here, have entered from the Mainland since 1997. Apart from changing the city's political complexion, this has considerable implications for public housing and government services, and makes one even more sympathetic for the young people who compete for them.

Another problem is air pollution. After 1997, air quality declined significantly because the government did not see it as a priority and liked to compare Hong Kong to cities in China rather than those in Europe or America, even though we call ourselves 'Asia's World City'. This also underlines another problem; collusion with big business and the failure to champion the ordinary person's quality of life against vested interests. Politically, Hong Kong has become polarised between the pro-establishment DAB party and the Pan-Democrats, who have become increasingly fragmented. In Legco, filibustering paralyses government business. People worry that their protests and antics will lead to less rather than more freedom.

Hong Kong's two main constitutional problems remain the election of the chief executive, which, thanks to a very conservative interpretation of the Basic Law by the National People's Congress, means that the CE in 2017 will still be elected by a vetting committee of 1,200. This hardly legitimises the CE's choice of ministers (or policy secretaries) and Exco appointees. It is disappointing for those liberals who saw Hong Kong as a possible laboratory for political reform in China. As the Chinese have always said about elections, they have nothing against them as long as they know who is going to win! The second problem is the functional constituencies, which may have been a good idea back in 1984 but are now unrepresentative and stuffed with vested interests.

Mainland tourism has fortunately been scaled back from its ridiculously high level of 50 million per year in 2013 when there were frequent clashes between locals and Mainlanders due to overcrowding and cultural differences. The hundreds of thousands of Mainland shoppers at Lunar New Year may help local business but at the same time, many of the things they buy are luxury products that locals simply cannot afford, e.g. handbags which cost a month's salary. Also upsetting for locals is small, friendly shops closing down to be replaced by expensive name-brand emporia. Provocative behaviour, such as eating noodles on the MTR or allowing their kids to relieve themselves on the streets are other causes of friction.

What is the future of Hong Kong? Over the last century it has always seen off the doomsayers who said it was in decline. In the fifties and sixties, it was a hardworking refugee community, followed by the golden years of economic success as an international finance centre and gateway to China. Like post-war Britain, Hong Kong is now searching for a new role. For the time being it retains its independent judiciary and freedom of speech. It is a treasury of professional and academic expertise. Maybe it can reinvent itself as the Riviera of China, where rich Mainlanders can own a villa and boat – but it now appears that these people feel too close to Big Brother for their fortunes to be safe, so have parked them in Singapore and other places. Hong Kong is also the conscience of China in that it is the only place in the country that commemorates the tragedy of 6/4.

The SAR government focuses on economic issues such as affordable housing, education and healthcare rather than rule of law, freedom of speech and conservation, which are perceived as 'Western values'. Similarly, they are not really concerned with public opinion as long, of course, as public order is maintained. In late 2015, five Causeway Bay booksellers disappeared and it was suspected that they had been illegally abducted by Chinese officials and taken to the Mainland. Admittedly, it was imprudent of them to be publishing gossip about senior Mainland officials but the implication of a midnight knock on the door for 'thought crimes' sent a shiver down the spine of Hong Kong people. A telling joke at the time was, 'What's the fastest way to China?' Answer: 'Open a bookshop!' People asked themselves about the credibility of 'one country, two systems' which is meant to operate for another thirty years until 2046.

When State Councillor Zhang Dejiang arrived in May 2016, 8,000 police were mobilised to protect him from any embarrassing protests. However, I sincerely hope that despite their conservative and authoritarian stance, China's leaders will be too smart and pragmatic not to make Hong Kong work successfully as China's most Westernised city. If Beijing were to trust the city a bit more, I'm sure it would respond with pride and patriotism. Should I be wrong, then many more HK professionals will leave for Canada and Australia and other countries.

Let's face it, nowhere is perfect and Hong Kong remains a great place to live. Over the last four decades, under the rule of four colonial governors and three local chief executives, I have seen Hong Kong transformed from a colonial outpost to a great world city. It is home for me and I always have a warm feeling upon return from other places. Of course, I am conscious of being a foreigner, of being different, of being 'a stranger in a strange land' – but it does not worry me. I am used to being the only *gwai lo* in a gathering. When I visit the UK, some of my friends tell me that I look Chinese – wishful thinking, perhaps? The Lion and the Dragon are no longer locked in a face-off. On the contrary, they should stand back to back to face the pressing development challenges of the post-Millennial world.

EPILOGUE

Many years ago, I visited Tibet and one evening was walking around the grounds of the Holiday Inn Hotel. Challenged by an armed Chinese soldier, I answered him in Cantonese. He stared at me and said *'Nei sik gong ngoh dei ge wa?'* – 'You can speak our language?' It transpired that he was from Canton and was desperate for someone to chat to in Cantonese. He told me that he was off duty soon and would take me to the Soldiers' Club to buy me a beer. The irony was that the only person he could find to speak Cantonese was a foreign devil! We spent the rest of the evening chatting and drinking. As we said goodbye after midnight he shook my hand vigorously. 'You not really *gwai lo,'* he said, 'you virtually Chinese!'

Hong Kong still enjoys its traditional advantages even though it is becoming homogenised with an increasingly confident and sophisticated Mainland. Although it has had its fair share of problems, the place nearly always bounces back. It is still the most convenient place in the world for many things, such as shopping and getting around. Its pace of life remains fast and everyone is always in a hurry. That is its culture. Everyone lives cheek-by-jowl and tolerates each other's foibles. The Chinese enjoy visiting Lan Kwai Fong at Halloween to gawp at the *gwai lo* dressed as vampires and ghouls. The foreigners enjoy taking part in Chinese festivals and dragonboat races.

During my forty years in China (not quite as long as my great-great grandfather's fifty years in India) I sincerely hope that I have forged connections between the cultures of Britain and China, promoting understanding, tolerance and goodwill.

Throughout its history, Hong Kong has acted as a bridge between the West and the East, and between foreigners and Chinese. I am glad to have acted as a bridge, first between the British and the Hong Kong Chinese during my career in the police and administrative service and subsequently between foreigners and Mainlanders on my many visits to China. 'Oh,' they say, with delight. 'You can speak our language!'

In 2013, I rented a small flat in the peaceful Guangdong town of Xinhui in order to write this book. Foreigners were rare and when I sat in small restaurants or teahouses, local people would approach and ask where I was from and what I was doing there. When they discovered I could speak Cantonese, they sat down to chat and share thoughts. Could I teach their children English? Were the Americans really going to fight with China? What was my favourite Chinese food? Some of them even asked if they could stroke the hairs on my arm. *'Wah!'* they said. Amazing!

As Kipling said:

> *East is East, and West is West, and never the twain shall meet,*
> *Till Earth and Sky stand presently at God's great Judgement Seat;*
> *But there is neither East nor West, Border, nor Breed, nor Birth,*
> *When two strong men stand face to face, tho' they come from the*
> *ends of the earth!*

FURTHER READING

A Concise History of Hong Kong, John M. Carroll, HKU Press, 2007.
Diamond Hill, Feng Chi-shun, Blacksmith Books, 2009.
Feeling the Stones, David Akers-Jones, HKU Press, 2004.
Governing Hong Kong, Steve Tsang, HKU Press, 2007.
Hong Kong Metamorphosis, Denis Bray, HKU Press, 2001.
Hong Kong Policeman, Chris Emmett, Earnshaw Books, 2014.
Hong Kong State of Mind, Jason Y. Ng, Blacksmith Books, 2014.
Hong Kong, Jan Morris, Random House, 1997.
Myself a Mandarin, Austin Coates, John Day Company, 1968.
On China, Henry Kissinger, Penguin, 2011.
Paper Tigress, Rachel Cartland, Blacksmith Books, 2014.
The Accidental Prawn, Guy Shirra, Sherriff Books, 2015.
The Opium War, Julia Lovell, Pica, 2011.
The Search for Modern China, Jonathan Spence, Norton, 1990.
Wan Chai, Arthur Hacker, Odyssey, 1997.

EXPLORE ASIA WITH BLACKSMITH BOOKS

From retailers around the world or from *www.blacksmithbooks.com*